THE SECRET
of
THE TORAH

A Translation of
IBN EZRA'S YESOD MORA

Translated and Annotated by
RABBI DR. H. NORMAN STRICKMAN

KODESH PRESS

THE SECRET OF THE TORAH:
A Translation of Ibn Ezra's Yesod Mora
Translated and Annotated by H. Norman Strickman

© Kodesh Press 2021

Hardcover ISBN:978-1-947857-55-1
Paperback ISBN: 978-1-947857-56-8

BACKGROUND IMAGE:
"Blue and Purple Cosmic Sky" by Felix Mittermeier

CENTER IMAGE:
"Ibn Ezra Reading the Stars": A scene of Ibn Ezra practicing
Astrology with an Arabic manuscripts being held by the men
that flank him to either side. Artist unknown, circa 1235

Kodesh Press LLC
New York, NY
www.kodeshpress.com
kodeshpress@gmail.com
sales@kodeshpress.com

Set in Arno Pro by Raphaël Freeman MISTD, Renana Typesetting
Printed in the United States of America

To
my loving wife, Zahava
my children, Ya'akov, Esther and Uri
my grandchildren, Danielle, Ben, and Lahav
my unforgettable father, Bentzion Strickman
and cherished mother Chayyah Strickman of blessed memory
My beloved father- and mother-in-law,
Moshe and Leah Berkowitz
of blessed memory

CONTENTS

INTRODUCTION TO THE SECOND EDITION

Rabbi Abraham ibn Ezra was one of the great thinkers produced by Spanish medieval Jewry. Though born in Spain, he composed most of his works in Italy, France, Germany, and England. While living in England, Ibn Ezra produced the *Yesod Mora Ve-Sod Torah*.

The *Yesod Mora* was one of the first books on Jewish philosophy written in Hebrew, and it influenced Jewish philosophy and the Kabbalah. It exposed many Jews who lived in Italy, France, and Germany who could not read Arabic to philosophic thought.

Rabbi Judah ibn Tibbon (c. 1120–1190), translator of R. Saadiah ben Joseph's (882–942) *Sefer Ha-Emunot Ve-Ha-De'ot*, wrote:

> The Jews living in exile in France and all the borders of Edom do not know Arabic. Books written in Arabic are like sealed books to them. They cannot approach them until they are translated into the Hebrew tongue … [this was so] until the wise man Rabbi Abraham ben Ezra came to their country and helped them … by composing short compositions. …

Similarly, Rabbi Jedaiah of Beziers (c. 1270–c. 1340) wrote of the great contribution that Ibn Ezra made to the intellectual development of French Jewry. He related the great joy which Ibn Ezra's arrival precipitated in their hearts.

Rabbi Jedaiah noted that Ibn Ezra "began to open the eyes of

French Jewry. He composed commentaries on the Torah and the prophets for them. Ibn Ezra pointed out the secrets to be found in the Torah. He wrote a work on the commandments and the secret of God's name. He explained the books of Kohelet and Job in accordance with philosophy. He wrote grammar books and works on mathematics, astronomy and the calendar."

It is worthy of note that Ibn Ezra's scientific writings extended beyond the Jewish community. Some of his astronomical and astrological works were translated into Latin and studied at European Universities. The content of these works had previously been inaccessible to the non-Arabic speaking world. His contribution to astronomy was acknowledged by the naming of a crater on the moon in his honor.

Many of Ibn Ezra's ideas have their parallel in Maimonides' *Guide for the Perplexed*. The noted historian Heinrich Graetz complained that in fourteenth-century Spain, "Maimonides' philosophical *Guide for the Perplexed* was entirely neglected and that instead of him Ibn Ezra became fashionable."

Some twenty-five years ago I decided to make Ibn Ezra's *Yesod Mora* available to the English-speaking community. The work was published by Jason Aaronson in 1995.

Since then several works dealing with the *Yesod Mora* have appeared. One is Joseph Cohen and Uriel Simon's critical edition and annotation of the *Yesod Mora* in 2007. Another is Dov Schwartz's annotated and critical edition of Rabbi Mordechai ben Eliezer Komtiyano's commentary on the *Yesod Mora*. They are excellent works that were not available to me when I worked on my first translation and annotation of the *Yesod Mora*. They would have made my work a lot easier had they been available to me when I did my original work. However, I used them when working on my revision of the *Yesod Mora*.

Last May, Rabbi Alec Goldstein called and told me that he had read my work and that he believed that the book should be reissued. Rabbi Goldstein eventually revealed to me that a friend of his, Rabbi Ben Kohanim, had read my work and had found it informative. I was very happy to hear Rabbi Goldstein's proposal. I seriously consider

Rabbi Goldstein's call as a sign from heaven telling me that it was time for a new generation of English-speaking Jews to be exposed to the *Yesod Mora*.

I want to thank Rabbi Goldstein for his efforts and for his undertaking the publication. I also want to thank him for his many excellent suggestions and learned comments that he made regarding the text of the work. I also want to express my appreciation to Rabbi Dr. Alan Yuter, to Mr. and Mrs. Marvin Libow, to Mr. Jules Gilder, and to the late Morris Balanson for their help in preparing the first edition of this work.

Above all I thank Hashem for keeping me alive to see a work which I published twenty-five years ago reborn.

I hope and pray that my work will continue to be a conduit for Rabbi Abraham ibn Ezra's voice to be heard by contemporary English-speaking Jews.

H. Norman Strickman
Petach Tikvah
January 2021

Introduction to the First Edition
ABRAHAM IBN EZRA: HIS LIFE AND WORKS

His Life

Rabbi Abraham ben Meir ibn Ezra was one of the outstanding scholars of medieval Andalusian Jewry. He was a noted poet, mathematician, astrologer, grammarian, and philosopher as well as one of medieval Jewry's greatest Bible commentators.

Abraham ibn Ezra was born in 1092 C.E.,[1] in Tudela, Spain, and died in 1167. It is unclear whether he died in London,[2] in Calahorra,[3] or in Rome.[4]

Little is known of Ibn Ezra's family life. He alluded to five sons (see

---

1. According to a statement found in several codices, Ibn Ezra died on a Monday, on the first day of Adar 1 4927 (January 23, 1167) at the age of seventy-five. If this date is accepted, then Ibn Ezra was born in 1092. See M. Friedlander, ed. and trans., *The Commentary of Ibn Ezra on Isaiah* (London, 1873), p. xxvii n. 54. However, Heinrich Graetz believes that Ibn Ezra was born between 1088 and 1089. See Heinrich Graetz, *Divre Yeme Yesra'el*, ed. and trans. S.P. Rabinowitz, vol. 4 (Warsaw: A. Alapin, 1916), p. 212.
2. E.Z. Melammed, *Mefarshei Ha-Mikra*, vol. 2 (Jerusalem: Magnes Press, 1978), p. 520.
3. Abraham Zakuta, *Sefer Ha-Yuchasin*.
4. L. Zunz, *Die Monatstage des Kalenderjares* (Berlin: 1872), p. 4. Quoted in Friedlander, p. xxvi n. 53.

Ibn Ezra on Exodus 2:1), but only one, Isaac, is known by name[5]; the other four probably died in infancy. A poet of note, who spent most of his life in the Near East, Isaac is reported to have converted to Islam and later returned to Judaism.[6] A heartrending lament by Ibn Ezra reveals that Isaac predeceased his father.[7] Ibn Ezra's wife died before 1140,[8] and he never remarried.

Abraham ibn Ezra lived in Spain until 1140 C.E., after which he wandered as an impoverished scholar until his death. It was during this period that most of his books were written. His travels included Rome, Lucca, Mantua, Verona, Narbonne, Beziers, Dreux, Rouen, Brent, and London.[9]

Unsettled conditions,[10] wanderlust, and poverty[11] contributed to Ibn Ezra's leaving Spain. Concerning his poverty, he lamented:

> I cannot become rich, the fates are against me
> Were I a dealer in shrouds, no man would ever die,
> Ill-starred was my birth, unpropitious the planets,
> Were I a seller of candles, the sun would never set.[12]

His Poetry

Abraham ibn Ezra was a versatile poet. He composed liturgical poems (*piyyutim*, some of which are still recited in the synagogue ritual), secular poems of friendship and love, and verse on nature, astronomy,

---

5. For Isaac's biography see introduction to *Yitzchak ibn Ezra: Shirim*, ed. Menahem H. Schmelzer (New York: Jewish Theological Seminary, 1979).
6. See Chapter 3 of Al-Charizi's *Tachkemoni*. Quoted in *Ha-Shirah Ha-Ivrit Bi-Sefarad U-Ve-Provans*, ed. Chaim Shirman (Jerusalem and Tel Aviv: Bialik Institute and Devir, 1956), p. 112.
7. David Goldstein, *The Jewish Poets of Spain* (London: Penguin, 1965), p. 161.
8. *Ibn Ezra Al Ha-Torah*, vol. 1, ed. Asher Weiser (Jerusalem: Mossad Ha-Rav Kook, 1976), p. 9.
9. Melammed, pp. 519–520.
10. Caused by the wars between the Christians and the Muslims. See Weiser, p. 10.
11. Friedlander, p. xiv.
12. Ibid.

the seasons, the calendar, and religious and nationalistic subjects. In his nationalistic poems, Ibn Ezra gave vent to the suffering of Israel. He wrote:

> The God of Israel Thou wast of yore
> Thou wast their father
> And they were Thy children, but are they no more?
> Then why didst Thou for a thousand years forget them?
> And enemies from all around beset them.
> Dost Thou not see, or is Thy hand so weak,
> That Thou canst not save those who help do seek?
> Redeemer there is none as near as Thou;
> Thy name from ever was Redeemer.
> So hasten, our God, redeem us now.[13]

His religious poems reveal a deeply spiritual man. He wrote:

> In Thee, my God, is my desire,
> In Thee, my passionate love and fire.
> To Thee my reins, to Thee my heart,
> To Thee my soul and spirit dart.
> To Thee my hands, to Thee my feet,
> From Thee doth my form complete.
> My blood, my bones, they are all Thine,
> My body and image divine.
> To Thee belong my eyes and thought,
> The form and pattern Thou hast wrought.
> To Thee my soul, to Thee my might,
> Thou art my trust and my delight.[14]

---

13. Meyer Waxman, *A History of Jewish Literature* (New York: Bloch, 1960), p. 234.
14. Ibid., p. 233.

His Bible Commentary

Ibn Ezra's most notable achievement was in the field of biblical exegesis; his commentary on the Pentateuch is his most enduring creation, ranking second in popularity to Rashi's work.

Ibn Ezra began his commentaries on the Bible in Rome in 1140 C.E.[15] and continued this work for the rest of his life. He probably composed commentaries on the entire Bible, but his work on Early Prophets, Chronicles, Proverbs, Jeremiah, Ezekiel, Ezra, and Nehemiah is no longer extant.

Ibn Ezra's commentary on the Bible was a major contribution to biblical exegesis. It is based on the rules of Hebrew grammar and focuses on the plain meaning of the text. In the introduction to his commentary on the Pentateuch, Ibn Ezra wrote: "I will not show favoritism to anyone when it comes to interpreting the Torah. I will, to the utmost of my ability, try to understand grammatically every word and then do my best to explain it."[16]

Although Ibn Ezra held that, generally speaking, the Bible is to be taken at face value, he made an exception for those verses that contradict reason. He thus believed that all verses that refer to God in human terms are not to be taken literally[17] but are to be interpreted metaphorically: "We know that the Torah spoke in the language of man, for it was given to humans who speak and hear" (Ibn Ezra on Genesis 1:26).

Ibn Ezra respectfully differed with the Rabbis of the Talmud in instances in which he believed that their interpretations contradicted the literal meaning of the text. However, in cases that had halakhic relevance, Ibn Ezra maintained that the law transmitted by the Rabbis was true in itself, but that the Sages had used the biblical verse under

---

15. Graetz, p. 218.

16. *Ibn Ezra's Commentary on the Pentateuch, Genesis (Bereshit)*, trans. H. Norman Strickman and Arthur Silver (New York: Menorah, 1988), p. 17. Annotated.

17. "Far be it from us to believe that God has an image" (Ibn Ezra on Genesis 1:26; see also *Yesod Mora* 12:2).

discussion as a means of formulating the laws. Ibn Ezra thus maintained, contrary to the rabbinic Sages, that "be fruitful and multiply" (Genesis 1:28) is not a command but a blessing, and that the Sages merely used this verse as a mode for the transmission of a law passed on to them (Ibn Ezra on Genesis 1:28).

Commenting on Exodus 23:2, Ibn Ezra noted that the Rabbis interpreted *aharei rabbim le-hattot* ("after a multitude to pervert justice") to mean that legal disputes are to be solved in accordance with the majority opinion of a legally constituted court of law (*Sanhedrin* 2a), after which he argued that this is not the literal meaning of the verse. Ibn Ezra then said that the Sages used this text as a sign by which to remember the above-noted *halakhah*.

In some cases, Ibn Ezra observed that a law which the Talmud derives from a biblical verse is really rabbinic in origin. For example, Exodus 23:19 reads, "You shall not seethe a kid in its mother's milk." According to the Rabbis, this verse prohibits the cooking of any kosher meat and milk (see *Hullin* 113b). Ibn Ezra insisted that the Pentateuch prohibits only the cooking of a kid in its mother's milk and that the other prohibitions are rabbinic (see Ibn Ezra on Exodus 23:19).

When Ibn Ezra offered an interpretation of a verse that differed with the *halakhah*, he usually added a note to the effect that the *halakhah* is to be followed because it is independent of the verse or because one is obligated to follow the rabbinic enactments since "the minds of the Sages were greater than our minds." Ibn Ezra did not want his literal approach to undermine the *halakhah* or to serve as a support for anti-halakhic sectarians.

Thus, Ibn Ezra was infuriated when shown a commentary on the Bible with a view that reckoned the beginning of the biblical day with the morning, not the night before, as maintained by *halakhah*. Ibn Ezra feared that this commentary might cause the Sabbath to be desecrated by suggesting that work might be permitted on the eve of the Sabbath. He wrote a book titled *The Sabbath Epistle* (*Iggeret Ha-Shabbat*) to refute the notion that the biblical day begins in the morning. Ibn Ezra cursed the author of the aforementioned commentary, who may have been Samuel ben Meir, Rashi's grandson, with the imprecation, "May the hand of him who wrote this wither, and may his eye be darkened."[18]

Ibn Ezra's commentaries influenced all subsequent major Bible commentators. Indeed, he is quoted in the commentaries of Abraham Maimonides, Nahmanides, Bahya ben Asher, Levi ben Gershom, and Abravanel as well as other exegetes, philosophers, and scholars. Maimonides is reported to have charged his son not to pay attention to any Bible commentaries other than those of Ibn Ezra.[19]

The *Yesod Mora*

Although Ibn Ezra's reputation is primarily based on his Bible commentaries, he was also a philosopher of note. Indeed, every survey of medieval Jewish philosophy has either a chapter or some pages devoted to Ibn Ezra's philosophy.

Ibn Ezra's philosophical ideas are scattered throughout his biblical commentaries. They are the focus, however, of his *Sefer Yesod Mora Ve-Sod Torah (Treatise on the Foundation of Awe and the Secret of the Torah)*.

The *Sefer Yesod Mora Ve-Sod Torah* (henceforth *Yesod Mora*) was composed by Ibn Ezra in London in the summer of 1158 or 1159. Ibn Ezra composed it in four weeks during the months of Tamuz and Av. The *Sefer Yesod Mora* and the above mentioned *Iggeret Ha-Shabbat* were the last works produced by Ibn Ezra.[20] The *Yesod Mora* was the first major book on Jewish philosophy to be written in Hebrew. Indeed, in its time it was one of the few philosophical books available to those who did not understand Arabic. [21]

---

18. See "Sefer Ha-Shabbat," in *Yalkut Ibn Ezra*, ed. Israel Levin (New York and Tel Aviv: Israel Matz Hebrew Classics, and I. Edward Kiev Library Foundation, 1985). See also Graetz, p. 228.

19. The authenticity of Maimonides' charge has been challenged. See *Chumash Im Pirush Mehokekei Yehudah*, ed. Y.L. Krinsky (New York: Reinman Sefarim Center, 1975), p. 18.

20. Joseph Cohen and Uriel Simon, *R. Abraham ibn Ezra: Yesod Mora Ve-Sod Torah*, Bar Ilan 2007, p. 16:

21. The *Yesod Mora* had considerable influence on the *Hasidei Ashkenaz*. See

Unlike Saadiah Gaon, Judah Ha-Levi, and Maimonides, Ibn Ezra did not offer a polemical justification for writing his work.

Saadiah claimed that he wrote his *Sefer Ha-Emunot Ve-Ha-De'ot* for his co-religionists who were faltering in faith. Thus Saadiah wrote:

> I will begin this book, which it is my intention to write, with an exposition of the reason why men, in their search for Truth, become involved in errors and how these errors can be removed so that the subject of the investigation may be fully removed so that the object of their investigation may be fully attained; moreover, why some of these errors have such a powerful hold on some people that they affirm them as the truth, deluding themselves that they know something.[22]

Rabbi Judah Ha-Levi, Ibn Ezra's contemporary and friend, wrote the *Kuzari* to defend Judaism from the attacks by Muslims, Christians, philosophers, and heretics: "I was asked to state what arguments I could bring to bear against the attacks of philosophers and followers of other religions which differ from ours and against the sectaries who differ from the majority of Israel."[23]

Maimonides wrote his *Moreh Nevukhim* for those Jews who were disturbed by what they saw as a conflict between philosophy and religion. Thus Maimonides wrote:

> The object of the treatise is to enlighten a religious man who has been trained to believe in the truth of our holy law, who conscientiously fulfills his moral and religious duties, and at the same time has been successful in his philosophic studies. Human reason has attracted him to abide within its sphere; and he finds it difficult to accept as correct the teaching based

Sifrut Ha-Musar Ve-Ha-Derush, ed. Yosef Dan (Jerusalem: Keter, 1973), p. 121.

22. Saadiah Gaon, "The Book of Doctrines and Opinions," in *Three Jewish Philosophers*, ed. Alexander Altmann (New York: Atheneum, 1969), p. 25.

23. Judah Ha-Levi, "Kuzari," in *Three Jewish Philosophers*, ed. I. Heinemann (New York: Atheneum, 1969), p. 25.

on a literal interpretation of the Law.... Hence he is lost in perplexity and anxiety.[24]

The purpose of the *Moreh Nevukhim* is to resolve this perplexity and anxiety.

The composition of the *Yesod Mora* was apparently not motivated by any such purpose. Ibn Ezra explained that he wrote this work in response to a request for a book explaining the commandments:

> The awe-inspiring God knows my heart's sincerity. For I did not compose this book to show that I mastered the sciences or to glorify myself by showing that secrets have been revealed to me. Neither did I write it in order to argue with our ancient Sages, for I surely know that they were wiser and more God-fearing than I. I composed this book for a revered and noble individual whom I taught the books that I wrote for him. I troubled myself to compose a book for him dealing with the commandments only because of my great love for him, for I found him to a person of integrity whose fear of the Lord exceeded that of most men.[25]

The Sciences

Ibn Ezra opened the *Yesod Mora* with an evaluation of the various branches of knowledge. He noted that man's rational soul separates human beings from the rest of the animal kingdom. This soul is a *tabula rasa* when first placed in the body. It is put there in order to be developed. If a human being cultivates his rational soul properly, then it acquires eternal life.

In the words of Ibn Ezra: "The soul is destined to return to God

---

24. Moses Maimonides, *The Guide for the Perplexed*, trans. M. Friedlander (London: Pards, 1904), p. 2.

25. *Yesod Mora* 2:4. The individual referred to was most probably Joseph ben Ya'akov, one of Ibn Ezra's patrons. Ibn Ezra had earlier expressed his gratitude to Joseph ben Ya'akov in an introductory poem to the *Yesod Mora*, where he wrote: "As I finish, I thank God and his friend;/Joseph the son of Jacob for the gift of his hand."

the glorious who gave her. She was placed in the body to be shown the Lord's work, to study the works of her Master and to observe His commandments" (Introduction to *Yesod Mora*).

"Man's soul is unique. When it is first placed in the body... it is like a tablet set before a scribe. When God's writing is inscribed upon this tablet... then the soul clings to God both while it is yet in man and later after it leaves the human body" (*Yesod Mora* 10:2).

Ibn Ezra claimed that all branches of wisdom are rungs in the ladder that leads to true wisdom (Introduction to *Yesod Mora*). And "Wisdom is the form of the supernal soul which does not perish when the body dies" (Ecclesiastes 7:12).

Ibn Ezra then analyzed the role of traditional learning in the development of the soul. He maintained that the various branches of Torah study have value in the development of the rational soul but are in and of themselves insufficient for its full development.

Ibn Ezra opened the *Yesod Mora* with an analysis of the study of the *Mesorah*. He found the work of the Masoretes very valuable, for they "preserved Scripture in its original form without any additions or deletions" (*Yesod Mora* 1:1).

Nevertheless, a person who has mastered the *Mesorah* but does not understand the meaning of Scripture is like a person who holds a medical book in his hands and knows all that there is to know about its page makeup but does not comprehend its contents. Similarly, "One who has mastered the *Mesorah* but has not studied any other wisdom is like a camel that carries a load of silk. It is of no use to the silk and the silk is of no use to it" (*Yesod Mora* 1:1).

Ibn Ezra then addressed the study of grammar. He stressed the importance of the knowledge of grammar, for one cannot fully understand the text of the Torah without it. Furthermore, one who knows grammar will be able to express himself more elegantly in prose and in poetry. However, since the value of grammar is its being a tool with which one decodes Scripture, one should not spend one's entire life studying it or in grammatical scholarship. In fact, Ibn Ezra indicated that more than sufficient grammar books have already been written (*Yesod Mora* 1:2).

Ibn Ezra then discussed the study of the Bible. He observed that there are people who devote their entire life to the study of Scripture and believe that they have reached the highest level of human perfection because they devote all of their abilities to this discipline. Ibn Ezra argued that devotion to the text of the Pentateuch alone is insufficient for the understanding of God's law, for while it is true that the Torah "is the source of life and the basis of the commandments, it is beyond the ken of any scholar to fully comprehend even one precept of the Torah if one does not first master the oral law" (*Yesod Mora* 1:3). This appears to be, at least in part, an anti-Karaitic polemic.

The study of Scripture, specifically for the Prophets and the Writings, also has its drawbacks, for while it is true that some commandments are clarified by these sources, the results are meager when compared to the effort expended in their study. It is ironic that a man who owes his fame to his reputation as a Bible commentator claimed that the rewards of scriptural study are small "in comparison to the effort expended in knowing the names of the Israelite cities; the accounts of the judges and kings; how the Temple was constructed, and how the one which is yet to be built is to be made; and the words of the prophets, some of which have already come to pass while others relate to the future. We can ascertain the meaning of some of the latter by research. In other instances, we grope walls as do the blind. One commentator offers one interpretation and another a different one" (*Yesod Mora* 1:3).

Ibn Ezra said: "Even if we know the entire book of Psalms [what have we gained?]. For though written with Divine inspiration, it contains no prophecies for the future. The same is so with Job, Solomon's work, the five Scrolls, and the book of Ezra" (*Yesod Mora* 1:3).

Ibn Ezra then discussed the study of the Talmud (*Yesod Mora* 1:4). According to Ibn Ezra, there are scholars who view knowledge of the Talmud as the ultimate wisdom. Ibn Ezra noted that these scholars do not bother to study the *Mesorah*; they also consider the study of grammar a waste of time and neglect the study of Scripture (*Yesod Mora* 1:4).

Ibn Ezra conceded that these scholars are somewhat justified in their approach, for the Talmud explains all the commandments, "which if a man do, he shall live by them." However, Ibn Ezra argued that as important as the study of the Talmud is, one must master additional sciences if one wants to master God's law completely and develop one's rational soul.

Thus, a student of the Talmud must know Scripture and its grammar (*Yesod Mora* 1:4). For the scholar who has not mastered these disciplines will not be able to understand properly the verses of the Torah quoted in the Talmud. He will not know whether these verses are being interpreted literally or midrashically. Hence, without a knowledge of Scripture and its grammar, one cannot fully comprehend the Talmud (*Yesod Mora* 1:4).

Ibn Ezra argued that one cannot properly comprehend the Talmud if one does not know the sciences, for there are many passages in the Pentateuch and the Talmud that are either incomprehensible or given to misinterpretation by one who has no prior knowledge of the sciences (*Yesod Mora* 1:4–7).

The passages to which Ibn Ezra referred are those portions of the Bible and Talmud that deal directly with the sciences or those that must be understood allegorically (*Yesod Mora* 1:4–6).

Ibn Ezra clearly believed that talmudic scholars who are ignorant of the sciences cannot properly understand certain parts of the Bible and Talmud. In fact, he held that they probably misinterpret these passages.

The fact is that Ibn Ezra did not value talmudic learning as an end in itself. He prized it only insofar as it taught a person how to fulfill his obligations to man and God.

Ibn Ezra criticized scholars who devote all of their efforts to the study of talmudic passages that have no practical relevance. Thus, Ibn Ezra criticized those who devote all their time to the study of the order of *Nezikim* (the Order that deals with damages). He argued that "One judge ... is sufficient to straighten out that which is crooked." As to the value of the study of these laws per se, Ibn Ezra wrote that "If all of Israel were righteous, there would be no need for the order of *Nezikim*" (*Yesod Mora* 1:8).

Ibn Ezra maintained that one must master philosophy and the physical sciences if one wants to develop one's soul completely. He taught that a person can comprehend "the mystery of the soul, the secret of the heavenly angels, and the concept of the world to come as taught in the Torah, the prophets, and the Sages of the Talmud" only after he masters the natural sciences, logic, mathematics, and the "science of proportions" (*Yesod Mora* 1:5).

When a person knows the sciences and the secrets of God's Throne and the Chariot and knows God, his soul cleaves to God while he is yet alive and continues clinging to God after it leaves his body (*Yesod Mora* 10:2).

One may ask, "If the development of the soul depends upon the knowledge of philosophy and the natural sciences, what need is there for the Torah?" Ibn Ezra did not openly raise this question. The *Yesod Mora*, however, clearly answers it.

According to Ibn Ezra, the desires of the flesh impede the development of the soul. Ibn Ezra believed that one of the primary purposes of the *mitzvot* is to prevent man's corporeal nature from dominating the body and thereby hindering the development of the rational soul. The *mitzvot* do this by restricting man's appetites (*Yesod Mora* 10:2).

Ibn Ezra explained that a Nazirite who concludes his or her term must bring a sin offering for descending in spirituality by once again enjoying wine, a drink that stirs one's sexual passions (*Yesod Mora* 10:2).

In addition to the above, the *mitzvot* of the Torah provide instructions that, if followed, ensure an individual's well-being. Indeed, the Torah's negative *mitzvot* may be compared to the prohibitions laid down by a physician (*Yesod Mora* 7:3). In fact, Ibn Ezra held that a person is not rewarded for observing negative commandments. The reward of observing a negative commandment lies in the avoidance of the evil that falls upon a person who commits any act that the Torah prohibits (*Yesod Mora* 7:3).

The Commandments

According to the Talmud, there are 613 *mitzvot* in the Torah (*Makkot* 23b). Most of the post-talmudic scholars take this talmudic statement literally. A number of them composed lists of the 613 commandments. Although these scholars disagree as to which of the laws mentioned in the Torah are to be included, they all accept the concept of 613.[26]

Ibn Ezra was ambivalent on the concept of 613 commandments. On the one hand he believed, "In reality there is no limit to the commandments" because each mitzvah of the Torah has infinite implications. In the words of the book of Psalms, "I have seen an end to every purpose; but Your commandment is exceedingly broad" (Psalm 119:96) (*Yesod Mora* 2:3). On the other hand, Ibn Ezra claimed that if we count only the "categorical commandments," the "rational commandments," and commandments dealing with eternally binding rituals, then the commandments are no more than [even] one tenth of six hundred and thirteen (*Yesod Mora* 2:3).

Ibn Ezra did not list the 613 commandments found in the Torah. In fact, he never referred to them again in the *Yesod Mora*. Hence, it is quite possible that Ibn Ezra never seriously entertained the concept of 613 commandments.[27] He considered it a homily.[28]

Ibn Ezra explained that the *mitzvot* are divided into positive and negative commandments (*Yesod Mora* 7:1). He noted that the commandments are observed in the following ways: (1) belief; (2) speech; and (3) action (*Yesod Mora* 7:2).

Mitzvot observed by belief include: (1) belief in the existence of God; (2) belief that God brought the Israelites out of Egypt; (3) loving God; (4) cleaving to God; and (5) loving one's neighbor (*Yesod Mora* 7:10).

Mitzvot observed by speech include: (1) reciting grace after meals;

---

26. Gerson Appel, *A Philosophy of Mizvot* (New York: Ktav, 1975), p. 26.
27. "Among others who voiced doubt concerning the tradition [of 613 commandments] were Judah ibn Bal'am...and Ibn Ezra" (Appel, p. 204 n. 4).
28. See *Makkot* 23b: Rabbi Simlai taught: "There were 613 *mitzvot* stated to Moses in the Torah, consisting of 365 prohibitions corresponding to the number of days in the solar year, and 248 positive *mitzvot* corresponding to the number of a person's limbs." This statement is part of a sequence of homilies on the commandments.

(2) praying; (3) reciting *Hallel*; (4) teaching Torah to one's children; and (5) discussing the contents of the Torah (*Yesod Mora* 7:11).

Mitzvot that are observed by deeds include: (1) offering sacrifices; (2) eating *matzah* on Passover; (3) building a *sukkah* on Sukkot; (4) giving charity; (5) sounding the *shofar* on Rosh Hashanah; and (6) fasting on Yom Kippur (*Yesod Mora* 7:12).

Ibn Ezra explained that while some commandments are observed only by belief, faith must permeate the observance of all commandments. Indeed, he argued, "If belief is lacking, then the observance of the commandments is meaningless" (*Yesod Mora* 7:2). Ibn Ezra's views on this point coincide with that of his older contemporary, Bahya ibn Pekuda (c. 1050–c. 1120). Bahya composed a work called *Hovot Ha-Levavot* (*Duties of the Heart*), which, as its name implies, stresses the importance of inwardness.

Ibn Ezra's emphasis on faith is in direct contradiction to the views of many modern Jewish thinkers. The latter tend to emphasize action over faith. It stands in stark contrast to the position of such men as Moses Mendelssohn, who held that Judaism is a system of revealed legislation. According to Mendelssohn and his followers, it is the act, not the belief, which is paramount.

Mendelssohn argued that there isn't a single commandment "which says: 'You shall believe' or 'You shall not believe.' But they all enjoin 'You shall do' or 'You shall not do.' One can't command faith because we do not accept any decrees other than such that arrived at by way of conviction. All the divine behests are directed at man's will and power of action."[29]

This was not the opinion of Ibn Ezra or other medieval Jewish thinkers. The medieval Jewish thinkers held that that Lord seeks the heart. In fact, they drew up articles of faith. The great Jewish minds of the Middle Ages ruled that one who denies any of the basic

---

29. Moses Mendelssohn, *Jerusalem* (Berlin: Welt Verlag, 1919), p. 81. Quoted in *The Modern Impulse of Traditional Judaism*, ed. Zevi Kurzweil (New York: KTAV, 1985), p. 9.

articles of the Jewish faith places himself outside the pale of the Jewish people.[30]

Ibn Ezra distinguished between three types of *mitzvot*:

1. Rational laws. "These laws are not contingent upon place time or any other thing" (*Yesod Mora* 5:1). These laws "were known via reason before the Torah was given through the agency of Moses [at Sinai]" (*Yesod Mora* 5:1). Examples of such laws are: you shall not murder, you shall not steal, you shall not commit adultery, honor your father and your mother, and the like. These laws are the fundamental laws of the Torah.

2. Symbolic precepts. Commandments that serve as reminders of the rational laws or of precepts that Israelites, both men and women, are obligated to be conscious of at all times. The Sabbath, which recalls creation, is one example (*Yesod Mora* 5:2).

3. Esoteric commandments (*Yesod Mora* 8:1). These commandments possess a purpose that only a few can fathom. The reasons that Ibn Ezra gives for this class of commandments include concern for the health of the body, concern for the health of the soul, living in accordance with the laws of nature, and various astrological motifs (*Yesod Mora* 9).

Ibn Ezra believed that there is a reason for all the commandments of the Torah (*Yesod Mora* 8:1). Unlike Saadiah Gaon and Judah Ha-Levi, he did not divide the *mitzvot* into *shimiyot* (traditional commandments) and *sikhliyot* (rational commandments). Like Maimonides after him, Ibn Ezra maintained that all *mitzvot* possess a coherent teleology.

Ibn Ezra believed that an individual is obligated to observe all the commandments, even if he does not understand their purpose or function:

---

30. Menachem, Kellner, *Dogma in Medieval Jewish Thought* (Oxford: Oxford University Press, 1986).

A person who refuses to observe [the laws] until he knows the reason for their [observance] will remain without guidance. He will be like a child who refuses to eat bread until he first knows how the ground was plowed, the grain planted, harvested, winnowed, cleansed, ground, sifted, kneaded, and baked. If a child acts thusly, he will surely die of starvation....

The correct thing for a child to do is to eat normally, and as he grows, to ask a little at a time until all of his questions are answered. Similarly, an intelligent person can ultimately learn the very many clearly stated reasons which the Torah itself offers for the precepts (*Yesod Mora* 8:1).

There are commandments, however, for which the Torah gives no reason, and "only one man in a thousand knows" the reasons for them (*Yesod Mora* 8:1).

Ibn Ezra named his work *Sefer Yesod Mora Ve-Sod Torah* (*Treatise on the Foundation of Awe and the Secret of the Torah*). *Yesod Mora* is parallel and rhymes with *Ve-Sod Torah*. Furthermore, in the first chapter of the *Yesod Mora*, Ibn Ezra spoke of *yesod ha-Torah ve-sod ha-mora* (the foundation of the Torah and the secret of awe; see *Yesod Mora* 1:3). It thus appears that *Treatise on the Foundation of Awe and the Secret*[31] *of the Torah* is another way of saying *Treatise on the Reasons for the Mitzvot of the Torah*.[32]

---

31. It should be noted that Ibn Ezra's use of the word "secret" does not apply only to the mystical and esoteric. It also applies to mundane facts that a person is not always aware of. Thus, "the secret of the Torah" refers to both down-to-earth and esoteric explanations of the *mitzvot*.

32. Ibn Ezra identified the fear of God with the negative commandments. Thus, Ibn Ezra wrote:

"The words 'to fear the Lord your God' (Deuteronomy 14:23) though stated in the positive encompass all negative precepts" (*Yesod Mora* 2:5).

"I found one verse which embodies all the commandments. The verse is, 'You shall fear the Lord your God; and Him shall you serve' (Deuteronomy 6:13). Now 'You shall fear' takes in all negative

There may be a secondary meaning to the title *Sefer Yesod Mora Ve-Sod Torah*. According to Ibn Ezra, a human being should choose cleaving to God as his life's goal. This, as noted above, is accomplished by the development of the soul. According to Ibn Ezra, the soul can reach its fullest potential only if a human being avoids the pleasures of the body. This can be accomplished only by following the laws of the Torah. Hence, the title *Sefer Yesod Mora Ve-Sod Torah* may allude to the following: The Foundation of Awe (i.e., cleaving to God) is the secret of the Torah. In other words, the observance of the Torah sets the stage for the development of the soul, which leads to a permanent relationship with God.

---

commandments pertaining to the heart, lips, and deeds. It is the first step that one climbs in one's ascents to the service of the glorious God" (*Yesod Mora* 7:12).

Hence, it is possible that *Treatise on the Foundation of Awe and the Secret of the Torah* means, strictly speaking, "Treatise on the Reasons for the Negative and Positive Commandments of the Torah."

ACKNOWLEDGMENTS

This translation is based on J. Baer's edition of the *Yesod Mora* (Frankfurt am Main and Leipzig, 1840). However, in a number of instances, the translation follows other readings. When it does, the sources are indicated in the footnotes. I found M. Creizenach's German translation of the *Yesod Mora* very helpful. I likewise, as noted above, found the works of J. Cohen, U. Simon, and Dov Schwartz very helpful. I have corrected a number of errors in the earlier edition and welcome comments regarding this version.

In addition, the following editions were consulted:

1. Levin's edition of the *Yesod Mora* in his *Yalkut ibn Ezra* (New York and Tel Aviv, 1985). Levin's edition is based on three manuscripts and three printed editions. I found Dr. Levin's comments on the text of Ibn Ezra most enlightening and helpful.

2. Stern's edition of the *Yesod Mora,* along with his commentary *Livyat Chen* (Prague, 1833). I found Stern's commentary extremely useful in interpreting the *Yesod Mora.*

3. Waxman's edition of the *Yesod Mora* (Jerusalem: Chokhmat Yisrael, 1931).

4. When I did my work on the *Yesod Mora* more than twenty years ago, Joseph Cohen's and Uriel Simon's excellent scientific edition of the *Yesod Mora* (Bar Ilan, 2002) was not yet published. The aforementioned would have been very helpful. However, I consulted their work in preparing this edition.

Ibn Ezra's
Ode of Thanks

Everything is full of the glory of the One God who is without
    beginning;

However, it is beyond the ability of Man to describe Him.

The heart of the intelligent will know its Creator by His
    works;[1]

For the one who denies Him is in truth His witness.[2]

To the people whom He created for His glory and Name;

On Mount Sinai without revealing His image,[3] He showed
    His fire and flame.

To His appointed and faithful messenger; He gave His Law
    and Teaching.[4]

I of broken spirit have applied myself to understand His
    charge;

I have found its basis and secret written.[5]

---

1. By studying nature, man can learn something about God: "The heavens
declare the glory of God, and the firmament shows His handiwork" (Psalm
19:2).
2. The very existence of man bears witness to a creator. Thus, the very body
of the one who denies God testifies to the Lord's existence.
3. Cf. Deuteronomy 4:14.
4. Hebrew, "*Talmud.*" The reference is probably to the oral law, the Talmud.
5. In the Torah. See *Yesod Mora* 1:3.

A house for His Law will I build;
The fear of God have I set as a support for its pillar
As I finish I thank God and His friend Joseph the son of
  Jacob, for the gift of his hand.[6]

---

6. For his financial support, Ibn Ezra often dedicated his works to patrons.

IBN EZRA'S INTRODUCTION

B ehold the book called *The Foundation of Awe and the Secret of the Torah*,[1]

Written by Abraham the son of Meir ibn Ezra the Spaniard.

Behold, I have begun to speak.

It is my intention to expostulate at length; For I need a firm foundation.

With the help of the One who lowers and raises;[2]

I arrange twelve chapters.[3]

The Soul and Immortality

I begin by saying that aside from man's supernal, rational soul, a human being has no preeminence over a beast (cf. Ecclesiastes 3:19). She [the soul] is destined to return to the glorious God who gave her [to human beings]. She was placed in the body to be shown the Lord's work [i.e., creation], to study the works of her master, and to observe His commandments.

---

1. *Sefer Yesod Mora Ve-Sod Torah.*
2. God. See 1 Samuel 2:7.
3. Lit., "Gates." The reference is to the twelve chapters that make up *Yesod Mora.*

Every branch of knowledge gives life to the one who acquires it.[4] Now there are many sorts of knowledge, each one of which is helpful [in achieving immortality]. All of wisdom's categories are rungs in the ladder that leads to True Wisdom [which leads to immortality]. Happy are they whose hearts have been opened. At their end, they will flow to God and His goodness.

4. Eternal life. According to Ibn Ezra, eternal life is gained by acquiring wisdom. Ibn Ezra writes, "Wisdom is the form of the supernal soul, which does not perish when the body dies" (on Ecclesiastes 7:12).

Chapter 1

THE VARIOUS BRANCHES OF KNOWLEDGE

1. The *Mesorah*

There are learned Jews whose entire wisdom consists of knowing the words of the Masoretes.[1] They understand all their glorious signs [such as *peh* for an open chapter] and their lovely hints [the shorthand notations used by the Masoretes]. They know all open and closed chapters [i.e., whether a new section starts on the same line or a new line], all words that are read one way but written another way [i.e., *kerei* and *ketiv*],[2] all full and deficient spellings,[3] the large and small letters,[4] the suspended letters,[5] the letters that have dots above them

---

1. The sages who transmitted the text and general format of Scripture, such as spelling, vowels, accents, and cantillation notes, and break up of chapters and verses.
2. For example, *yishgalennah* (Deuteronomy 28:30) is read as if written *yishkavennah*.
3. At times a word is spelled only with its consonants. At other times the vowel letters (*alef, hei, yod,* or *vav*) are included in the spelling.
4. Some letters are written larger than others, for example, the *bet* in *bereshit*, "In the beginning" (Genesis 1:1). Others letters are written smaller than others, for example, the *alef* in *va-yikra*, "And [God] called" (Leviticus 1:1).
5. Four letters are written suspended between the line, for example, the *nun*

1

(e.g., Genesis 33:4), and the number of verses, words, and letters of each and every book in Scripture.[6]

The truth of the matter is that the Masoretes performed a valuable service. They can be compared to the guardians of a city's wall,[7] for it was due to their efforts that the Torah of God [i.e., the five books of Moses] and the Holy Scriptures [the Prophets and Writings] were preserved in their original form without additions or deletions. An intelligent person should acquaint himself with some of their teachings. However, he should focus on the meaning of Scripture [rather than just these Masoretic nuances], for the words [of Scripture] are like bodies, and their meanings are like souls. If one does not understand the meaning [of Scripture], all of his efforts [spent mastering the *Mesorah*] are vain and meaningless. He is like a man who holds a medical book in his hand and troubles himself to find out how many pages are in the book, how many columns are on each and every page, how many letters are in each column. For all of this, he will not be able to heal any illness. One who possesses knowledge of the *Mesorah* but has not studied any other wisdom is like a camel that carries a load of silk. It is of no use to the silk and the silk is of no use to it.

2. Grammar

There are others whose entire wisdom is limited to the knowledge of grammar. They know all the conjugations and their parts and which letters serve as prefixes and suffixes and root letters (see *Yesod Mora* 11:2). They know the meanings of all the Hebrew nouns and the various types of intransitive and transitive verbs. They also know the letters and words that serve as prepositions and how the verbs are connected to them.

---

in *menasheh* (Judges 18:30), the *ayin* in *mi-ya'ar* (Psalm 80:14), the *ayin* in *resha'im* (Job 38:13) and the *ayin* in *me-resha'im* (ibid. 15)

6. For example, the Masoretes report that the Pentateuch contains 5,845 verses, 79,856 words, and 400,945 letters.

7. Cf. "Rabbi Akiva says: The *Mesorah* is a fence around the Torah" (*Avot* 3:17).

The truth of the matter is that the study of grammar is a wonderful science, for the one who possesses it knows how to speak elegantly in his prose and in poetry. Many things [i.e., meanings] in Scripture become clear after grammatical analysis. The same holds true for the [Torah's] commandments.

For example, the Pentateuch states, *ve-ahavta le-re'akha ka-mokha* ["you shall love to your neighbor as (you do to) yourself"] (Leviticus 19:18). It does not state, *ve-ahavta et re'akha* [which would be the proper way to say "love your neighbor"], as in *ve-ahavta et Adonai Elohekha* ["and you shall love the Lord your God"] (Deuteronomy 6:5). There is irrefutable proof that there is a difference between *ve-ahavta le-re'akha* and *ve-ahavta et re'akha*. For Scripture writes with regard to the stranger, *ve-ahavta lo kamokha* [translated literally: "And you shall love to him as to yourself"] (Leviticus 19:34).[8]

The clause *va-ahavtem et ha-ger* ["you shall love the stranger"]

---

8. Leviticus 19:16–17 reads:

    You shall not go up and down as a talebearer among your people; neither shall you stand idly by the blood of your neighbor: I am the Lord. You shall not hate your brother in your heart; you shall surely rebuke your neighbor, and not bear sin because of him. You shall not take vengeance, nor bear any grudge against the children of your people, but *you shall love your neighbor as yourself; I am the Lord.*

    Most translations render *ve-ahavta le-re'akha kamokha* as, "and you shall love your neighbor as yourself," or something similar. Some commentators are of the opinion that the *lamed* of *le-re'akha* is superfluous (see Ibn Ezra on Leviticus 19:18); that is, it has no meaning and is not to be taken as a preposition. They interpret *ve-ahavta le-re'akha* as if it were written *ve-ahavta re'akha kamokha* (which is *ve-ahavta et re'akah kamokha* without the accusative particle *et*).

    Ibn Ezra disagreed and took pains to point out that the two forms differ because there are commentators who hold that both forms have the same meaning. He argued that *ve-ahavta le-re'akha kamokha* is similar to *ve-ahavta lo* (the stranger) *kamokha* (Lev. 19:34); in both cases a prepositional *lamed*, meaning "to," follows the verb *ve-ahavta*. Ibn Ezra interprets *le-re'akha* to mean: "for your neighbor." He interprets *ve-ahavta lo kamokha* as: "you shall care for him (the stranger) as you care for yourself" for

(Deuteronomy 10:19) does not refute this assertion, because the word *kamokha* ["as yourself"] does not appear in it, and *va-ahavtem et ha-ger* ["love the stranger"] (Deuteronomy 10:19) is connected to what is written above it. I have explained the aforementioned in its appropriate place.[9]

---

he believes that Scripture would not command a Jew to actually love a stranger as he loves himself.

According to Ibn Ezra *ve-ahavta le-re'akha kamokha* is not an independent clause. It is connected to the "neighbor" mentioned earlier in the passage. Scripture is to be interpreted as follows: Do not take vengeance; do not bear grudges, but act lovingly toward your neighbor. See Ibn Ezra on Lev. 19:18, where he writes: "I believe that the meaning of *ve-ahavta le-re'akha kamokha* is: One should love that which is good for one's neighbor as he loves that which is good for himself." In other words, one should care for his neighbor as he cares for himself.

Maimonides seems to interpret likewise. He writes, "One is commanded to love every fellow Israelite even as he loves himself, for it is said, *ve-ahavta le-re'akha kamokha*." He goes on to explain, "One is, therefore, obliged to speak in praise of his neighbor and to be considerate of his money, even as he is considerate of his own money or desires to preserve his own honor" (*Hilkhot De'ot* 6:3). Hence Scripture deliberately used the former, rather than the latter in Leviticus 19:18.

Ibn Ezra implies that there is a difference between the commandment to love God and the commandment to love one's fellowman. The commandment to love God, consists of a verb (*ve-ahavta*) and a direct object (*et Adonai*). It commands one to cleave to God. See also Ibn Ezra on Deuteronomy 6:5: "You should love Him to the utmost in any way that you are able...Your heart should be totally committed to the love of God." The commandment to love one's fellow man consists of a verb (*ve-ahavta*) and a preposition (*le-*). It commands man to act lovingly towards his fellow human being.

9. The phrase *va-ahavtem et ha-ger* appears to be parallel to *ve-ahavta le-re'akha*, in which case there would be no difference between *ve-ahavta le-re'akha* and *ve-ahavta et re'akha*. However, Deuteronomy 10:19 does not say "and you shall love the stranger *as yourself*," which proves that they are not the same. Rather, *ve-ahavta le-re'akha kamokha* parallels *ve-ahavta lo kamokha* (Leviticus 19:34). Hence, Leviticus 19:18 should be compared to Leviticus 19:34, rather than to Deuteronomy 10:19.

The truth of the matter is that it is good for an intelligent person to study this science [i.e., grammar]. However, one should not devote one's entire life to it by poring over the works of Rabbi Judah [ibn Hayuj], the first grammarian, the ten books of Rabbi Marinus,[10] and the twenty-two books of Rabbi Samuel the Nagid.[11] Concerning these, Solomon said, "of making many books there is no end" (Ecclesiastes 12:12).

3. Scripture

There are others who constantly meditate upon the Torah, the Prophets, and the Writings. They also study the Aramaic translation of Scripture. They believe in their hearts that they have reached the highest level [of human perfection] because they search for the meaning of Scripture with all of their abilities.[12] The truth of the matter is that the Torah is

---

Scripture states: "For the Lord your God...loves the stranger, in giving him food and raiment" (Deuteronomy 10:17–18). It then goes on to say *va-ahavtem et ha-ger* (lit., "love the stranger"). According to Ibn Ezra, *va-ahavtem et ha-ger* should not be taken as an independent clause meaning "love the stranger," but as a dependent clause meaning "You shall therefore love the stranger." In other words, Scripture is telling us, since God acts lovingly toward the stranger, it is our duty to equally do so.

See Ibn Ezra on Deuteronomy 10:18: "He [God] similarly loves the stranger and sustains him when he relies on Him. Now since God loves the stranger, you too are obligated to love him."

10. Jonah ibn Janah, the noted eleventh-century spanish grammarian.

11. A noted halakhist, poet, grammarian, and statesman (993–1056).

12. Ibn Ezra's remarks seem to be directed at the Karaites. (See Simon Uriel, *Four Approaches to the Book of Psalms* [New York: State University of New York Press, 1991, pp. 202–210.) Indeed his comments here and polemics against the Karaites in his introduction to the Pentateuch are similar and in many cases, identical. The tone here is totally different, however. In his introduction to the Pentateuch, Ibn Ezra calls the Karaites distorters, and the ones "whose loins totter." Here he merely points out that the study of Scripture is not the be-all and end-all of learning. Hence, it is possible that the reference here is not to the Karaites but to those to whom the Talmud refers to as *ba'alei mikra*, people whose learning primarily consists

the source of life and the basis of all the commandments. However, it is beyond the ken of any scholar to fully know even one precept of the Torah if he doesn't master the contents [lit., "words"] of the oral law. For example, Scripture states, "You shall not do any manner of work [on the Sabbath]" (Exodus 20:9). Now, who will explain to us how many primary categories of "work" exist? Who will define their extensions?[13] Furthermore, who will delineate the dimensions of the *sukkah*?

The sum of the matter is that all the commandments require the explanations transmitted by our fathers. How much more so do we need tradition to inform us whether the festivals are contingent upon the mean conjunction of the new moon,[14] its true conjunction, upon the area where the moon is about to be seen,[15] or upon the actual sighting of the moon. Now all this varies depending on longitude and latitude, the area of the earth from which the arc of vision[16] is measured, and whether the lunar sphere inclines to the right or left of the line of the zodiac.

---

of Scripture. It is noteworthy that although Ibn Ezra is known to posterity as a great Bible commentator, it is obvious from the *Yesod Mora* that he considered himself more than a "mere" commentator on Scripture.

13. According to the Mishnah (*Shabbat* 7:2), there are thirty-nine categories of "work" prohibited on the Sabbath, and it is to these that Scripture refers when it says, "You shall not do any manner of work" (Exodus 20:9). Each one of the thirty-nine categories of work listed has extensions. For example, it is prohibited to plant on the Sabbath. Planting is extended to include watering, pruning, or doing anything to help a plant in its growth.

14. The festivals fall on specific dates, which are contingent on when the new moon falls. New moon is determined by the conjunction of the sun and moon. "The moment that the moon would have the same longitude as the sun, if both moved uniformly" (W.M. Feldman, *Rabbinical Mathematics and Astronomy* [New York: Sefer Hermon Press, 1978], p. 123). See Maimonides, *Hilkhot Kiddush Ha-Hodesh* 6:1.

15. The reference is possibly to a given area where it is calculated that the moon will first be visible.

16. "The difference in altitudes between the sun and the moon" (Feldman, p. 160). See also Maimonides, *Hilkhot Kiddush Ha-Hodesh*, chap. 17.

We need tradition to tell us from which spot on Earth to calculate the birth of the new moon,[17] for the science of astronomy has established beyond a shadow of a doubt that there are four full hours between the time that the sun first shines upon Jerusalem and upon this island [England].[18]

There are also many other commandments, such as "Circumcise therefore the foreskin of your heart" (Deuteronomy 10:16),[19] whose meaning cannot be ascertained from the Torah. We can arrive at their meaning only by using our powers of reason.[20]

A scholar should also know Scripture [i.e., Prophets and Writings], for many commandments are clarified by Scripture's narratives [lit., "words"]. We thus learn the meaning of the precept "You shall not eat with the blood" (Leviticus 19:26) from Saul's charge to Israel.[21] We similarly learn the meaning of "The fathers shall not be put to death

---

17. The new moon is seen at different times in different places. The question thus arises: Which spot on Earth determines the new moon? Maimonides writes: "The observation of the new moon [for the purposes of its legal sanctification] may take place only in the Land of Israel." Hence, "we have computed all these calculations on the basis of the city of Jerusalem and the localities which surround it in a circumference of about six- or seven-days journey. For it was here that the people used to watch for the new crescent and then go and testify before the court [in Jerusalem]" (*Hilkhot Kiddush Ha-Hodesh* 3:8).

18. Ibn Ezra wrote the *Yesod Mora* in London.

19. Reason tells us that we are not to take this statement literally. See the third way of interpreting Scripture in Ibn Ezra's introduction to the Pentateuch.

20. In addition to studying Torah, man must also develop his intellectual capacities. Without this ability, one cannot properly interpret the Torah. In his introduction to the Pentateuch, Ibn Ezra wrote "Man's intelligence is the angel which mediates between him and his God."

21. King Saul said to the men in his army: "Bring me hither every man his ox, and every man his sheep, and slay them here [on the altar] and eat: and sin not against the Lord in eating with the blood" (1 Samuel 14:34). From 1 Samuel 14:34, it is learned that the meaning of Leviticus 19:26 is that one is not permitted to slaughter any animal and eat of its flesh without first sprinkling its blood on the altar. See Ibn Ezra on Leviticus 19:26.

for the [sins of the] children" (Deuteronomy 24:16) from the story [lit.,
"words"] of Amaziah.[22] However, the result is meager in comparison to
the effort expended[23] in knowing the names of the Israelite cities, the
accounts of the judges and kings, how the first Temple was constructed
[i.e., its intricacies; see 1 Kings 7], how the one which is yet to be built is
to be made, and the words of the prophets, some of which have already
come to pass while others relate to the future.[24] We can ascertain the
meaning of some of the latter by research [hence there is value in
studying them]. In other instances, we grope walls as the blind do.
One commentator offers one interpretation and another a different
one. Even if we know the entire book of Psalms, which consists of
hymns and prayers [what have we gained?]. For though written under
divine inspiration, it contains no prophecies for the future.[25] It is the
same with the book of Job, Solomon's books [Proverbs, Ecclesiastes,

---

22. See 2 Kings 14:5–6. King Amaziah executed those who assassinated his
    father, but he did not punish their children. Scripture tells us that Amaziah
    acted in accordance with the rule of Deuteronomy 24:16, which states,
    "The fathers shall not be put to death for the children, neither shall children
    be put to death for the fathers, every man shall be put to death for his own
    sin."
23. Very few commandments are explained in the Prophets and the Writings.
24. Ibn Ezra, like many medieval Jewish thinkers, did not value the study of
    history. Indeed, many of them viewed the study of history as a waste of
    time. See B. Lewis, *History, Remembered, Recovered, Invented* (Princeton,
    NJ: Princeton University Press), pp. 21–27. Ibn Ezra valued the study of the
    Prophets and Writings only insofar as it explained or threw light on the
    laws of the Torah, helped one to master Hebrew, or predicted the future.
25. According to Uriel Simon, this comment is directed at the Karaites. The
    Karaites believed that one could ascertain the time of the coming of the
    Messiah from a study of Psalms. Simon notes: "In other words, Ibn Ezra
    is here arguing, first, that our understanding of the book of Psalms is far
    from being as complete and comprehensive as the Karaites claim, and
    second, that it contains only poems and prayers, which, for all that they
    are prophetic, are not – because of their nature as prayers and poems –
    future-oriented prophecies in the sense of detailed prognostic prophecies
    of the Messianic era, as the Karaite *pesher* would find in them" (Uriel

and Song of Songs], the Scrolls [Ruth, Lamentations, and Esther], and the book of Ezra.

Likewise, the date of the Messiah's appearance cannot be ascertained from the book of Daniel [contrary to what many people think]. For as I have explained in its proper place, Daniel himself did know it.[26] If we were to study these books day and night, we would not learn how to observe even one commandment that would enable us to inherit the world to come. The Sages, therefore, said, with regard to the study of Scripture, that "it is meritorious and it is not meritorious" (*Bava Metzia* 33a).

An intelligent person should rather learn the rules [lit., "the secret"] of the Holy Tongue from Scripture.[27] For it enables a person to understand the Foundation of the Torah and the Secret of Awe.[28]

The Aramaic translation [of the Torah, Targum Onkelos] is also of use [in helping us to comprehend the Pentateuch], even though it does not always follow the plain meaning of the text.

4. Talmudic Study

On the other hand, there are many scholars who never studied the *Mesorah*. They similarly consider the study of grammar to be a waste of time. They have also not read Scripture. It goes without saying that they have not studied its concepts. These people, from their youth, have studied only the explanation of the Mishnah known as the Talmud.

The above-noted scholars follow various paths (see sections 7–8).

Simon, *Four Approaches to the Book of Psalms* [New York: State University of New York Press, 1991], p. 209).

26. See Ibn Ezra on Daniel 11:31: "Daniel did not know the end time" (that is, Daniel did not know when the Messiah would come).

27. In other words, one should study the Prophets and the Writings in order to perfect one's knowledge of Hebrew grammar rather than to learn ancient history or to ascertain the date of the Messiah's coming.

28. An allusion to Ibn Ezra's *Yesod Mora Ve-Sod Torah* ("The Foundation of Awe and the Secret of the Torah"). One must know Hebrew well in order to study the sources of Judaism.

All of these paths are correct [for they lead to knowledge of God's laws]. The Talmud explains all the commandments, which if a man does, he shall live by them (cf. Leviticus 18:5). However, it is unseemly for an intelligent person to be ignorant of the knowledge of Scripture. When a student of the Talmud, who does not know Scripture, comes across a biblical quotation, he will not know its source. Furthermore, he will not know whether the verse is being explained according to its plain meaning, is being interpreted midrashically, or is being used to support a rabbinic enactment (*asmakhta*). For by utilizing their great wisdom and casuistical powers, the Sages were able to derive new meanings from biblical texts [lit., "things from things"]. In reality, the talmudic Sages knew the plain meaning of the text better than all subsequent generations.[29] Clearly, a person who has not studied Scripture will be unable to understand [lit., "to read"] the verse [quoted by the Talmud, and he will not properly understand it].

It is also necessary for one to know grammar. For it helps one to understand many things in the Torah that the early Sages who were learned in all the sciences left unexplained. Their successors [who are ignorant of these sciences] understand only what the Sages clearly explained. There are also things in the Talmud that they do not know how to interpret. The following is an example: "At times the conjunction of the moon and sun come at longer intervals. At times the conjunction of the moon and sun come at shorter intervals" (*Rosh Hashanah* 25a).[30] They similarly do not understand the meaning of "the birth of the new moon before midday" (*Rosh Hashanah* 20b)[31]

---

29. Hence, we follow their interpretation of Scripture when it is consistent with a passage's literal sense. A person ignorant of the knowledge of Scripture, however, will accept a midrashic interpretation as the literal meaning of the text.

30. "The length of a lunation, or synodic month [synod, a meeting between sun and moon] is not constant.... At those times of the year when the sun's true motion is rapid...the month is longer than the mean synodic period. When the sun's motion is slow, the month is shorter" (Feldman, p. 123).

31. If the conjunction between the sun and moon takes place before midday,

and the meaning of "the moon is hidden[32] from us [in Babylonia for twenty-four hours, six from the old moon and: eighteen from the new moon]. From them [in the Land Israel] it is hidden six hours from the new moon and eighteen from the old moon."[33]

5. Astronomy, Geometry, Psychology, and Logic

It is impossible for an intelligent person to know all of the above (in section 4), unless he studies astronomy and learns the orbits of the sun and moon. Furthermore, a person cannot know astronomy if he does not study geometry. For geometry is "like a ladder set upon the earth and the top of it reaching heaven" (Genesis 28:12). When one masters astronomy and the circuits of the [sun and moon; Heb., *tekufot*], he comes to know the works of the glorious God. The Sages also said, "Whoever does not calculate the circuits [of the sun and moon] and [that of the] planets, concerning him, Scripture states, 'But the deeds of the Lord, they regard not'" (Isaiah 5:12; *Shabbat* 25a). Furthermore, if a person does not know geometry, he will not be able to comprehend the proofs offered in tractate *Eruvin* for the Sabbath boundaries.[34] Neither will he be able to comprehend the forty-nine measures of Rabbi Nathan.[35] Similarly, an intelligent person who did not study psychology will not understand the five ways in which a human being's soul is similar to its Creator.[36] One cannot know the

---

then the moon may be seen close to sunset. If it occurs after midday, then the moon cannot be seen close to sunset.

32. The reference is to the moon's invisibility at the end of the month.

33. *Rosh Hashanah* 20a–b. Lit. "from us" and "from them."

34. One is not permitted to walk on the Sabbath two thousand cubits beyond the last house in town. The Talmud discusses the various shapes these two thousand cubits may take. For examples, see Mishnah, *Eruvin* 5:2–7.

35. The reference is apparently to a mathematical work dealing with, among other things, the dimensions of the Tabernacle and its furniture. Cf. Rashi on Exodus 27:5; *Sukkah* 8a.

36. Cf. *Berakhot* 10a: "Five times did David say, Bless the Lord, O my soul. In reference to what was it said? He said it in reference to the Holy One, blessed be He, and in reference to the soul. For just as the Holy One, blessed

latter if one has not studied the very intricate sciences dealing with the heavens and the earth.[37] An intelligent person must also study logic,[38] for it is the scale employed by every science.[39] The ancients exhorted us a long time ago, "Be eager to study the Torah; know what to answer an unbeliever."[40]

6. Esoteric Rabbinic and Biblical Dictums

There are many things in the words of our Sages that require proof [that what they said was correct] and interpretation.[41] For example, the statements "He who is awake at night [and turns his heart to vanity has his blood on his own head]" (*Avot* 3:4) and "He who drinks borrowed water [has his blood on his own head]" (*Pesahim* 11a) pertain to the physical sciences [and therefore those who know the physical sciences can explain them]. The reference to Igrath the daughter of Mahalath relates to the laws of astronomy.[42] The

---

be He, fills the entire world, so does the soul fill the entire body; just as the Holy One, blessed be He, sees but cannot be seen, so does the soul see, but cannot be seen; just as the Holy One, blessed be He, feeds the entire world, so does the soul feed the entire body; just as the Holy One, blessed be He, is pure, so is the soul pure; and just as the Holy One, blessed be He, dwells in a place secret from all, so does the soul dwell in a secret place."

37. Levin reads: "The very intricate science dealing with the nature of the heavens." According to Ibn Ezra, man is a microcosm. He held that a person cannot understand the microcosm if he has no understanding of the macrocosm. See Ibn Ezra on Genesis 1:26.

38. Heb. *Hokhmat ha-mivta*. According to Ibn Ezra *Avot* 2:19 applies this idiom to the study of logic.

39. All knowledge is based on logical thinking.

40. *Avot* 2:19. By knowing the rules of logic one will know how to defend Judaism.

41. Many rabbinic statements are not to be taken at face value. One must know logic and the sciences in order to interpret them adequately.

42. Or astrology. Igrath the daughter of Mahalath is the queen of demons. Cf. *Pesahim* 112b: "Do not go out alone on the nights of neither Wednesday nor Sabbaths because Igrath the daughter of Mahalath, she and 180,000 destroying angels go forth, and each has permission to wreak destruction.

statement to the effect that the moon spoke evil of the sun is linked to the science of astronomy.[43]

Many matters in Scripture also require interpretation. It thus must be pointed out that Kohelet speaks of the four elements [lit., "roots"], namely – heaven, earth, wind, and dust.[44] Thus:

- "The sun also rises" (Ecclesiastes 1:4) refers to heaven [or fire];
- "And the earth abides forever" (Ecclesiastes 1:3) [refers to earth, i.e., dust][45];
- "And the wind returns again to its circuits" (Ecclesiastes 1:6)[46] [which refers to air] and does not stop, and,
- "All the rivers run into the sea" (Ecclesiastes 1:7) [referring to water] refer to the other three elements.

These four elements are [also] mentioned in the chapter [of the Torah] dealing with creation. We thus read, "[In the beginning God created]

---

independently." This statement alludes to the evil influence that Saturn exerts on those nights. Cf. *Reshit Hokhmah*, ed. R. Levi and F. Kantirah, p. 4.

43. Cf. *Hullin* 60b. "R. Simeon b. Pazzi cited an apparent contradiction [in Scripture]. A verse says, 'And God made the two great lights' (Genesis 1:16), and then continues, 'The greater light...and the lesser light' (Genesis 1:16). The moon said unto the Holy One, blessed be He, Sovereign of the Universe, Is it possible for two kings to wear one crown?' God answered, 'Go and make yourself smaller.'"

The story alludes to the fact that after the moon is full, it begins to wane. See *Yesod Mora Ve-Sod Torah*, edited by Joseph Cohen and Uriel Simon. Bar Ilan Press, 207. P. 82.

44. The four elements are earth, water, air, and fire. In this instance, heaven refers to fire because there is a sphere of fire above the firmament. Similarly, earth here refers to water, because most of the earth is covered with water, or because "the sphere of water is next to the sphere of the earth." See Chapter 10.

45. The reference is to the element earth. Ibn Ezra earlier employed the term earth as a synonym for water. He now employs it as a synonym for dust.

46. Some texts read: The word ruah [wind] certainly does not refer to a side. The word *ruah* also has the meaning of a side. Hence the comment.

the heaven [i.e., fire] and the earth" (Genesis 1:1); and "God's wind [air] blowing over the water" (Genesis 1:2).

[The four elements are also mentioned in the book of Isaiah. Isaiah asks:] "Who has measured the waters in the hollow of his hand, and meted out heaven with the span, and comprehended the dust of the earth in a measure. Who has meted out the wind [ruah] of the Lord?" (Isaiah 40:12–13, translated literally).

They are also mentioned in [Psalm 104]:

- "Who stretches out the heavens like a curtain" (Psalm 104:2);
- "Who did establish the earth upon its foundations" (Psalm 104:5);
- "Who makes winds your messengers" (Psalm 104:4); and
- "Who lays the beams of your upper chambers in the waters" (Psalm 104:3).

The four elements are also mentioned in [Psalm 33]:

- "He gathers the waters of the sea together as a heap" (Psalm 33:6);
- "Let all the earth fear the Lord" (Psalm 33:8), which follows [lit., "and he already mentioned" in an earlier verse]:
- "By the word of the Lord were the heavens made, And all the hosts of them by the breath [ruah, 'wind'] of His mouth" (Psalm 33:6; where "heavens" represent fire, and ruah represents air).

The four elements are also [mentioned in the book of Job]:

- "When He makes a weight for the wind, and metes out the waters by measure" (Job 28:25);
- "For He looks to the ends of the earth, and sees under the whole heaven" (Job 28:24).

They are also alluded to in [the book of Proverbs]: "Who has ascended up into heaven and descended? Who has gathered the wind in his fists? Who has bound the waters in his garment? Who has established all the ends of the earth?" (Proverbs 30:4).

Scripture similarly states:

- "The measure thereof is longer than the earth, and broader than the sea" (Job 11:9; earth and sea are two of the four elements).
- Another verse states, "Have you surveyed unto the breadths of the earth" (Job 38:18) [both verses stress the difficulty of mastering the sciences].

However, all these things are clear to the intelligent.

Similarly, many other things require explanation. We can thus demonstrate beyond the shadow of a doubt that what is noted at the end of the book of Psalms ["Praise the Lord from the earth ... Fire and hail," Psalm 148:7–8], namely, that fire and hail are "earthly" elements [and not "heavenly elements"], is true.[47] The same is the case with the statement to the effect that the waters are upon the heaven.[48] Likewise, the statement that the lights [i.e., the sun and moon], and the stars are in one firmament (Genesis 1:17) requires explanation.[49] Whatever Scripture says is all true.[50]

---

47. See Ibn Ezra on Psalm 148: "The Psalmist calls upon the elements out of which the earth was created to praise God. He then delineates the elements. They are fire and hail, snow and vapor, stormy wind. We thus see that fire and hail are 'earthly' elements even though they seem to come from the sky."

48. Cf. "And you waters that are above the heavens" (Psalm 148:4). Ibn Ezra believed that there is a sphere of water above the firmament. Hence Scripture can speak of waters that are above the heavens, for heavens in the later verse refers to the firmament and not the heaven wherein the heavenly bodies are constituted. See Ibn Ezra on Psalm 148:4. Also see next note.

49. For in reality the sun, moon, and stars are not in the firmament but in the heaven, which is above the firmament. See Ibn Ezra on Genesis 1:1, where he explains that that the sun, moon, and other luminaries "are called lights in the firmament because they are visible there," that is, they shine through the firmament and thus appear to be there. However, they are not actually there.

50. Whatever Scripture says concerning the world is true, but at times, it requires interpretation. For not everything is to be taken literally.

7. Rabbinic Scholars

The talmudic scholars of our generation follow various paths. There are those who study the Talmud to know what is permitted and what is prohibited. Others study it for its homilies [Hebrew, *midrashim*]. They also create new homilies of their own and search for a reason for every complete and incomplete spelling.[51]

I will now lay down a rule [regarding homilies based on changes in spelling or wording]: Know that the prophets do not preserve the exact wording when they repeat something. They only preserve its substance. For that is what is important.[52] For example:

- We find that Eliezer actually used the term *hagmi'ini* ["give me to drink"] when speaking to Rebekah [at the well] (Genesis 24:17). However, he quoted himself as saying *hashkini* ["give me to drink"] (Genesis 24:43) [when he spoke to Rebekah's family].

- Isaac said to Esau, "that my soul may bless you before I die" (Genesis 27:4). However, Rebekah quoted him as saying, "and I will bless you before the Lord before my death" (Genesis 24:7).

- We find the terms *yefot mareh* ["well favored"] (Genesis 41:2) and *yefot to'ar* ["well favored"] (Genesis 41:18) used in describ-

---

51. Many Hebrew words are spelled with or without a *vav*, a *yod*, or an *alef*. Some aggadists offer meanings for the various spellings. Ibn Ezra believed that these meanings are "fit for children." See Ibn Ezra's introduction to his commentary on the Pentateuch.

52. From a literal point of view, it is a waste of time to seek reasons for the various changes in spelling and wording in Scripture. Ibn Ezra writes, "Note that words are like bodies and their meanings are like souls. The body is, as it were, a vessel for the soul. Hence all the wise men of all nations are in the habit of preserving the ideas conveyed by a word and not concerned with changes in wording when the meaning remains one and the same" (on Exodus 20:1).

ing Pharaoh's dream.[53] However, we do not find these terms used in Joseph's interpretation of the dream.[54]

• Balak requested of Balaam, *arah li* ["curse me"] (Numbers 22:6). However, Balaam quoted him as saying, *kavah li* ["curse me"] (Numbers 22:11).

• Moses tells us, "And Israel sent messengers unto Sihon king of the Amorites, saying: Let me pass through your land; we will not turn aside into field, or into vineyard" (Numbers 21:21–22). However, Moses later changed his wording and said, "Let me pass through your land; I will go along by the highway...You shall sell me food for money" (Deuteronomy 2:27–28).

• It is written, "Now therefore let Me alone, that My wrath may wax hot against them, and that I may consume them" (Exodus 32:10). However, when Moses described this event [the golden calf] a second time, he quoted God as saying, "Let Me alone, that I may destroy them, and blot out their name" (Deuteronomy 9:14).

• Similarly, in the first account [of the golden calf] we are told that God said, "and I will make of you a great nation" (Exodus 32:10). However, in the second account [of the golden calf] we are told that the Lord said, "And I will make of you a nation mightier and greater than they" (Deuteronomy 9:14).[55]

• There are many other such instances. Thus, we find that "Remember" (Exodus 20:8) and "Observe" (Deuteronomy

---

53. The first use occurs in Scripture's description of Pharaoh's dream. The second occurs when Pharaoh repeats the dream to Joseph.

54. Joseph refers to the kine as *tovot* ("good") rather than as *yefot mareh* ("well favored") or *yefot toar* ("well favored").

55. The last two sentences are omitted in the Stern and Waxman editions. However, they are in the Creizenach and the Levin editions. Creizenach adds a line pointing out a discrepancy between Genesis 31:3 and Genesis 32:10.

5:20) interchange in the decalogue.[56] We also find "you shall not covet" (Exodus 20:14) and "neither shall you desire" (Deuteronomy 5:18) interchanging.

- *Ed shaker* [false witness] (Exodus 20:13) and *ed shav* [false witness] (Deuteronomy 5:17) also interchange.

- *Avnei shoham* [onyx stones] does not have a *vav* prefaced to it [when God commanded Israel to donate the stones in Exodus 25:7]. However, Moses altered its form and placed a *vav* before it [saying *ve-avnei shoham* when he conveyed God's command to Israel in Exodus 35:9].

- *Lo tinaf* ["You shall not commit adultery"] (Exodus 20:13) similarly interchanges with *ve-lo tinaf* ["Neither shall you commit adultery"] (Deuteronomy 5:19).

- There are many other additions and omissions in the [second version of the] Decalogue.[57]

The intelligent person will understand why this is so [Moses in some cases used his own formulation when repeating God's word].

8. Study for Practical Purposes

There is a type of scholar who studies the Talmud for self-glorification.[58] He therefore devotes all of his time to the order of *Nezikin*

---

56. There are two versions of the Decalogue in Scripture, one in Exodus and one in Deuteronomy. They differ in wording. Exodus reads, "Remember the Sabbath day"; Deuteronomy reads, "Observe the Sabbath day."

57. Ibn Ezra listed them in his commentary on Exodus 20:1.

58. To be a judge. The medieval Jewish philosophers did not value talmudic learning as an end in itself. They prized it only insofar as it taught a person how to fulfill his obligations to man and God. Hence, they did not value the study of those parts of the Talmud that did not have practical relevance. For example, Rabbi Bahya ibn Pekuda, in his introduction to *Hovot Ha-Levavot* (*Duties of the Heart*), quoted the following response of a sage who was asked a theoretical question on a point of law: "You who ask concerning a point which will not harm anyone, if he does not know it – do you know the things which you are obligated to know... that you

["Damages"].[59] He is also paid for teaching the simple [those who cannot study on their own] and for setting the crooked straight [for deciding cases in which one person injured another]. However, if all of Israel were righteous, there would be no need for the order of *Nezikin* [for people would not harm each other]. Furthermore, there are commandments that are not incumbent on each and every individual. One person can serve as an agent and fulfill the precept on behalf of many. Such is the case with the one who sounds the shofar on Yom Kippur (proclaiming the start of the Jubilee year, Leviticus 25:9) and on Rosh Hashanah (lit., "the Day of Remembrance") (Numbers 29:1), the one who offers the daily burnt offering (Numbers 28:1–8) and the additional offerings [of Sabbaths and festivals] (Numbers 29:1–39), and the one who reads the Torah on the Day of Assembly [*Hakhel*] (Deuteronomy 31:12). Similarly, one judge rather than many judges is sufficient to straighten out that which is crooked [i.e., there is no need for many experts on the laws of *Nezikin*, since one judge per community is sufficient].[60]

---

spend time in speculations on curious legal problems, which will neither advance your knowledge or faith, nor correct faults in your character." He went so far as to claim that the talmudic Sages never troubled their minds with theoretical aspects of ritual or civil law. It should also be noted that Maimonides' *Mishneh Torah* omitted all the talmudic dialogue and debate and that he stated in his introduction to *The Guide for the Perplexed* that after one knows what is permitted and what is prohibited (i.e., talmudic law) he should then study metaphysics. The kabbalists had a similar notion, except that they substituted the study of Kabbalah for the study of Aristotle's metaphysics.

59. The Talmud is divided into six orders. One of them is called *Nezikin* and deals with theft, injury, lost objects, partnership, oaths, judges, law courts, and related topics.

60. Ibn Ezra explicitly writes *shofet ehad*, "one judge," even though the general rule is *dinei mamonot ba-sheloshah* – monetary matters require three judges.

9. The Purpose of Life

Man is obligated to perfect himself, to acquaint himself [Hebrew *le-hakkir*] with the commandments of the Lord who created him and to act correctly.[61] Man will then know his Creator.

Similarly, Moses says, "Show me now Your ways, that I may know You" (Exodus 33:13). The prophet says, "Let not the wise man glory in his wisdom" (Jeremiah 9:22), that is, in any sort of wisdom: "But let him that glory, glory in this" (Jeremiah 9:23), namely, "That he understands, and knows Me" (Jeremiah 9:23). The Torah states, "Know this day, and lay it to your heart [that the Lord, He is God in heaven above and the earth beneath; there is none else]" (Deuteronomy 4:39). David says, "Know the God of your father, and then serve Him with a whole heart" (2 Chronicles 28:9), for this is what man was created for. After a person has perfected himself he should, if he can, perfect others [i.e., he should help others perfect themselves].

The ancient Sages of blessed memory knew the secret of "the Chariot"[62] and the *Shi'ur Komah* ["Dimensions of the Height"].[63] Far be it, far be it for them to have ascribed a body to God [as a literal reading of *Shi'ur Komah* implies]. It is only that their words, like the words of the Torah, require explanation.[64] For we read in the Torah, "Let us make man in our image, after our likeness" (Genesis 1:26).

---

61. Ibn Ezra reads *le-hakhin ma'asav*. Stern edition reads *le-havin ma'asav*.
62. Heb. *Merkavah*. An ancient esoteric doctrine centered on Ezekiel's vision of God's Throne-Chariot. Cf. Ezekiel 1; *Hagigah* 11a; Maimonides' *Guide for the Perplexed* 3:7. See also "Appendix C (Ma'aseh Merkavah)," in G. Scholem, *Jewish Gnosticism, Merkabah Mysticism, and Talmudic Tradition* (New York: Jewish Theological Seminary, 1960).
63. A mystical work giving the dimensions of God. Most scholars believe it to have been composed in the Geonic period. However, Saul Lieberman believes it to be a tannaitic Midrash on Song of Songs. See Gershom G. Scholem, *Jewish Gnosticism, Merkabah Mysticism, and Talmudic Tradition* (New York: Jewish Theological Seminary, 1960), Appendix D.
64. The Torah and the Prophets speak of God in human terms. However, we do not take these terms literally. This is also the case with the words of the rabbinic Sages.

Also, we read in the prophecy of Ezekiel, "And upon the likeness of the throne was a likeness as the appearance of a man upon it above" (Ezekiel 1:27). The prophet further says, "And from the appearance of his loins and downward" (Ezekiel 1:28). I will give you a hint at the end of this book regarding a secret which will enable you to understand all of these things (see chapter 12:3).

There is a Gaon who wrote a work per the opinions of the philosophers and called it the *Sefer Ha-Yihud*.[65] However, very little in it is correct. [For the Gaon maintains] that God only knows Himself.[66] In other words, he said, God does not know us. The Gaon thought that the Knower (God) is not the known and the Knowledge.[67]

---

65. "The Book of Unity," a work dealing with the unity of God. The book is no longer in extant. See Cohen and Simon, p. 88, *Sefer Ha-Yihud*, note 124. Ibn Ezra is vague. Our interpretation of what Ibn Ezra claims to be the opinion of the *Sefer Ha-Yihud* follows the explanation of Rabbi Komtiyano and Simon and Cohen. Others render differently. See Simon and Cohen and I. Levin.

66. These thinkers believed that God does not change. They believed that learning new things causes change in the learner. Hence they believed that God does not learn new things. In fact they believed that God knows only Himself. This is the belief of Aristotle. Ibn Ezra claims that the Gaon accepted this belief. It is very strange for a Gaon to hold such a belief. Perhaps this is Ibn Ezra's point. The Gaon did not understand the implication of Aristotle's statement.

67. He did not know that the Knower, the known, and the Knowledge are one and the same when it comes to God. Hence knowledge does not add to His being. See Ibn Ezra on Exodus 34:6: God alone is the Knower, the known [the content of His thought] and the known [the object of His thought]." Also see Maimonides, *Hilkhot Yesodei Ha-Torah* 2:10: "The Holy One, blessed be He, does not know with a knowledge which is external to Him in the way that we know, for ourselves and our knowledge are not one. Rather, the Creator, may He be blessed, He, His knowledge, and His life are one ... Were He to ... know with a knowledge that is external from Him, there would be many gods, Him, His life, and His knowledge. The matter is not so. Rather, He is one from all sides and corners, in all manners of unity. Thus, you could say, "He is the Knower, He is the Subject of Knowledge, and He is the Knowledge itself. All is one ... Thus, He does not recognize

The notion that God created the world when a desire to do so newly came upon Him[68] belongs in the same category [because God is unchangeable].

The general rule is: how can a person seek to know what is beyond him when he does not [first] know his own soul or body?[69] However, only when one knows the natural sciences and their proofs, learns the categories that are the "guardians of the walls"[70] taught by the science of logic, masters the science of astronomy with its absolute proofs based on mathematical knowledge, and comprehends the science of geometry and the science of proportions,[71] can one ascend to the great level of knowing the mystery [lit., "secret"] of the soul, the secret of the supernal angels and the concept of the world to come (as taught in) the Torah, the Prophets, and by the Sages of the Talmud. Such an individual will grasp and perceive the deep secrets – a few of which I will explain – that are hidden from the eyes of most people.

Rabbi Saadiah Gaon composed the *Sefer Emunot Ve-De'ot*. There are righteous gates (chapters) in it. However, it also contains gates (sections) that are incomprehensible.[72]

---

and know the creations in terms of the creations as we know them, but rather He knows them in terms of Himself. Thus, since He knows Himself, He knows everything, for the existence of everything else is dependent on Him..." (translated by Eliyahu Touger, Chabad website; also see *Guide* 1:65).

68. This seems to be the opinion of Saadiah Gaon. See *Sefer Emunot Ve-De'ot*, ch. 1 (end). Ibn Ezra also takes issue with Saadiah Gaon in the introduction to his commentary on the Pentateuch.

69. Ibn Ezra implies that the author of the *Sefer Ha-Yihud* did not know this.

70. The walls of reason. Its study prevents man from thinking and speaking nonsense.

71. Heb. *Hokhmat Ha-Arakhin*, one of the categories of medieval science. See "*Erekh and Hokhmah*," in J. Klatzkin, *Otzar Ha-Munahim Ha-Flosofiyim*. See also H.A. Wolfson, "The Classification of Sciences in Medieval Jewish Philosophy," in *The Hebrew Union College Jubilee Volume* (Cincinnati: Hebrew Union College, 1925). Also see Ibn Ezra's *Reshit Hokhmah*.

72. So Komtiyano, Simon and Cohen's version. Other editions read: Rabbi Saadiah Gaon composed the *Sefer Emunot Ve-De'ot* (The Book of

I will now backtrack, and insofar as I am able to, speak on the commandments. May God guide me in straight paths. For there is no guide like the Lord (Cf. Job 36:22).

Beliefs and Opinions). It contains many chapters, but his words are not comprehensible.

Chapter II

CLASSIFYING AND ENUMERATING THE COMMANDMENTS

1. The Categories

O how glorious is the science of logic. It begins with the knowledge of the five terms.[1] For [the science of logic teaches that] there is a supreme category that includes inferior categories and their parts. Now an inferior category that is close to the supreme category is called "a supreme kind," while a subcategory that is close to its parts is referred to as "an inferior kind." Thus, the word *matter* refers to a supreme category, for it includes stones, stars, metals, plants, and living creatures. However, the term *living creature* is a supreme kind, for it takes in fowl, cattle, man, and fish. On the other hand, the word *man* takes in individuals, such as Reuben and Simeon. Hence, it forms an inferior kind.

---

1. The Aristotelian "Predicables," the five ways in which a predicate may be related to a subject. They are genus, species, differentia, proprium, and accidens. Cf. Ronald Jager, *Essays in Logic from Aristotle to Russell* (Englewood Cliffs, NJ: Prentice Hall, 1963), p. 3. See also W.D. Ross, *Aristotle* (Cleveland: Meridian Books, 1961), pp. 60–61. Ibn Ezra made this point here because he wanted to stress that one must be acquainted with the rules of logic before one attempts to classify the commandments.

2. Classifying the Unclean Fowl

We find that the number of prohibited fowl listed in the Torah portion *Shemini* is twenty (Leviticus 11:13–20). However, in the Torah portion *Re'eh Anokhi*, their number is twenty-one (Deuteronomy 14:12–18). The ancient Sages said that the *ra'ah* (glede) is to be identified with the *da'ah* (kite).[2] They also said (*Hullin* 63b) that the *ayyah* (falcon, mentioned in both places) is the same as the *dayyah* (kite).[3]

Rabbi Marinus [i.e., Jonah ibn Janah] asked: If the *ayyah* and *dayyah* are one and the same, why count it twice [in the same verse]? Our Sages[4] said that Scripture referred to it by two names so as not to give anyone an opportunity to open his mouth [i.e., in order to remove any doubt]. However, if this is so, then Scripture should mention each one of the fowl by all of its names. The truth of the matter is that God spoke only in language that people understand [and God would not confuse people by referring to the same object by two names in one verse].

The answer to our question is found in the science of logic. For

---

2. In Leviticus 11:14, the *da'ah* is listed among the unclean fowl and the *ra'ah* is not mentioned. In Deuteronomy 14:13, however, the *ra'ah* is listed and the *da'ah* is omitted. The talmudic Sages identified the *da'ah* with the *ra'ah* in order to harmonize both lists. Cf. *Hullin* 63a.

3. Mentioned in Deuteronomy 14:13 but not in Leviticus 11. By identifying the *ayyah* with the *dayyah*, the Sages explain why the *dayyah* is not listed in Leviticus. They argue that it is listed under the name of *ayyah*. In addition, if we identify the *ayyah* with the *dayyah*, the number of prohibited fowl in Deuteronomy is decreased to twenty. The number of prohibited fowl listed in Leviticus is thereby equal to the number listed in Deuteronomy.

4. See *Hullin* 63b. Some editions read, "Rabbi Solomon," the reference being to Rashi. See Rashi on Deuteronomy 14:13, who writes: "*Ayyah*, *dayyah*, and *ra'ah* are names for the same bird. Why is its name called *ra'ah*? Because it sees very well [*ra'ah* can mean 'see']. Why does Scripture employ three names when prohibiting this fowl? In order not to give an opponent any opportunity to disagree, so that the one who wishes to prohibit should not call it *ra'ah*, and the one who wishes to permit it will say, 'This one is named *dayyah*,' or 'This one is named *ayyah*,' and Scripture did not prohibit this one."

da'ah [mentioned only in Leviticus] is a supreme kind that includes both the *dayyah* and the *ra'ah* [mentioned in Deuteronomy]. The word *tzippor* ("birds") in "but the birds divided he not" (Genesis 15:10) is similar. It includes both "the turtle dove and the young pigeon" (Genesis 15:9). Similarly, Scripture states, "And the high places of Isaac shall be desolate" (Amos 7:9). However, elsewhere it reads, "The high places also of Aven shall be destroyed" (Hosea 10:8).[5] Furthermore, two letters [in the words *ra'ah* and *dayyah*] are each taken from the word *da'ah*.[6]

When studying all arts and sciences, one does not seek to know all the particulars, for it is not in man's capacity to know their ultimate number. The particulars are constantly being destroyed and their number changes from moment to moment. It is only the group [i.e., kind or species] that exists forever.

3. Counting the *Mitzvot*

I found it necessary to mention the various categories before I discussed the precepts because I saw a number of sages counting the 613 commandments in different ways. Some of them list the prohibition of seething a kid in its mother's milk once. Others count it as three commandments because it is written three times in the Torah (Exodus 23:19; 34:26; Deuteronomy 14:21). Now our Sages interpreted each one of the latter.[7] There are many other such instances [where the Torah repeats a law a number of times].

Some count the particulars and the categories.[8] Others count only

---

5.   The reference is not to two different high places. For "the high places of Isaac" is a supreme kind and "the high places of Aven "an inferior kind.

6.   *Da'ah* is spelled *dalet, alef, heh*. *Ra'ah* is spelled *resh, alef, heh*. *Dayyah* is spelled *dalet, yod, heh*. This shows that the *ra'ah* and the *dayyah* are types of the *da'ah*.

7.   According to talmudic Rabbis, one verse prohibits the cooking of meat in milk, another eating meat cooked in milk, and a third denying any benefit from meat cooked in milk. Cf. *Hullin* 115b.

8.   As separate precepts. If the Torah issues a categorical prohibition and later lists its particulars, they count both the general statement and the

the particulars in some instances and only the categories in others. Some count a commandment that comes in two formulations with one meaning twice.[9] From the standpoint of true inquiry, there is no limit to the commandments.[10] Indeed, the poet states, "I have seen an end to every purpose; But Your commandment is exceeding broad" (Psalm 119:96). However, if we count only the categories, the fundamental commandments [Hebrew, *ikkarim*, see ch. 5], and the precepts that are eternally binding, then the commandments are no more than [even] one tenth of six hundred and thirteen.[11]

4. Reason for the Composition of the *Yesod Mora*

The awe-inspiring God knows my heart's sincerity. For I did not compose this book to show that I mastered the sciences or to glorify myself by showing that secrets have been revealed to me. Neither did I write it in order to argue with our ancient Sages, for I surely know that they were wiser and more God fearing than me. There are likewise great wise men in this generation. On the contrary, I composed this

---

particulars as independent commandments. For example, Scripture states, "You shall not do any manner of work [on the Sabbath]" (Exodus 20:10). It then goes on to say, "You shall kindle no fire throughout your habitations upon the Sabbath day" (Exodus 35:3). These sages count the above as two different commandments.

9. Numbers 15:38 states, "Speak unto the children of Israel, and bid them that they make them throughout their generations fringes in the corners of their garments." Deuteronomy 22:12 states, "You shall make yourself twisted cords upon the four corners of your covering." Some scholars count the aforementioned as two separate commandments.

10. For the implications of each and every commandment are limitless. See Gerson Appel, *A Philosophy of Mizvot* (Hoboken, NJ: KTAV, 1975), p. 204: "Among others who voiced doubt concerning the tradition [that there are 613 commandments was] Ibn Ezra in his *Yesod Mora*." See also E. Levine's introduction to his edition of Ibn Ezra's commentary to the Pentateuch.

11. According to Ibn Ezra's calculations, there are only about sixty *mitzvot* in the Torah. See Yosef Cohen and Uriel Simon (eds.), *R. Abraham Ibn Ezra, Yesod Mora Ve-Sod Torah* (Bar Ilan, 2007), p. 96, fn. 24

book for a revered and noble individual[12] with whom I studied the books that I wrote for him. I took the trouble to compose a book for him, dealing with the commandments, because of my great love for him. I found him to be a person of integrity, whose fear of the Lord exceeded that of most men.

5. The Supreme Category; the supreme kind and the inferior kind

There is a supreme category [in Scripture] that takes in all positive and negative precepts, namely the charge, "To keep for your good the commandments of the Lord" (Deuteronomy 10:13).

The statement "And you shall serve the Lord your God" (Exodus 23:25) encompasses all positive fundamental commandments and their reminders[13] relating to the heart, mouth, and deeds.[14]

The words "to fear the Lord your God" (Deuteronomy14:23), though stated in the positive, encompasses all negative precepts [hence it, too, is a supreme kind]. It commands a person to fear God and to refrain from touching a woman with whom he is prohibited to have sexual relations. It requires a person to act like a servant who fears to do evil in the presence of his master [so too should someone be literally afraid of God's wrath]. For there are others who follow their lust.[15] They neither fear the king [i.e., God], nor are they worried that

---

12. Joseph ben Jacob. See Ibn Ezra's Ode of Thanks prefaced to the *Yesod Mora* and the notes thereto.
13. Acts that serve to remind a person of the fundamental commandments.
14. Ibn Ezra held that the commandments are divided into three groups: commandments that pertain to thought, precepts that pertain to speech, and commandments that pertain to deeds. The first category contains precepts, such as the love of God, the fear of God, and loving one's neighbor. The second category includes commandments, such as reading the *Shema* and reciting grace, and prohibitions against bearing false witness and taking God's name in vain. The third category includes the positive and negative precepts in Scripture that entail acts, such as wearing phylacteries and placing a *mezuzah* on one's doorpost, and prohibitions against murder, theft, and adultery.
15. Levin reads: For if he satiates his lust and is alone he fears not the king.

the king might learn what they did. Neither do they care about the dirt and the shame or that they will acquire an evil name.[16]

The statement "After the Lord your God shall you walk" (Deuteronomy 13:5) takes in the obligation to practice acts of loving-kindness, to be righteous, and to love peace [hence it, too, is a supreme kind].

The prophet says [that the Lord requires of us] Only "to do justly, and to love mercy" (Micah 6:8) [which is also a supreme kind]. The aforementioned takes in "Honor your father" (Exodus 20:12); "You shall not murder" (Exodus 20:13); "You shall not commit adultery" (Exodus 20:13); "You shall not steal" (Exodus 20:13); "You shall not bear false witness against your neighbor" (Exodus 20:13); "You shall not covet" (Exodus 20:14); "Neither shall you deal falsely, nor lie one to another" (Leviticus 19:11); "Keep yourself far from a false matter" (Exodus 23:7); "nor favor the person of the mighty" (Leviticus 20:15); "neither shall you take a gift" (Deuteronomy 16:19); "You shall not oppress your neighbor, nor rob him" (Leviticus 19:13) "Just balances... shall you have" (Leviticus 19:36); "The wages of a hired servant shall not abide with you all night until the morning" (Leviticus 19:13); and "You shall not take vengeance, nor bear a grudge" (Leviticus 19:18); "a perfect and just measure shall you have" (Deuteronomy 25:15); "you shall leave them for the poor and for the stranger" (Leviticus 19:10); "If you lend money to any of My people [...you shall not be to him as a creditor]" (Exodus 22:24); "You shall not afflict any widow, fatherless child" (Exodus 22:21); "you shall not wrong [a stranger]" (Leviticus 19:33) and many other similar laws.

"And to walk humbly with your God" (Micah 6:8) includes all modes of behavior, statutes, and laws taught to us by God.

6. Commandments That Are No Longer Observed

There are many commandments whose time has passed. What need is there to count them among the six hundred and thirteen

---

16. According to Ibn Ezra, "to fear the Lord your God" is directed to people who do not understand that sin is intrinsically evil. It is directed to people who keep from sinning only out of fear of the Lord.

commandments?[17] Among the obsolete commandments are "And you shall take a bunch of hyssop…and none of you shall go out of the door of his house until the morning" (Exodus 12:22); "let no man go out of his place on the seventh day [to gather manna]" (Exodus 16:29); "you shall leave none of it until the morning" (Leviticus 22:30); and "Be ready against the third day" (Exodus 19:15).

[The same applies] to the commandments dealing with the construction of the Tabernacle,[18] and the manner of its journey (Numbers 41:34, 10:11–29), the banners (Numbers, ch. 2), and the sending forth of the unclean (Numbers 5:1–4).

[The same is the case with the commandment regarding the] use of a spade [to cover excrement] and the setting aside of a place in the camp [for people to relieve themselves] (Deuteronomy 23:14–15).

[The same also applies to the precepts commanding us] to wage war against enemies who no longer exist (Numbers 31:2, Deuteronomy 23:16–18), to utter the blessings and the curses (Deuteronomy 11:26–32, 27:11–26), to set up an altar on Mount Ebal (Deuteronomy 27:5), to plaster the stones (Deuteronomy 27:1–2), to write the Torah,[19] to set aside cities of refuge (Numbers 35:9.34), and to wage war against Amalek (Deuteronomy 25:17–19).

7. Instructions Not Included in the Count of 613

Some commandments were given to Moses alone [and thus are not to be counted in the list of 613 commandments]. Thus, when God made the covenant with Israel, He told Moses, "An altar of earth you shall make unto Me" (Exodus 20:21). Similarly, the commandments to hew out the tablets (Exodus 34:1) to erect the Tabernacle (Exodus 26:30, 40:1–2), to celebrate seven days of consecration (Leviticus 8:32), to anoint the Tabernacle (Exodus 30:26–29), to anoint Aaron (Exodus

---

17. See rule 3 of Maimonides' *Sefer Ha-Mitzvot*: "One should not count commandments that are not practiced in every generation [among the 613 commandments]."
18. Cf. Exodus 25–31; 35:4–39:43.
19. Upon the stones. Deuteronomy 27:3 (Stern).

29:7, 30:30, 40:15) and his sons (Exodus 30:30, 40:15), to place the *urim* and *tummim* upon the breastplate (Exodus 28:30), to place the tablets of the covenant in the ark (Exodus 25:21, Deuteronomy 10:2), and to make a copper serpent [lit., the incident of the copper serpent] (Numbers 21:8–9).

The same is the case with other commandments. Examples of the aforementioned are beating the fire pans into plates [lit., "the beaten plates"] (Numbers 17:3), the priests' placing the Torah close to the outside of the ark (Deuteronomy 31:26), setting aside a jar of manna (Exodus 16:32–34), and placing Aaron's staff in front of the ark (Numbers 17:25).

8. Supreme and Inferior Categories

Some commandments form a supreme category. "None of you shall approach to any that is near of kin to him" (Leviticus 18:6) is an example. On the other hand, the law prohibiting a man to uncover the nakedness of his father and mother (Leviticus 18:7) is an inferior category. Scripture begins [the list of those people with whom one is specifically prohibited from having sexual relations] by stating, "[The nakedness of your father and the nakedness of your mother shall you not uncover:] she is your mother [you shall not uncover her nakedness]" (Leviticus 18:7). The Torah therefore states, "You shall not uncover the nakedness of your father's sister: she is your father's near kinswoman" (Leviticus 18:12)[20] and "You shall not uncover the nakedness of your mother's sister for she is your mother's near kinswoman" (Leviticus 18:13).[21]

Those who counted the commandments counted every prohibited sexual act[22] as a separate commandment [even though they are all

---

20. That is, the nakedness of your father's sister falls into the category of the nakedness of your father.

21. That is, your mother's sister falls into the category of the nakedness of your mother.

22. Such as sexual relations with a sister, a brother, a son, a daughter, and so forth. The prohibited sexual acts are listed in Leviticus 18:7–21.

included in the supreme category of "None of you shall approach to any that is near of kin to him" (Leviticus 18:6)] because the penalties imposed by the law courts for their violation differ in some cases. The word *karet* ("cut off") includes them all.[23]

Now they [those who counted commandments] considered the prohibition to eat the flesh of unclean cattle (Leviticus 11:1–9, Deuteronomy 14:3–8), twenty types of fowl (Leviticus 11:13–19, Deuteronomy 12:11–18), creatures that swarm upon the earth (Leviticus 11:29–30), swarming things that fly (Leviticus 11:20–21, Deuteronomy 14:19), and things that swarm in the water (Leviticus 11:20–21, Deuteronomy 14:19) as one commandment.[24]

We know that the uncleanliness of the eight creeping things (Leviticus 11:29–30) is very strict.[25]

Scripture states, "and of their carcasses you shall not touch" (Leviticus 11:8) because[26] the swine, the rock-badger, the hare, and the camel

---

23. Leviticus 18:29 concludes, "For whosoever shall do any of these abominations, even the soul that do them shall be cut off from among their people." Thus, they ultimately receive the same penalty. Hence, as opposed to "those who counted the commandments," they should all be counted as one commandment.

   Heb. *karet*, lit., "cut off," is "a penalty inflicted by God...Some say that *karet* refers to death before the age of fifty-two. Others say it means the eradication of one's name via the death of one's children" (Ibn Ezra on Genesis 17:14).

24. They "considered the prohibition to eat flesh of unclean cattle, twenty types of fowl, creatures that swarm upon the earth, swarming things that fly and things that swarm in the water as one commandment," i.e., as one collective commandment, even though they counted each prohibited sexual act as a separate commandment.

25. A person who touches any of the eight creeping things "when they are dead" becomes unclean. Hence Scripture lists them by name.

26. According to the Torah, the carcass of whatsoever goes upon its paws, among all beasts that go on all fours (Leviticus 18:27) renders a person unclean. The question thus arises, Why then does Scripture single out the swine, the rock-badger, the hare, and the camel? – hence Ibn Ezra's comment.

each have one kosher sign.[27] The meaning of "and of their carcasses you shall not touch" is, being that you are holy, do not touch any carcass that will defile you. The same applies to fish.

Scripture states, "and their carcasses you shall have in detestation" (Leviticus 11:11) [do not touch them]. Scripture thus mentions them [i.e., the carcasses of fish], as it mentions all the other carcasses [in Leviticus 27]. The one who touches them does not incur the penalty of *karet* or stripes [the penalty incurred for eating unclean cattle, birds, or fowl].[28]

9. Commandments to Be
Observed Only Under Certain Conditions

There are certain negative commandments whose violation one can rectify [lit., "do"] and be free of guilt. For example, the Torah states, if at all possible, "you shall let nothing of it [the Paschal Lamb] remain until the morning" (Exodus 12:10). Scripture then goes on to say that should some of the Paschal Lamb remain until the morning then, "you shall burn it with fire" (Exodus 12:10). Similarly [concerning a woman who has been widowed without children], "her husband's brother shall go in unto her" (Deuteronomy 25:5) is not an obligatory commandment [for he has the option of refusing to marry his sister in law; see Deuteronomy 25:7–9]. If the husband's brother wants to "go in unto her," it is well with him and he shall receive his reward [for so doing]. However, if he refuses to do so, the law court will not force him [to perform the levir's duty].

---

27. The swine has split hooves. The rock-badger (Heb., *shafan*), hare, and camel chew their cud. Hence, one might think that their carcasses do not defile.

28. Simon and Cohen emend the text. They read: "The one who touches them does not incur the penalty of stripes [the penalty incurred for eating unclean cattle, birds, or fowl]. There is thus no reason to mention them by name."

10. Prohibited Sexual Behavior

There are additional categories of prohibited acts of sexual intercourse (in Scripture).[29] There is a prohibition that is limited to a specific kind, and there is a prohibition that also applies to other species. The prohibition against a man's having intercourse with another man (Leviticus 18:22) and the prohibition against having intercourse with any type of beast is an example (Leviticus 18:23). The last mentioned even applies to fowl. However, Scripture speaks about that which is most common [which is why the verse mentions "beasts" rather than "fowl"]. The Pentateuch thus states, "And God remembered Noah, and every living thing [nefesh hayyah], and all the cattle that were with him" (Genesis 8:1) [but does not mention fowl]. The aforementioned verse specifies animals [nefesh hayyah, "every living thing"] and cattle because they [unlike fowl] are important creatures, for they [land animals] were created on the same day as man [while fowl were created on the fifth]. Likewise, the law stating "and an ox or an ass fall therein [into a pit that a person has opened]" (Exodus 21:23) speaks of that which is most prevalent at this time [i.e., in the time of Moses]. The same law applies to horses, mules, and camels [even though they are not listed in Exodus 21:23].

There is also a prohibition relating to a female not of one's kind [i.e., a nonhuman female], such as a female beast (Leviticus 18:23).

There are also prohibitions against ever having intercourse with various types of human females, namely, the wife of one's father, one's sister, and one's daughter (Leviticus 18:8–10).

There are prohibitions that are in force only as long as a certain individual lives. The proscription of a married woman [only applies while her husband is alive, Leviticus 18:20], the proscription of a woman who is obligated to marry her brother-in-law,[30] and the prohibition

---

29. Lit. "There is another type of category pertaining to prohibited sexual acts." Scripture does not only prohibit the uncovering of the nakedness of one's father and mother. It also forbids other acts of sexual intercourse.

30. See Leviticus 18:16. If brother dies without children, then one of the surviving brothers marries his widow (Deuteronomy 25:5). According to

to have intercourse with the sister of one's wife[31] are examples of the aforementioned.

There is also a law prohibiting intercourse with a woman who is not of the Jewish faith. This proscription is removed if the woman accepts Judaism [lit., "with a woman who is not of the nation of the one who sleeps with her until she turns to his law"]. For Orpah returned to her people and to her god (Ruth 1:15).[32] However, Ruth said, "your people shall be my people, and your God my God" (Ruth 1:17) [that is, she accepted the God of Israel. Otherwise, Boaz would not have married her]. One who has intercourse with the above-mentioned, that is, with a woman who has not purified herself from her uncleanliness[33] to profess the unity of God, gives of his seed to the idols.[34]

There is also a law prohibiting one to fornicate with a woman,[35] whether she be a virgin or a widow, whom he is permitted to marry.[36]

There is also a prohibition against having intercourse with one's wife all the days "of the impurity of her sickness" (Leviticus 12:2, 18:19) and while she sits "in the blood of impurity" (Leviticus 12:1–6)[37] after giving birth to a male or female.

Jewish law, such a widow cannot remarry until the ceremony of *halitzah* is performed.

31. Leviticus 18:18. A man may marry his deceased wife's sister.
32. The implication being that she previously accepted the God of Israel. Otherwise, Elimelech's sons would not have married her. See Ibn Ezra on Ruth ch. 1.
33. That is, has not rejected idolatry, a play on 2 Samuel 11:4.
34. The Bible does not expressly prohibit having intercourse with a non-Jewish woman. However, since Scripture, in numerous places, exhorts Jews to bring up their children to worship the Lord, Ibn Ezra argues that it stands to reason that one is prohibited from having sexual relations with a non-Jewish woman, for she will bring up any children born of this union to be idol worshipers.
35. Maimonides derived this prohibition from Deuteronomy 23:18.
36. A high priest cannot marry a widow, hence Ibn Ezra's qualification.
37. Some editions read "blood of her purity."

11. Conditional Commandments

Some sections of the Torah are written in the form of commandments, but they are not really obligatory precepts. The section dealing with the "beautiful captive" (Deuteronomy 21:10–14) is an example. An Israelite is not permitted to take a captive woman to wife until he fulfills all the conditions stated in Scripture.

Do not be amazed that Scripture states [at the outset of the "captive woman" section], "and you shall desire her and you shall take her to you to wife" (Deuteronomy 21:11) [which appears to be a command]. For the Torah speaks of the captor's intention.[38] It is like the case of Pharaoh. For Scripture speaks of Pharaoh's designs when it says, "so I took her to be my wife" (Genesis 12:19).[39] The Torah similarly speaks of Balak's intention when it says that "Balak arose and fought against Israel" (Joshua 24:9).[40] "And after that you may go in unto her, and be her husband" (Deuteronomy 21:13) is conclusive proof of [that "and you shall take her to you to wife" means "and you want to take her to wife." For all the conditions that must be fulfilled before having sexual relations with the captive woman follow].

The following are the terms of the captive woman: Since the captor intends to take her to wife, he must bring her into his home and not leave her in the care of anyone else. The captive woman has to shave her head, and pare her nails (Deuteronomy 21:12) like a leper.[41]

Scripture does not have to note that she has to purify herself "with the waters of sprinkling"[42] because it is elsewhere written, "you and your captives [shall purify yourselves]" (Numbers 31:19).

---

38. Its meaning is "and you want to take her to you to wife." Indeed, the Jewish Publication Society renders, "and thou hast a desire unto her, and want to take her to thee to wife."

39. Pharaoh never touched Sarah. Hence, "so I took her to be my wife" means "so I intended to take her to be my wife."

40. Balak never fought Israel. Hence, "and fought against Israel" must be understood as "intended to fight Israel."

41. The leper shaves his head before undergoing the ritual of purification. See Leviticus 14:8.

42. Sprinkled on one purifying himself after coming in contact with the dead.

The captive woman "shall put the raiment of her captivity – which she wore when serving idols – from off her" (Deuteronomy 21:13), as it is written, "and change your garments" (Genesis 35:2).[43]

The captive woman shall "bewail her father and her mother a full month" (Deuteronomy 21:13), whether they were killed [in the war in which their daughter was taken captive]] or if they are still alive. The purpose of this delay [i.e., waiting thirty days] is to give her captor time to reverse himself and not take her. One who takes a daughter of Israel and does not have to fulfill all these conditions is behaving much better than this lusting captor.[44]

The above-discussed section of the Torah has no obligatory commandment aside from the precept "you shall not deal with her as a slave" (Deuteronomy 21:140).

12. Optional Benedictions

The same applies to benedictions.[45] There are benedictions that we are required to recite before performing obligatory precepts. On the other hand, there are benedictions praising God for permitting us to engage in a given act under certain conditions [in other words, the

---

See Numbers 19:1–22.

43. The complete verse reads, "Then Jacob said to his household, and to all that were with him: Put away the strange gods that are among you, and purify yourselves, and change your garments." Ibn Ezra in Genesis 35:2 explains that the washing of garments was to be done because one is obligated to wear clean garments when going to pray in a place designated for entreaty. He seems to say the same in Deut. 12:13 for there he notes that Scripture reads "and she shall put the raiment of her captivity off from her" because the raiments are filthy. Here he explains "and she shall put the raiment of her captivity off from her" as due to her wearing them while worshiping idols.

44. Thus, "and you shall take her to you to wife" and the conditions that follow cannot be construed as a command.

45. In the previous section, Ibn Ezra observed above that not all precepts are obligatory. He now goes on to say that the same applies to benedictions. Some are obligatory, and some are not.

commandment is not obligatory]. The benediction recited before ritually slaughtering an animal is an example of the aforementioned. If one pronounces this benediction before slaughtering the Passover offering, then one is uttering a blessing over a precept that must he observed [for one is obligated to bring a Passover offering]. It is akin to the blessing recited before circumcision. However, [if one recites a blessing before slaughtering an animal for food, then one is reciting a blessing over an optional act], for God did not command us to ritually slaughter animals. He merely prohibited the eating of flesh coming from an animal whose blood was shed in any way but that prescribed by Jewish law [i.e., *shehitah*].

The blessing recited before ritual slaughter is thus like the marriage blessing uttered under the nuptial canopy, wherein one notes that God has prohibited sexual relations with certain parties and those to whom we are betrothed but permitted us to have sexual relations with those to whom we are married.[46] Now, one who pronounces a benediction before ritually slaughtering an animal and goes on to examine its carcass and to remove the fat and sinews from it and then praises God after eating its flesh, is assured of his reward. If he does not do all of the above, then punishment awaits him.[47]

However, none of these acts are obligatory,[48] for there is no commandment to eat meat. There is no doubt that one who fasts and keeps himself from eating meat, as Daniel did (1:8–16), will receive a greater reward from God.[49] The same applies to one who fasts every

---

46. Ibn Ezra did not believe that there was a biblical obligation to marry.
47. If person kills an animal nonritually and eats its flesh, or if he ritually kills an animal and eats of its flesh without inspecting the carcass or removing the fat and sinews therefrom, he commits a sin and will be punished by being flogged.
48. Ritual slaughter, inspection of the carcass, and removing the fat and sinews are not obligatory commandments.
49. He will receive a greater reward than the one who eats meat and makes a blessing over it. Here Ibn Ezra shows himself partial to asceticism. Fasting is a greater religious act than reciting a blessing over food.

day and does not recite grace after meals.[50] Similarly, a Nazirite is not obligated to recite Kiddush and Havdalah or to drink four cups of wine at the Seder. The obligation for the aforementioned is only upon one who drinks wine.

I make mention of the above because I heard that a pious scholar used to wander in the streets searching for someone with a fowl so that he [the pious scholar] might ritually slaughter it.[51] The pious scholar's mind was on the blessing [rather than on the act of ritual slaughter]. He wanted to fulfill the daily quota of a hundred blessings.[52]

13. Negative Statements that Explain Commandments Are Not to Be Counted as Commandments

Some of the composers of Azharot[53] listed admonitions whose real purpose is to explain precepts, as negative commandments. The following are examples:

- "That his heart turn not away" (Deuteronomy 17:17) [which explains why a king cannot have many wives].

- "Nor cause the people to return to Egypt" (Deuteronomy 17:16) [which explains why a king cannot have many horses].

- "And that the breastplate be not loosed from the *ephod*" (Exodus 28:28). The meaning of the latter is, "When they shall bind the

---

50. A person who fasts every day and consequently does not recite grace after meals will receive a greater reward than one who eats and daily blesses God for providing him with food.

51. Which implies that there is an obligation to ritually slaughter an animal. Hence, the pious scholar ran looking for an opportunity to serve this commandment.

52. Cf. *Menahot* 43b: "Rabbi Meir says, A man is obligated to recite a hundred blessings each day."

53. The *Azharot* ("Exhortations") are liturgical poems devoted to the enumeration of the 613 commandments. The numerical value of the word "Azharot" is 613. The poems take their names from the first composition of this type, which opens with the line "Exhortations did You give to Your people of old."

breastplate [to the *ephod*] it shall not be moved" [from the breastplate].

- The verse which reads: "That he not die" (Exodus 28:35), like the verses quoted above, explains a preceding commandment [i.e., it explains why bells are to be attached to the bottom of Aaron's robe].

If it were not for tradition, then "they [the staves] shall not be taken from it [the ark]" (Exodus 25:15) would properly belong among the above.[54]

14. Confusing Optional and Obligatory Commandments

[Among the composers of the Azharot,] there are those who include optional acts among the commandments. They thus list "you may give it [i.e., anything that dies of itself] unto the stranger that is within your gates; or you may sell it unto a foreigner" (Deuteronomy 14:21) as a precept [even though he is permitted to dispose of the carcass in any manner he desires]. "You shall cast it [i.e., flesh torn by beasts] to the dog"[55] (Exodus 22:30) is similarly [optional], for its meaning is tied to "And you shall be holy men unto Me" (Exodus 22:30). The meaning of the verse is, "it is unfit for you to eat meat that has been torn. Give it rather to the dog that watches your sheep." Hence, the *lamed* of *la-kelev* [to the dog] is vocalized with a *pattah*.[56] The same would appear to be

---

54. According to the plain meaning of the text, this statement merely amplifies the first part of the verse that reads, "The staves shall be in the rings of the ark." However, Jewish tradition teaches that this is a separate prohibition in its own right: "Rabbi Elazar says, One who removes the staves from the ark is punished with stripes, for it is said, 'they shall not be taken from it'" (*Yoma* 72a).

55. According to Ibn Ezra, you do not have to necessarily cast the meat to a dog. Some opinions, however, held that "you shall cast it to the dog" is a commandment. See Azharot of Ibn Gabirol, who lists *ve-tet neveilah la-ger* among the 613 *mitzvot* (Simon and Cohen). Also See Tosafot, *Yoma* 31b, s.v. *lav de-nevelah*.

56. The *pattah* denotes the definite article. Thus, *la-kelev* means "to the dog,"

the case with "you shall make them serve forever" (Leviticus 25:46), were it not for a specific tradition [to the contrary].[57] [This tradition must be accepted] because we have received all the commandments from the patriarchs.[58] There is no difference between the words of the Torah and their words with regard to the commandments.[59] For they, too, were given unto us [at Sinai].

They [the Rabbis] received the tradition from their fathers and their fathers [received it] from the prophets. It [i.e., the Tradition] was all given by God via the hand of Moses.

15. Errors Made by the Authors of the Azharot in Computing the Commandments

I will now give you an example of one commandment that they [the composers of the Azharot] considered to be two, namely, "Remember

---

whereas *le-kelev* means "to a dog."

57. The verse can be translated "you shall make them serve" or "you may make them serve." According to the plain meaning, the verse appears to indicate that one may keep non-Hebrew slaves in perpetual bondage, but if one wishes to, one may free them. Rabbinic exegesis concludes that it is an imperative, and it is forbidden to free them. According to the Talmud, Leviticus 25:46 teaches that one must keep non-Hebrew slaves in perpetual servitude: "Rav Judah said in the name of Samuel, whoever frees his [non-Jewish] slave violates the positive commandment, 'you shall make them serve forever'" (*Gittin* 38b).

58. The Sages of the Talmud. They are referred to as *avot*, "fathers" or "patriarchs." Cf. *Pirkei Avot*.

59. Ibn Ezra held that with regard to practical observance, the rabbinic interpretation of a biblical text has the same status as that which is explicitly written in the Torah. Hence, if the Rabbis tell us that Leviticus 25:46 is a commandment and that the verse is to be understood as "you shall make them serve forever" rather than "you may make them serve forever," we accept the talmudic interpretation as if it were clearly and unambiguously so written in Scripture. When it comes to non-halakhic interpretations, however, then one may follow an independent course. See the first approach to biblical interpretation in Ibn Ezra's introduction to the Pentateuch.

the Sabbath day, to keep it holy" (Exodus 20:8) and "Observe the Sabbath day, to keep it holy" (Deuteronomy 5:12).[60]

Now "sanctifying the Sabbath" (Exodus 20:8, Deuteronomy 5:12), "calling the Sabbath a delight," "not following one's wonted ways on the Sabbath," "not pursuing one's affairs, nor speaking thereof on the Sabbath" [all mentioned in Isaiah 58:13] are all many commandments [relating to the Sabbath].[61] However, the thrust behind all of these commands is "you shall not do any manner of work [on the Sabbath]" (Exodus 20:9).[62]

One must keep in mind, during the days of the week, when the coming Sabbath falls.[63] He must keep this in mind.[64] Thus, "remember" means the same as "keep" [and they are one and the same commandment].

The Sabbath is sanctified, as explicitly stated in Jeremiah (17:22, 24) by not doing work on that day.[65] "Sabbath delight" (cf. Isaiah 58:13) refers to the body's rest from toil. One is not to pursue one's affairs nor speak thereof on the Sabbath, for doing so might lead one to do work on the Sabbath.

---

60. They count "Remember the Sabbath day to keep it holy" (Exodus 20:8) and "Observe the Sabbath day to keep it holy" (Deuteronomy 5:12) as two separate commandments. However, according to Ibn Ezra, they are one and the same precept.

61. Yet they are not counted as separate commandments. However, employing the logic of those who count "Remember" and "Observe" as two separate *mitzvot*, we should also count all the precepts in Isaiah 58:13 as separate commandments. See *Shabbat* 11a and 11b.

62. Ibn Ezra's point is that the precepts in Isaiah 58:13 are all subsumed by Exodus 20:9.

63. Ibn Ezra interprets Exodus 20:8 to mean that one is obligated to remember the Sabbath during the other days of the week.

64. Ibn Ezra interprets Deuteronomy 5:12 to mean that one must keep the day on which Sabbath falls in mind all the days of the week.

65. This explains "to keep it holy" (or "to sanctify it") in Exodus 20:8 and Deuteronomy 5:12.

16. The Problem with the Azharot

Among the Azharot we find "Circumcise therefore the foreskin of your heart" (Deuteronomy 10:16) among the positive commandments and "and be no more stiff-necked" (Deuteronomy 10:16) among the negative precepts. I asked the great men of our generation to explain to me the meaning of these verses [since these verses cannot be taken literally]. Their response was to dismiss me with a broken reed, the way they do with students who do not have a mind [lit., "heart"] that can discern between truth and falsehood.[66]

Now those who wrote the Azharot are like a person who counts the number of herbs written in medical books without knowing the benefit of each and every herb.[67] What benefit does he derive from knowing their names?

Scripture sometimes employs two terms with regard to a commandment. "Remember, forget you not [how you provoked the Lord your God to wrath in the wilderness]" (Deuteronomy 9:7) is an example. However, an author of Azharot considered "Remember" and "forget you not" to be two different commandments [and counted them as such]. I will explain the latter verse in its proper place. Many other such commandments are found in the Torah without anyone paying attention.

---

66. They apparently gave Ibn Ezra an aggadic interpretation. In his commentary on Deuteronomy 10:16, Ibn Ezra explained that to circumcise one's heart means to purify one's heart. In his commentary on Exodus 32:9, he explained that to be stiff-necked means to refuse to respond to those who call on him to repent. He similarly explains the above later on in Chapter 7.
67. In his introduction to the *Sefer Ha-Mitzvot*, Maimonides also noted that many of the Azharot were written by poets, not rabbis.

Chapter III

COMMANDMENTS THAT BRANCH OUT

1. The Nazir

Some commandments consist of basic regulation [lit., "root"], along with its hedges.[1] The Nazirite who must abstain from wine and strong drink (Numbers 6:3) for the duration of his Nazirite vow, because wine eliminates reasoning and increases lust is a case in point. Thus, Daniel fasted and did not drink wine on Passover (Daniel 10:3–4).[2] For the obligation to [drink wine on Passover] is rabbinic.[3]

---

1. Secondary regulations that "protect" the primary object of the precept. For example, a Nazirite is primarily prohibited from drinking wine. However, the Torah also prohibits the Nazirite from drinking any grape extract as a "hedge."
2. See Ibn Ezra 10:2–5: "In those days I, Daniel, was mourning three whole weeks. I ate no pleasant bread, neither came flesh nor wine in my mouth, neither did I anoint myself at all, till three whole weeks were fulfilled." Scripture then goes on to say that in the four and twentieth day of the first month Daniel saw a vision. The above indicates that Daniel mourned for twenty-one days and that his mourning ended after he saw an encouraging vision. Counting back twenty-one days from the twenty-fourth day of the first month brings us to the third day of the first month. Thus Daniel did not drink wine from the third day of Nissan until the twenty-first day of Nisan, meaning he did not drink wine at the Passover Seder.
3. Ibn Ezra apparently held that the Bible would not command a person

Now, God prohibited the Nazirite from taking vinegar [of wine] and the partaking of any liquor of grapes, pressed grapes, or grape stone (Numbers 6:3–4). Furthermore, [the Torah says that] a razor shall not come upon the head of a Nazirite (Numbers 6:5) so that he does not make himself attractive to women.[4] A Nazirite who abstains only from wine will not be completely holy to God. He will be so only by abiding by all of the aforementioned commandments. This is the reason [for the additional prohibitions].

The ancients did the same with the prohibition of eating on the Day of Atonement.[5] Now abstaining from food is the essence of a fast. Indeed, whenever Scripture speaks of afflicting the soul [lit., "whenever the word 'affliction' is connected to the soul"] the reference is to fasting,[6] for the power of the lusting soul[7] is in the liver.[8] We thus read, "Because your soul desires to eat meat" (Deuteronomy 12:20); "And his soul desires food" (Job 33:20);[9] "And the soul that eats of it" (Leviticus 7:18).

"Why have we fasted, and You do not see? Why have we afflicted our soul, and You take no knowledge?" (Isaiah 58:3), wherein the second half of the verse, which repeats what is written in the first half of the

---

to drink wine, for wine induces passion. Hence, he points out that the obligation to drink wine on Passover is of rabbinic origin.

4. Ibn Ezra's interpretation of the law prohibiting a Nazirite to cut his hair. The Torah itself does not offer any reason for this prohibition.

5. The Bible states with regard to the Day of Atonement, "you shall afflict your souls" (Leviticus 16:29). According to Ibn Ezra, this means "you shall abstain from food." However, the Rabbis also prohibited one to drink, wash, anoint oneself, wear shoes, or engage in sexual relations on the Day of Atonement. See Yoma 76a.

6. In other words, the fundamental meaning of "and you shall afflict your souls" (Leviticus 16:31) requires fasting.

7. Or "vegetable soul." According to Ibn Ezra, there are three souls in the body: a rational soul, an animal soul, and a vegetable soul. See Chapter 7.

8. And suffers when food is denied to the body. Hence, Scripture speaks of the affliction of the soul.

9. Translated according to Ibn Ezra.

line, also proves that affliction of the soul refers to fasting. "Is such a fast that I have chosen? The day for a man to afflict his soul?" (Isaiah 58:5) and "And satisfy the afflicted soul [with food]" (Isaiah 58:10) are additional proof that afflicting the soul is another term for fasting.

I have already explained why the *bet* of *ba-tzom* ["in the fast"] in "I afflicted my soul in the fast" (Psalm 35:13) is vocalized with a *pattah*.[10]

The Sages said that [in addition to eating], drinking is also prohibited on the Day of Atonement, because Scripture states, "And you shall eat before the Lord your God ... the tithe of your corn, of your wine, and of your oil" (Deuteronomy 14:23) [we thus see that Scripture considers drinking wine as eating; see *Yoma* 76a].

The book of Daniel tells us, "neither did I anoint myself at all" (Daniel 10:3).[11] It then goes on to say, "you did set your heart to understand, and to afflict [*le-hitanot*] yourself before your God" (Daniel 10:12).[12] The word "soul" is not mentioned [for Daniel ch. 10 does not deal with fasting].

Now, it is also prohibited to bathe on the Day of Atonement (*Yoma*

---

10. Rather than with a *sheva*. "I afflicted my soul in the fast" is difficult. If it means "I fasted," why add in "the fast"? Ibn Ezra answers that "in the fast" refers to a specific fast. For the *pattah* beneath the *bet* indicates the definite article. See Ibn Ezra on Ps. 35:13: The *bet* of *ba-tzom* ("in fasting") is vocalized with a *pattah*. [A *bet* so vocalized indicates the direct object: *ba-tzom* (with fasting) thus means, "in *the* fast."] Ps. 35:13 reads: "But as for me [David], when they were sick, my clothing was sackcloth, I afflicted my soul with fasting." According to Ibn Ezra the meaning of the verse is: when they were sick I afflicted my soul in *the fast* that was called on their behalf.

11. During three weeks of mourning. We thus see that one who refrains from anointing himself is afflicting himself. The Rabbis prohibited anointing oneself on the Day of Atonement.

12. Heb. *le-hitanot*, lit. "to afflict," is another form of the root of the word *ve-initem*, "and you shall afflict," which, when connected to the word *nefesh*, means "to fast."

76b). However, the Rabbis said that one who has a seminal emission should bathe himself.[13]

How apt are the words of the ancients who said, "And be careful to perform a minor precept just as well as a major one" (*Avot* 2:1)[14] and "The reward of a precept is the precept itself" (*Avot* 4:2).[15]

2. The Decalogue

Behold, the first five statements of the Decalogue relate to God.[16] They are connected to the heart [i.e., directed at man's intelligence] and are the most important [of the ten statements].[17] The Sixth Commandment, which opens the series of statements dealing with interpersonal relationships, begins with "You shall not murder" (Exodus 20:13). This commandment is the most important of the statements dealing with man's relationship to his fellow man.

I will now state a general rule. The death penalty and the punishment of excision are imposed only for violations of negative commandments. For the violator of a negative commandment angers God much more than a person who is too lazy to observe a positive commandant [lit., "to do what he is commanded]. I have not found

---

13. On the Day of Atonement. See *Yoma* 77b. We thus see that bathing is not an essential part of fasting. Otherwise, the Sages would not permit a person who had a seminal emission to bathe.
14. Ibn Ezra apparently takes a minor precept to refer to the above-noted rabbinic laws pertaining to Yom Kippur. It is also possible that he equally applies it to the "hedges," which the Bible itself built around certain laws.
15. Ibn Ezra understands this to mean "the reward [for keeping the hedges] of the commandment is [that the fundamental] commandment [itself is preserved]."
16. Since this chapter deals with laws and their hedges, Ibn Ezra points out that the same is true of the Decalogue. It is the most important part of the Torah. For the rest of the laws in the Torah are extensions of the statements found in the Decalogue.
17. These five commandments relate to one's mind. Later on, Ibn Ezra points out that the commandments dealing with the heart are the most important precepts of the Torah.

the penalty of excision inflicted as a punishment for the violation of a positive commandment except for circumcision (see Genesis 17:14), for circumcision is a lifelong sign of the covenant in the body, [and for not eating the Passover sacrifice, as mentioned in the next paragraph]. The law requires that it [i.e., circumcision] be performed once. The obligation to circumcise a newborn child falls on the father or on the head of the Bet Din. However, if the child was not circumcised and does not have himself circumcised when he grows up, then he incurs the penalty of excision.

The penalty of excision is also incurred by one who refrains from offering the Passover sacrifice, for the recollection of the Exodus is the root of all the commandments.[18] Hence following "You shall make for yourselves no molten gods" (Exodus 34:17), Scripture states, "The feast of unleavened bread shall you keep" (Exodus 34:18). Similarly, the answer given by the Torah to "What mean the testimonies, and the statutes, and the ordinances mean?" (Deuteronomy 6:20) is, "We were Pharaoh's bondmen in Egypt [and the Lord brought us out of Egypt with a mighty hand]" (Deuteronomy 6:21).

3. A Commandment Which
Takes in All Positive Commandments

I will now allude to a commandment [reading "Cursed is he who does not confirm the words of this law to do them" (Deuteronomy 27:26)"]. The aforementioned includes all positive precepts.[19] It is a precept, the violation of which is punished by the penalty of excision.[20]

When we searched for a reason as to why certain individuals are cursed, we found that they are cursed for acts done in secret (see

---

18. The commandments serve to recall the Exodus. Here, too, Ibn Ezra points out a commandment that branches out. Indeed, all other commandments are based on it.
19. Thus it, too, is a basic law with many branches.
20. According to Ibn Ezra "cursed" means "God will excise him or her." Furthermore Ibn Ezra is of the opinion that this penalty is meted out to all who refuse to obey the commandments.

Deuteronomy 27:15–26). Thus, Scripture begins the list of those who are cursed with one [who makes an idol and sets it up in secret] (Deuteronomy 27:15). Indeed, it is clear that most of the offenses for which one is cursed are done in secret.[21] The reason why someone who has relations with his sister or mother-in-law is cursed (Deuteronomy 27:22–23) is that a person may be alone with them without anyone's suspecting [that they are engaging in sexual activity].

Similarly, one who has relations with an animal is cursed (Deuteronomy 27:21), because the animal cannot speak [and therefore has no recourse for redress].

At the end of the list of curses, Scripture states, "Cursed be he that does not confirm [in secret to anger God] the words of this law to do them" (Deuteronomy 27:26), for if he does so in public, the Bet Din will either force him to comply [with the positive commandments] or penalize him [if he refuses to obey or violates the law].

It therefore seems that the meaning of "these" [in "Do not defile yourself in all of these things [be-khol elleh]"] (Leviticus 18:24)[22] is ["one of these"], for it is similar to the word "these" in "If one who is unclean by a dead body touches all of these" (Haggai 2:13) [where "all of these" means "any of these"].

The sacrifice offered for a sin committed in error (see Leviticus 4:2) proves that a person who deliberately and brazenly sins in public profanes the name of God.[23] Indeed, we see that the entire congregation of Israel violated the precept "you shall keep alive nothing that

---

21. Scripture curses those who commit incest and bribery and remove landmarks. These offenses are usually committed only in secret.

22. Literal translation. Since Ibn Ezra deals with sexual violations mentioned in Deuteronomy 27:15–26, he also comments on the sexual acts prohibited in Leviticus 18:1–23. His point is that we should not take "Do not defile yourself in 'all of these' things" (Leviticus 18:24) literally as meaning that one should not violate all the sexual acts that precede this verse because Deuteronomy 27:26 indicates that violating one of them incurs a curse. In other words, kol elleh is to be rendered "one of these" or "any of these," but not "all of these."

23. If an inadvertent act contrary to the will of God is sinful, so much more

breathes" (Deuteronomy 20:15) in order not to profane the name of God [when they spared the Gibeonites; see Joshua 9:26]. They acted in this manner because of the oath that they had taken [to not harm the Gibeonites; see Joshua 9:15].

---

so when the act is performed with intention. Deliberate acts which are not atoned for bring down God's wrath on the perpetrator.

Chapter IV

COMMANDMENTS CONTINGENT ON TIME, PLACE, AND GENDER

1. Commandments Depending on Particular Circumstances

Some precepts, such as the commandments to provide burnt offerings,[1] shewbread (Exodus 25:30), wine for libations,[2] and oil for the lights,[3] are incumbent on the congregation. Other commandments, such as the laws pertaining to high priests (Leviticus 21:10–13), ordinary priests (Leviticus 21:1–15), and the Levites (Numbers 3:5–10, 8:23–26), are obligatory for specific families [in this case, the family (tribe) of Levi]. There are many such commandments. A number of commandments, such as the laws relating to a king (Deuteronomy 17:16–20), a Nazirite (Numbers 6:1–21), a leper (Leviticus 13–14), and the unclean,[4] apply to specific individuals [i.e., kings, lepers, the unclean, etc.]. Family origin plays no role in these laws.[5]

---

1. Offered daily and on new moons and festivals. Cf. Exodus 29:38–42; Numbers 28; 29.
2. Which accompanied the sacrifices. See Leviticus 23:13.
3. Kindled every evening in the Temple. See Exodus 25:6, 35:14; Leviticus 24:2.
4. Leviticus 5:2–3; 6:13; 7:21; 15:1–33; Numbers 9:10–12; 19:9–22.
5. Some laws apply only to priests, hence Ibn Ezra's qualification.

Most of the commandments encompass both men and women. Others, such as the laws relating to circumcision (Genesis 17:10–14, Leviticus 12:3), nocturnal emissions (Deuteronomy 23:10–11), the firstborn (Exodus 13:2, 11–12, Numbers 18:15), the redemption of the firstborn (Numbers 13:13, 18:15–16), and primogeniture [lit. "receiving a double share," see Deuteronomy 21:15–16], apply only to males.

Some precepts, such as the laws dealing with a menstruant (Leviticus 15:19–20, 25:30), childbirth (Leviticus 12:1–8), a suspected adulteress (Numbers 5:11–31), the seduction of a young virgin (Exodus 22:15), and the vows of a married woman and a minor (Numbers 30:4–16), apply only to females.

Some commandments, such as the burnt offerings (Leviticus 1:17), the additional offerings [offered on festivals], and the three pilgrimages (Exodus 24:14–17, Deuteronomy 16:16–17), are contingent on an outside factor, namely, the place chosen by God [these commandments are not solely dependent on our will to observe them. Rather, they require the existence of the Temple]. There are many such commandments.

Among the commandments that depend on outside factors are [the following]:

- If we have a son we must circumcise him.

- If our son is a firstborn we must redeem him (Exodus 13:13, Numbers 18:15).

- If we plant a tree, we are prohibited to eat its fruit for three years. However, we may harvest its fruit in the fourth year (Leviticus 19:23–24, Deuteronomy 20:6).

- If we have a field or a vineyard, we must tithe its produce (Deuteronomy 14:22–27).

- If we lend money, then we must not act like creditors (Exodus 22:24).

- If we suspect our wives of adultery, then we must act according to the law (Numbers 5:11–31).

- If we have male or female slaves, or if someone takes a woman,[6] we must follow the procedures laid down by Scripture (Exodus 12:44, 20:10, 21:2–11, 32; Deuteronomy 5:14, 15:12–18, 23:16–17).

There are many similar precepts. Most of them consist of laws and ordinances [Heb. *dinim u-mishpatim,* i.e., laws dealing with interpersonal relationships].

Some commandments are contingent on time. Examples of the latter are circumcision, which is to be performed on the eighth day following birth (Genesis 17:12, Leviticus 12:3) and vows of valuations (Leviticus 27:2–8) which differ [in number] from a month old to age five (Leviticus 27:6), from age five to age twenty (v. 5), and from age twenty to age sixty (v. 3).

The observance of many precepts, such as circumcision (*Pesahim* 4a, *Megillah* 20a, *Yevamot* 72b) and the burnt offering (*Tamid* 3:2–3, *Zevahim* 10:1, *Pesahim* 5:1) is limited to daytime. Others, such as the eating of the Paschal Lamb (Exodus 12:8–11) and the counting of the *omer* (Leviticus 23:15, *Menahot* 66a) are limited to nighttime. Some, such as the lighting of the lamps [in the Temple] (Exodus 27:21) and the entrance of the unclean into the camp (Deuteronomy 23:12), are observed between day and night [i.e., at dusk]. The latter is also the deadline for the sacrifice of the Paschal Lamb (Exodus 12:6). The observance of other commandments, such as reciting the *Minhah* prayers (*Berakhot* 27b) and the time when the Paschal Lamb may first be slaughtered (*Pesahim* 61a), commences at noon.

Some commandments, such as the Sabbath, are observed once a week (Exodus 20:8–10, Deuteronomy 5:12–14). Others, such as Shavuot (Exodus 34:22, Leviticus 23:3, Deuteronomy 16:10), Yom Ha-Zikkaron (i.e., Rosh Hashanah, the New Year; Leviticus 23:24–25), Yom Kippur (Leviticus 23:26–32), and Shemini Atzeret (v. 36), are observed once a year.

Other commandments are observed for seven days. The eating of

---

6. If someone marries a woman. See Cohen and Simon, p. 120.

matzot, which according to the plain meaning of the text is obligatory for seven days,[7] is an example of the latter because Scripture mentions the Paschal Lamb and then says, "seven days shall you eat unleavened bread therewith... that you may remember the day when you came forth out of the land of Egypt" (Deuteronomy 16:3). Scripture thus points out that *matzot* are to be eaten for seven days because the Israelites ate *matzot* for seven days [following their departure from Egypt], for the cloud went before Israel day and night [from the moment they left Egypt] until Pharaoh drowned.[8] Moses [alone, without the cloud accompaniment] – as I have already explained in its place (see Exodus 12:15, 22) – then caused Israel to journey until the Tabernacle was erected.[9]

The same is the case with the seven days of Sukkot (Leviticus 23:42–43) and the lighting of the Hanukkah lamps for eight days (*Shabbat* 21b). It is also the same with the reading of the Scroll of Esther in its proper time [on the eve and day of Purim; *Megillah* 2a, 4a], the reading of the entire Hallel (Psalms 113–118) in eighteen days and one night,[10] the reading of half of the Hallel[11] on every new moon (*Taanit* 28b) and [the last] six days of Passover (*Arakhin* 10a–10b), counting the *omer* for seven weeks (Leviticus 23:15–16), and the sanctification of the seventh and the fiftieth year (Leviticus 27:1–12).

There are many commandments that are not dependent on any outside factor or on a specific time. They are obligatory for all Israelites who have reached the age of commandment observance [age twelve for a female and thirteen for a male]. These commandments apply

---

7. In contrast to the rabbinic opinion, which holds that the obligation to eat *matzot* is limited to the first night of Passover. See *Pesahim* 120a.

8. On the eve of the seventh day. During these seven days, Israel had no time to bake leavened bread.

9. This sentence has nothing to do with the reason for eating *matzot* for seven days. Ibn Ezra inserted it merely for informational purposes.

10. The eighteen days are: eight days of Sukkot, eight days of Hanukkah, the first day of Passover, and the day of Shavuot. The one night is the first night of Passover.

11. Psalms 113–118 with the exclusion of Psalms 115:1–11 and 116:1–11.

to all, whether they are male or female, king or priest, poor or rich, healthy or plagued. They oblige both [native-born] Israelites and proselytes. There is one law for all. These commandments are fundamental precepts [Hebrew, *ikkarim*, lit., "roots"].

Chapter v

THE FUNDAMENTAL
COMMANDMENTS

1. Commandments Based on Reason

The fundamental commandments [mentioned at the end of chapter 4] are those precepts that are implanted in the heart.[1] They are not contingent on place, time, or anything else. They are called *pikkudim* ["charges"] because they are like a deposit [*pikkadon*] placed in the hands of a bailee for safekeeping [for they come from man's rational soul, which is placed in the body as a deposit to be ultimately withdrawn]. King David therefore says, "The charges [*pikkudei*] of the Lord are right" (Psalms 19:9).[2] The *pikkudim* were known by reason before the Torah was given through the agency of Moses.

There are many such precepts. The Decalogue is an example, with the exclusion of the Sabbath [which is a law known only by tradition rather than reason].

The *pikkudim* [though previously known by reason] were repeated

---

1. Rational laws that can be discovered through reason, for example, not to murder, not to steal, and so forth.
2. For they are based on reason. God is the source of reason and He deposited (*pakad*) some of His reason in human beings in the form of commandments, called *pikkudim*. It is worthy of note that Rabbi Judah Ha-Levi identifies wisdom with God. He writes: "God is called 'wise in heart' (Job 9:4) because He is *etzem ha-hokhmah* [the essence of wisdom]."

by Moses. Scripture speaks of the *pikkudim* when it states, "and [Abraham] kept My charge, My commandments, My statutes, and My laws" (Genesis 26:5).[3] For if our father Jacob knew the law regarding all of those with whom one is prohibited to have sexual relations, he would not have married two sisters at one time.[4] We therefore interpret "for all these abominations[5] have the men of the land done" (Leviticus 18:27) as referring to most of the prohibited sexual acts – such as male homosexuality, which is contrary to God's will and is an abomination contrary to the laws of nature.[6] The same applies to a man or a woman practicing bestiality (Leviticus 18:23) and to engaging in sexual relations with very close relatives. Therefore, "that is near unto him" (Leviticus 21:3) should be connected to "his sister," who is the daughter of his father and mother.[7] The verse is similar to "and Israel saw the Egyptians dead upon the seashore" (Exodus 14:30).[8] Abraham therefore said, "And moreover she is indeed my sister, the daughter of my father, but not the daughter of my mother" (Genesis 20:12).[9]

---

3. Ibn Ezra clearly implies that the patriarchs observed only the rational laws. This is contrary to the opinion of the rabbinic sage Rav, who held that Abraham observed the entire Torah (*Yoma* 28b). See Ibn Ezra on Genesis 26:5: "The statutes spoken of in our verse [that the Torah says that Abraham kept] refer ... to statutes based on reason."

4. The fact that Jacob married two sisters, in violation of Leviticus chs. 18 and 20, shows that this rule is a traditional, rather than a rational law.

5. Reason dictates that one may not do anything contrary to the laws of nature.

6. However, it does not apply to such acts as taking two sisters or engaging in any other sexual act not prohibited by reason.

7. Leviticus 21:3 permits a priest to defile himself for "his dead sister, a virgin, that is near to him." According to Ibn Ezra, this phrase should be interpreted as if written "for his dead sister that is near unto him, a virgin." According to Ibn Ezra, "that is near unto him" refers to a full sister. A half-sister is not considered a near relative.

8. Exodus 14:30 is to be understood as if written "and Israel standing on the seashore saw the Egyptians dead." We thus see that at times the words in a verse have to be rearranged for clarity. See Ibn Ezra on Exodus 14:30.

9. Hence, Abraham did not violate any of the Torah's rational laws, because

The fact that the Bet Din does not punish [for this sin] is proof of this [that marrying two sisters is not prohibited by reason].[10]

Should someone ask "Why does the law differentiate between a sister and a brother?"[11] Perhaps he can tell us why it distinguishes between a virgin[12] and a non-virgin,[13] but does not do so in the case of a brother.[14]

2. Commandments Which
Remind Us of the Fundamental Precepts

Some commandments serve as reminders of the fundamental precepts. For example, the Sabbath commemorates creation [and belief in creation is a fundamental concept]. Likewise, not permitting one's slave to work on the Sabbath recalls the Exodus from Egypt (see Deuteronomy 5:14–15). Similarly, the Paschal Lamb, the *matzot*, the bitter herbs, the *sukkah*, the *mezuzah*, and the *tefillin* worn on the hand and head [all serve as reminders]. Likewise, the *tzitzit* [serve as reminders; see Numbers 15:41]. This is so [that the *tzitzit* serve as reminders] even though the lack of blue thread [which serves as a memorial] does not keep one from fulfilling the precept.[15] We also

---

a half-sister is not prohibited by rational law.

10. This is the reading in the Levin, Waxman and other editions of the *Yesod Mora*, p. 327. By "the Bet Din does not punish [for this sin]" Ibn Ezra probably means that the Bet Din does not inflict the death penalty for having sexual relations with a sister as it does for other sexual violations, such as adultery.

   Other texts read, "there is no penalty of *karet*." The latter reading contradicts Lev. 20:17. See Cohen and Simon, p. 125.

11. Lit. "Why a sister and not a brother?" In other words, why does Scripture permit a priest to defile himself to a dead sister only when she is a full sister but does not make this requirement of a brother?

12. A priest may defile himself to a sister who is a virgin (Leviticus 21:3).

13. A priest may not defile himself to a sister who is not a virgin (see Leviticus 21:3).

14. A priest may defile himself to his brother whether married or not.

15. One of the fringes was blue. See Numbers 15:38. According to Ibn Ezra, it

find that the lack of bitter herbs does not prevent one from fulfilling the precept of eating *matzot* [even though both must be eaten on the eve of Passover; see Exodus 12:8].

For it is the blue that serves as a memorial. Hence, the robe of the *ephod* was entirely blue (Exodus 28:32), and the holy plate of the holy crown (Exodus 39:30)[16] was tied with a blue thread (Exodus 39:31).

Now, the person who envelops himself in a *tallit* [only during prayer] does not fully observe the commandment.

In reality, one is obligated to do so [i.e., to wear fringes] the entire day, for when a person is in the market and his eyes wander [lit., "and sees forms"], his heart lusts after what his eyes see much more than it does during prayer.

I note the above because I have seen many people who do not fear the Lord envelop themselves in a *tallit* [during prayer] in order to bring honor to themselves.

The *ephod* and the breastplate [of the High Priest; see Exodus 28:15] also serve as memorials.[17] The same is the case with the law prohibiting the eating of the sinew of the thigh vein [Hebrew, *gid ha-nasheh*] (Genesis 32:33). The latter too serves as a memorial. This law is in marked contrast to the law commanding the eating of the Paschal Lamb [which serves as a memorial].[18]

I will now explain [why it is prohibited to eat the sinew of the thigh vein].

When a father accepts something upon himself and his offspring, his son is obligated to obey his father. This is the reason why the people of Israel observe the days of Purim (Esther 9:28) and the

---

was this blue thread that served as a reminder of God's commandments. Cf. *Mishnah, Menahot* 4:1.

16. Heb. *tzitz nezer ha-kodesh*, etymologically related to the word *tzitzit*, "fringes."

17. I. Levin's edition adds, "I will explain their meanings later."

18. The point is that in one case, the prohibition serves as the memorial, while in the other, the eating serves as the memorial.

fasts [mentioned in Esther 9:31 and Zechariah 8:19]. If the son does not observe the latter, he violates the commandment of God who is All.[19]

The reason for not eating the sinew of the thigh vein is to perpetuate the memory of the loving-kindness that God showed to Jacob, who alone is our father. Unlike Abraham and Isaac, no one shares Jacob with us, for God chose Jacob whose descendants, unlike those of Abraham, were not intermingled with those whom God did not choose nor did he defile himself with their food or the wine of their feasts.[20] The aforementioned is in keeping with the way of the Torah, which notes, "Cursed be Canaan" (Genesis 9:25). The meaning of the latter is that the people of the children of Israel [i.e., Jacob], who is [one] of the sons of Shem, who is the father of all the children of Eber, shall trace their descent back to the one whom Noah blessed [Shem] (Genesis 9:26) and shall not intermingle with cursed seed.

The prophet says, "The Lord has also a controversy with Judah, and will punish Jacob" (Hosea 12:3). "And will punish Jacob" means that the Lord will punish the children of Jacob. The phrase "with Judah" is proof of this.[21] The prophet goes on to say, "In the womb he took his brother by the heel" (Hosea 12:4). This indicates that God gave Jacob the strength to grasp the heel of his brother Esau before he [Jacob] went out of the womb. The Lord did not do the same to any who were born.

The opinion of those who say that Jacob took hold of his brother's heel after he went out of the womb is incorrect. For Scripture states,

---

19. On Genesis 1:26, Ibn Ezra wrote, "God is One. He is the creator of all. He is all."
20. Abraham married Hagar the Egyptian, a Hammite (see Ibn Ezra on Genesis 10:21), and whose descendants include Ishmael and the children of Keturah and other concubines (see Genesis 25:1–6). Isaac's descendants include Esau. Unlike Abraham and Isaac, Jacob had descendants who are all included in the Jewish people.
21. The reference is not to the patriarch Jacob, but to the nation that descended from him. Judah parallels Jacob. As Judah refers to the people of Judah, so does Jacob refer to the people of Jacob.

"[And after that came forth his brother,] and his hand had hold on Esau's heel" (Genesis 25:26). If things were as they say, Scripture would have read, "And after that came forth his brother and his hand took hold of Esau's heel." Furthermore, Scripture states, "In the womb he took his brother by the heel, and by his strength, he strove with an angel" (Hosea 12:4), that is, Jacob strove with the angel and the angel could not overcome him [which is recalled by observing the prohibition of *gid ha-nasheh*].

Jacob is thus very exalted.[22] Furthermore [i.e., another reason for the prohibition of eating the sinew], from the standpoint of the science of medicine, every healthy [animal] organ strengthens its counterpart [in a human], and every weak organ harms it.[23]

Now since Scripture states "and the hollow of Jacob's thigh was strained" (Genesis 32:26), it goes on to say that it is therefore prohibited to eat the sinew of the thigh vein from that day forward.[24] Jacob's descendants are obligated to respect their father.

I had to expand on the above at length because it is in accordance with the plain meaning of the text. For the account of Jacob and the angel was mentioned in the Torah only because of the law prohibiting the eating of the sinew of the thigh vein (Genesis 32:33) [thus, the law was given to recall something that happened to Jacob]. The law regarding circumcision differs, for it is written, "And in the eighth day the flesh of his foreskin shall be circumcised" (Leviticus 12:3).[25]

---

22. The law prohibiting the eating of the sinew of the thigh vein recalls Jacob's strength.

23. The *gid ha-nasheh* being a weak organ, that is, an unhealthy organ, weakens its counterpart in the human body.

24. "Therefore the children of Israel eat not the sinew of the thigh vein...to this day" (Genesis 32:33) refers back to "and the hollow of Jacob's thigh was strained" (Genesis 32:26). In other words, Genesis 32:33 is to be understood as follows: Therefore – because the hollow of Jacob's thigh was strained – "the children of Israel do not eat the sinew of the thigh vein...to this day."

25. We do not circumcise our sons in memory of Abraham's having done so.

Concerning the orphan and the widow, Scripture states, "And you shall remember that you were a bondman in Egypt" (Deuteronomy 16: 12)[26] and do not lord over God's work.[27]

    Since the law is codified in Leviticus without mentioning Abraham, we see that the practice is independent of what happened to him.

26. Thus, this commandment, like many of those noted above (e.g., *sukkah*, *mezuzah*), serves to recall the Exodus.

27. By refusing to give the stranger, the widow, and the orphan their due. See Deuteronomy 16:11–12. Ibn Ezra refers to the widow, orphan, and stranger as God's work. The clause "and do not lord over God's work" is a paraphrase of, "and you shall observe and do these statutes."

Chapter VI
SOURCES OF THE COMMANDMENTS

1. The Written and Oral Laws

Some commandments are clearly explained in the Torah. However, there are precepts whose true meaning has come down to us through the holy transmitters of the Torah [the sages who transmitted the written and oral law from generation to generation; see *Avot* 1:1]. The latter received the tradition [of how these commandments are to be explained], sons from their fathers and students from their teachers.[1] It should be noted that were it not for tradition, one would be able to explain these commandments differently.[2] There are also commandments that we received from the Sages that are not mentioned in the Torah at all.

Let me state a general rule:

If it were not for the men of the great assembly and the Sages of the Mishnah and Talmud, the Torah of our God and its very memory

---

1. Ibn Ezra refers to commandments such as donning *tefillin* or not eating meat with milk. The law regarding the wearing of *tefillin* is based on Exodus 13:9, 16 and Deuteronomy 6:8, 18. The law prohibiting the eating of milk with meat is based on Exodus 23:19.
2. Thus, Exodus 23:19 might be taken literally, while Exodus 13:9, 16 and Deuteronomy 6:8, 18 could be interpreted symbolically.

would have perished. For these scholars properly analyzed everything in the Torah [lit., "in its place"]. They explained and clarified the precepts and statutes of the Torah for us in accordance with their tradition. At times, they find clear evidence for their traditions in the Torah. On other occasions, their support is Midrashic. At other times, they find mere supports [Hebrew, *asmakhta*] for their traditions [in the Torah].[3] One who is intelligent can discern when the Sages understand a text literally and when they do so midrashically, for all of their interpretations do not follow one course. God, who gave the Sages wisdom, will fully reward them [for preserving and transmitting the Torah].

The book of Jeremiah states, "Do not carry anything out of your houses on the Sabbath day" (Jeremiah 17:22). However, the Torah does not mention this.[4]

The commandments transmitted by the Sages [and interpreted by them in accordance with their tradition] that are mentioned in the Torah are numerous. There are likewise many precepts mentioned by the Sages that are not mentioned in the Torah.[5] I will now note some of the one and some of the other, namely, the one hundred blessings that one is obligated to recite every day,[6] the prayers,[7] grace

---

3. *Asmakhta* is rhetorical connection to Scripture. See, e.g., *Hullin* 64b: "It is actually a rabbinic law. The text quoted from Scripture is a mere support."

4. The Pentateuch does not mention that carrying an object between domains is an act prohibited on the Sabbath. We thus see that there were oral laws passed on from generation to generation.

5. Laws found in the oral law that are not mentioned in the Torah. Some of them are Biblical but explained and elaborated upon by rabbinic tradition others are rabbinic in origin.

6. See *Menahot* 43b. These blessings are not mentioned in the Torah. See next note.

7. The obligation to pray is not explicitly mentioned in the Torah. According to rabbinic interpretation, it is mandated by Deuteronomy 10:20. Cf. *Sifrei Devarim* 434 to *Ekev*. Also see *Berakhot* 21a. According to the Talmud (*Berakhot* 33a), the prayers and blessings were composed by "the men of

after meals,[8] the Hallel – which Rabbi Bahya[9] says is what "He is your glory [*tehillatekha*] and He is your God" (Deuteronomy 10:21) refers to, the recitation of the *Shema*, the *eruv*, Kiddush, Havdalah, the three Sabbath meals, and, according to some, the Sabbath candles.

The sounding of the shofar on the Day of Memorial [i.e., Rosh Hashanah] is similar, for were it not for tradition,[10] we would sound trumpets on Rosh Hashanah as we do on the new moon of Nisan,[11] which is the new moon preceding the season of spring.[12] The Rabbis [of the Talmud] therefore say that Rosh Hashanah is a day of judgment (*Rosh Hashanah* 1:2).[13]

The same applies to the *lulav* [the palm branches] on the festival of Sukkot [which the Rabbis interpret to be a separate precept in its

---

the great assembly." Maimonides rules that prayer is a biblical commandment (*Sefer Ha-Mitzvot*, Positive #5).

8. This precept is mentioned in Deuteronomy 8:10. However, its formulation is post-Mosaic. See previous note.

9. Bahya ibn Pekuda (c. 1050–1120), a *dayyan* at Saragossa. He is best known for his *Hovot Ha-Levavot* (Duties of the Heart). If we accept Rabbi Bahya's point of view, the obligation to recite *Hallel* is found in the Torah based on Deuteronomy 10:21.

10. Which teaches that there is a command to sound the shofar on Rosh Hashanah. See tractate *Rosh Hashanah* 32a–32b.

11. Trumpets were sounded on all new moons (see Numbers 10:10, *Sukkah* 55a, and Ibn Ezra on Leviticus 23:24). Ibn Ezra suggests that according to the literal meaning of the text, Leviticus 23:24 refers to trumpets and not a ram's horn. See Creizenach.

12. Lit. "the season of truth." Ibn Ezra refers to spring as the season of truth. According to Ibn Ezra, there is a propitious alignment of the heavenly bodies in the month of Nisan, which is the month which spring and all that it connotes fall. See Chapter 9.

13. The Rabbis say that the Torah singles out the first day of the seventh month as a day of sounding the shofar because Rosh Hashanah is a day of judgment. Rosh Hashanah was designated as a day of judgement because it precedes fall and the onset of winter which marks the decline and end of the year. It is the reverse of Nisan. Cohen and Simon, p. 47.

own right], For the Torah merely states, "And you shall take you [on the first day [of Sukkot] ... branches of palm-trees]" (Leviticus 23:40). Were it not for tradition, it would have a different meaning.[14] It is the same with the counting of the *omer*, for the Sages differentiated between "And you shall count for yourselves [plural]" (Leviticus 23:15) "and then shall [she, singular] number to herself" (Leviticus 15:28).[15] It is also the case with the law prohibiting the eating of torn meat.[16] This law is based on an important scientific fact relating to health.[17] The laws dealing with the seven days of the nuptial canopy, mourning, visiting the sick, burying the dead, the Hanukkah lights, the reading of the scroll of Esther, and the four cups of wine on Passover are similar.[18]

---

14. The verse could be interpreted as relating to the building and decoration of the festival booth.

15. According to rabbinic interpretation, each Israelite is obligated by the Pentateuch to verbally count the forty-nine days between the second day of Passover, when the *omer* is offered on Shavuot (see *Sifra, Emor* 12). Regarding the *omer* it is stated, "and you shall count for yourselves." Regarding the menstruant, it is stated, "and then shall [she] number to herself." The latter counts seven days from the flow's cessation, bathes, and is purified. In the latter case, the woman is commanded to keep track of the days but is not commanded to ritually count the days, unlike the counting of the *omer*. In other words, the counting of the *omer* is a precept. The counting of the seven days until purification is not a precept. However, were it not for the rabbinic tradition, we could similarly interpret Scripture's mandate to count fifty days from the day that the *omer* is brought.

16. See Exodus 22:30. According to rabbinic interpretation, torn meat refers to meat from an animal whose vital organs have been perforated. See *Hullin* 3:1 and 43a. Were it not for the rabbinic tradition, then Exodus 22:30 might be taken at face value.

17. Ibn Ezra believed that the Torah prohibited "torn" meat (*tereifah*) because it is unhealthy.

18. Some of these laws are known only through tradition. Others are based on traditional interpretation of Scripture.

I have already explained that the Rabbis utilize "and he shall inherit it" (Numbers 27:11) to support their tradition.[19]

---

19. The Hebrew text of Numbers 27:11 reads *ve-yarash otah* ("and he shall inherit it [feminine]"). The Rabbis translate this as "and he shall inherit her." They interpret this verse as teaching that "a man inherits his wife's property, but a woman does not inherit her husband's property (*Bava Batra* 111b). However, this is not the literal meaning of the verse, which deals with the disposition of a man's property should he die without leaving a son.

Chapter VII

THE NATURE AND PURPOSE OF THE COMMANDMENTS

1. Positive and Negative Commandments

One should carefully note that all the commandments are divided into positive and negative commandments.

This division of the commandments applies to all precepts, be they fundamental *mitzvot* (see ch. 5), be they precepts that are contingent on outside factors (ch. 4), be they precepts that serve as memorials (ch. 5), be they written laws, or be they laws known from tradition (ch. 6).

It should be noted that some of the negative commandments appear to be positive precepts but are really negative commandments. "Therefore, the children of Israel shall keep the Sabbath" (Exodus 31:16) is an example, for resting is not an act.[1] On the contrary, it refers to

---

1. Though this verse is written as a positive commandment, it is in reality a negative precept. The meaning of Exodus 31:16 thus is, "Wherefore the children of Israel shall not do any work on the Sabbath." Ibn Ezra believes that *tishbot* means, "cease working." Nahmanides and others say that the verse has a positive aspect namely "rest, and enjoy your rest." Ibn Ezra also believes that there is a positive aspect to Shabbat, as can be observed in his Shabbat *zemirot*. However, he is here dealing with *peshat*.

the cessation of work and rest from it, for it is written, "And He rested on the seventh day from all His work which He had made" (Genesis 2:2) before the Sabbath day so that He would not have to do any work on the Sabbath.[2] "And you shall afflict your souls" (Leviticus 16:31) is similar.[3] Its meaning is, do not enjoy yourself by indulging in eating and drinking, for affliction is the opposite of pleasure. Similarly, the meaning of "sanctify yourselves therefore, and be holy" (Leviticus 20:7) is, do not defile yourselves by eating anything despicable and innately harmful. Likewise, the Nazirite who abstains from wine is holy.[4]

2. How the Commandments Are Observed

All the commandments are observed in [up to] three ways, namely, by belief [in one's heart], by speech [lit., "mouth"], and by action.

The number one is found in every sum [i.e., all sums are made of ones]. Every commandment that is observed by speech or act similarly requires faith [i.e., the one thing that all commandments require is faith]. If belief is lacking, then the observance of the commandments is vanity and waste [i.e., meaningless and serves no purpose]. The Sages say God desires the heart (Sanhedrin 106b). God evaluates our minds [Heb. kelayot, lit., "the reins"] and investigates our heart. Scripture clearly states, "But the word is very close to you, in your mouth, and in your heart, that you may do it" (Deuteronomy 30:14). The afore-mentioned deals with the three ways in which the commandments are observed. The meaning of "in your mouth" is obvious [in referring to prayers and the recitation of the Shema with one's mouth]. "And

2. According to Ibn Ezra, "And He rested on the seventh day from all His work which He had made" means "And He rested on the seventh day from all His work which He had made before the Sabbath day." In other words, God did not create anything on the Sabbath. Thus, resting means not doing any work. That is, God completed His work before the Sabbath so that He did not have to do anything on that day. See Ibn Ezra on Genesis 2:2.
3. Like Exodus 31:16, it is syntactically similar to positive commandments but is in actuality a negative precept.
4. See Chapter 3. Levin reads, the one who abstains from wine is holy.

in your heart" refers to belief. "That you may do it" means that you should observe the commandments of God, which require that you act in a specific way. It is similarly written, "What does the Lord your God require of you, but to fear the Lord your God... with all your heart and with all your soul" (Deuteronomy 10:12). Likewise, David said, "He that has clean hands, and a pure heart; who has not taken My name in vain, and has not sworn deceitfully" (Psalm 24:4); "He that walks uprightly, and does righteousness, and speaks truth in his heart" (Psalm 15:2).

3. The Negative Commandments

It should be noted that an intelligent person has no difficulty in observing the negative commandments. This is so because God planted wisdom in the mind [lit., "heart"] for a person to use to protect himself from all harm. [God] may be compared to a physician who instructs a person who is unaware of which foods are harmful to him because of his physical constitution: "Do not eat anything that I have forbidden you to eat, for if you ingest these foods, you will become ill and die." No intelligent person desires to eat anything that will harm him. On the contrary, he will be disgusted by this food and abominate it, even though he has been told that it has an excellent taste, for an intelligent person eats to sustain his life. He does not seek life for the sake of eating,[5] as is the manner of the beasts who were not created to recognize and to study the truth, for they have no soul that continues to live after it separates from the body. Can't you see that the Torah states, "Let the earth bring forth, the living creature after its kind" (Genesis 1:24); "Let the waters swarm with swarms of living creatures" (Genesis 1:20). Scripture does not state this concerning man. On the contrary, it reads, "Let us make man" in the image of an angel (Genesis 1:26).[6] Now if an angel lives forever, so does he [man]

---

5. Maimonides similarly advises people "to eat and drink solely to keep [the] body and limbs' good health." See *Mishneh Torah, Hilkhot De'ot* 3:2.
6. Ibn Ezra's paraphrase of Genesis 1:26.

who is made in its image [in other words, it is only man and not beast that has an immortal soul].

Hence [i.e., since all negative commandments are naturally harmful to a human being], a wise man said that the four types of capital punishment imposed by the Bet Din [stoning, burning, decapitation, and strangulation; *Sanhedrin* 7:1], and similarly *karet* and death decreed by heaven, are inflicted for the violation of negative commandments,[7] whereas observance of the positive commandments is rewarded. However, the Sages offered proof from, "You shall not eat it; that it may go well with you, and with your children after you" (Deuteronomy 12:25)[8] that one who keeps himself from violating the negative commandments is rewarded.

Some say that the reward of ["that it may go well with you, and with your children after you" (Deuteronomy 12:25)] refers to the end of the verse, that is, "when you do that which is right in the eyes of the Lord" (Deuteronomy 12:25).[9] Others say that "that it may go well with you, and with your children after you" refers to the commandment "You shall not eat it" (Deuteronomy 12:25), which precedes it. [The meaning of "You shall not eat it" is: You shall not eat blood but instead] "you shall pour it out upon the earth as water" (Deuteronomy 12:24)[10]

---

7. No reward is given for abstaining from what the negative commandments prohibit because these acts are inherently harmful to humans. This is the opinion of the "wise man." However, the Sages disagree. See next note.

8. Cf. Mishnah, *Makkot* 3:15: "If a man keeps himself apart from blood which a man's soul abhors he receives a reward, how much more, if he keeps himself apart from robbery and incest which a man's soul longs after and desires, shall he gain merit for himself and his generations and the generations of his generations to the end of all generations."

9. That is, "that it may go well with you, and with your children after you" does not pertain to the prohibition of consuming blood. This view maintains that one is not rewarded for not violating negative commandments. Ibn Ezra does not identify those who put forward this opinion.

10. According to this opinion, the reward spoken of in Deuteronomy 12:25 refers to the positive commandment of pouring the blood on the ground. Here too, Ibn Ezra does not identify those who put forward this opinion.

so that it cannot be gathered and eaten by man [i.e., this is the primary thrust of the commandment], "for the blood is life" (Deuteronomy 12:23). The latter is known from the natural sciences [lit., "the science of nature"].

One would also be correct in saying that the commandment to fear God, which is a positive commandment, includes all positive and all negative commandments, for after stating to "fear the Lord your God" (Deuteronomy 10:12), Moses goes on to say, "to keep for your good the commandments of the Lord, and His statutes" (Deuteronomy 10:13) [i.e., there is a positive commandment to refrain from violating the negative commandments]. The "commandments" and "statutes" refer to the positive and negative commandments, for good befalls one who keeps himself from sinning because of his fear of the Lord.[11] The phrase "to keep for your good" includes both the good of this world and the good of the world to come. However, reward is given for the observance of the positive commandments, because one expends effort in fulfilling them [whereas one who refrains from a negative commandment merely avoids evil]. For example, such a person is like one who troubles himself, on the advice of a physician, to cook food that will make him healthy if he eats of it: "Behold, his reward is with him, and his recompense before him" (Isaiah 40: 10). The meaning of "for your good" is that you will be rewarded and you will escape punishment. Now the person who observes the instructions of the physician stays well [and the observance of the commandment is the built-in reward]. What the patient does neither helps nor injures his physician.[12] As Elihu said, "If you are righteous, what does that give

---

11. For he escapes punishment. Hence, "for your good" also applies to the negative commandments.

12. A human being's actions neither benefit nor harm God. This was the opinion of all the Medieval Jewish philosophers. "God is not a body and has no strength in the body, and has no shape or image or relationship to a body or parts thereof. This is why the Sages of blessed memory said with regards to heaven there is no sitting, nor standing, no awakeness, nor tiredness. This is all to say that He does not partake of any physical actions or qualities. And if He were to be a body then He would be like

Him?" (Job 35:7); "And if your transgressions are multiplied, what harm does that do to Him?" (Job 35:6).

4. Free Will

I will now give you a hint regarding an important secret [regarding free will].

We find that Scripture states, "O Lord, why do You make us err from Your ways" (Isaiah 63:17); "For You turned their heart backward" (1 Kings 18:37) [which implies that man does not have free will]. However, Moses said, "I have set before you today life and good, and death and evil." Similarly, Scripture states elsewhere, "Evil and good do not proceed out of the mouth of the Most High" (Lamentations 3:38) [which all imply that man does have free will]. In addition, our Sages said, "Everything is in the hands of heaven except for the fear of heaven" (*Niddah* 16b).

Note that a plant grown in soil that is tended is superior to a plant grown in soil that is not tended. Some soils are fertile, and some are infertile.[13]

I will now explain by means of a true example [from life].

Three powers are connected to human life. If you wish to, you may call them by the following three names: *neshamah* (soul), *ruah* (spirit), and *nefesh* (life).[14] The *nefesh* is the power of growth. It is located in

---

any other body and would not be God. And all that is written in the holy books regarding descriptions of God, they are all anthropomorphic" (Maimonides' commentary on the Mishnah, *Sanhedrin*; translated by Marc Mermelstein: http://www.mesora.org/13principles.html). Also See Ralbag's commentary on Nehemiah 1:7 and Ibn Ezra's quote from Job: "If you are righteous, what does that give Him?" (Job 35:7); "And if your transgressions are multiplied, what harm does that do to Him?" (Job 35:6).

13. Similarly, with people. Hence, a person is obligated to tend to his soul and body. The soil refers to the body and the plant to the soul. While ultimately God determines the original condition of the body, the individual has an obligation to tend to his body carefully, so that his soul can grow strong in him.

14. Man's three souls are first mentioned by Plato's *Republic*, Book 4. See also

the liver. The *nefesh* is found in humans, animals, and plants. The *nefesh* is corporeal, and it is that part of the psyche that desires food and sex. The *ruah* is located in the heart. It animates man and governs movement, the *ruah* is found in man and beast [but not in plants]. The *ruah* is corporeal. When the *ruah*, which is air-like, leaves the body, the person dies. The *ruah* grows in intensity [when stimulated]. It is that part of the psyche that waxes angry. The *neshamah* is the highest-ranking soul and its power is manifest in the brain.

5. Body and Soul

The nature and impulses of people vary. In some people, all three souls are powerful, while in others they are weak. In some, the two [i.e., weakness and strength] take turns. There is no need for elaboration. For the rational soul [*neshamah*] seeks what is beneficial for it in the works of God, for God is the source of its life. The *nefesh* seeks the pleasures of the flesh for its benefit. The *ruah* is intermediary. Now the brain needs the liver and the heart, and the liver and heart need the brain. In other words, each one of these organs needs the other. Hence, the Hebrews used the term *neshamah* both for the *nefesh* and for the *ruah* [sometimes *neshamah* refers specifically to the rational faculty, and sometimes it refers to any of the parts of the soul]. The souls are connected [lit., "tied"] to the body [so the body affects the soul, and the soul affects the body]. [For example,] if a person eats food that warms the blood, he will grow angry. We thus see that what the body does expresses itself in the *ruah*. If a person's body is temperamentally fit [and he is not easily agitated] and someone angers that person by saying or doing something, the energy of the *ruah* is activated in the heart and heats the body. The body is thus changed because of the *ruah*.

Solomon ibn Gabirol's *Mekor Hayyim* 5:13. Maimonides introduction to *Pirkei Avot*, ch. 1. Philo of Alexandria was probably the first authority to identify *neshamah, ruah,* and *nefesh* with reason (*logos*), spiritedness (*thymos*) and desire (*epithymia*); see *Special Laws* IV.92. See further: http://www.jewishencyclopedia.com/articles/13933-soul.

The intelligent person will satisfy his bodily needs in accordance with the requirements of his *neshmah* so that it does not change along with the changes of the body [so it is not adversely affected by the changes in the body].

6. Seeking Medical Aid

The great gift that God granted Israel was that they would not have any need of physicians alongside God if they observed the Torah. They would not have any reason to act like King Asa, who was criticized by Scripture for seeking the help of physicians (2 Chronicles 16:12).

The phrase *ve-rappo yerappei* ["and shall cause him to be thoroughly healed"] (Exodus 21:19) does not refute the above [i.e., that Israel would not have need of physicians if they observed the Torah]. For *ve-rappo yerappei* is not in the *kal* form.[15] On the contrary, *ve-rappo yerappei* is similar to *va-yerappei* ["and he repaired," lit., "and he healed"] in "and he repaired the altar of the Lord that was torn down" (1 Kings 18:30). It differs from *erpa* ["I heal," in the *kal* form] in "I [God] have wounded and I heal" (Deuteronomy 32:39) [which refers to inner wounds, i.e., to disease] and *tirpenah* ["shall heal"] in "He wounded and His hands shall heal" (Job 5:18).[16]

"The sun and the moon and the stars, even all the host of heaven... which the Lord your God has allotted unto all the peoples under the whole heaven" (Deuteronomy 4:19) is to be similarly interpreted.[17]

---

15. It is in the *pi'el*. Ibn Ezra explains in his commentary on Exodus 21:19 that a physician is prohibited from healing internal wounds. In other words, "and shall cause him to be thoroughly healed" is limited to external wounds. Internal wounds and illnesses are to be healed only by God. Hence, Scripture employs the *pi'el* form *ve-rappo yerappei* rather than the *kal* form that it does when speaking of God healing.

16. Ibn Ezra makes this point in a number of places in his commentary on Scritpure. However, this is not the accepted halakhic opinion. The accepted opinion is that there is an obligation to seek medical help when ill for all internal as well as external ailments.

17. Israel needs no one on Earth to help it fight disease because the Lord is Israel's physician. It also needs no aid from the heavenly forces in other

Similarly, "The Lord will punish the host of the high heaven on high" (Isaiah 24:21) refers to one who is under the influence of the stars [i.e., it does not refer to Israel]. The latter is dealt with by the science of astrology. However, God chose Israel for His very own portion. He removed Israel from the domain of the stars as long as they observe everything that the Lord commanded them in His Torah and stay within the domain of the Lord. The ancients therefore said, "Israel has no star" (*Shabbat* 156b). It is because of this that the Torah states, "so that we are distinguished [from other nations], I and Your people" (Exodus 33:15).[18] One should not argue and ask, "How can God change the laws of heaven?"[19] for lo and behold, the account of Noah shows this to be the case.[20]

7. The Good Person

All of the good [promised in Scripture] was set aside for all [individuals or nations] who are good. It is illogical to withhold the good from that which is mostly good because of a little evil in it. [Thus, good will befall a person who does mostly good even if he does some evil.] Now, fortune and misfortune befall a person according to his state. Therefore, every intelligent person has the power to choose good and the bad.[21] Hence, Scripture states, "There shall be no poor among you" (Deuteronomy 15:4) – only on the condition that all or most of

---

endeavors. For the meaning of Deuteronomy 32:29 is, unlike all other nations that are under the dominion of the stars, Israel is under the dominion of God.

18. Moses said this when he asked that Israel be led by God and not by an intermediary.

19. That is, if the stars decree that evil befall Israel, how can God alter the stellar decree?

20. According to Ibn Ezra, the flood came about by a deadly conjunction of the heavenly bodies (see his comments on Genesis 7:4). However, Noah was saved from the flood decreed by the stars. This shows that there is no contradiction between the fulfillment of the decree of the heavenly bodies and the saving of the righteous.

21. An intelligent person can determine whether good or evil will befall him.

the nation are good. It is therefore written, "if only you will diligently listen to the voice of the Lord your God" (Deuteronomy 15:5) [will there be no needy among Israel]. The individual [unlike the nation] benefits his soul after his latter end.[22]

8. Perfecting the Heart

Pay attention and note that all precepts written in the Torah, transmitted by tradition, or enacted by the patriarchs [i.e., Rabbis] aim at perfecting the heart. This is the case even though most of the commandments are observed by action or speech. Thus, Scripture states: "for the Lord searches all hearts, and understands all the imaginations of the thoughts" (1 Chronicles 28:9); "And to those who are upright in their hearts" (Psalm 125:4); "for the Levites were ... upright in heart" (2 Chronicles 29:34); "and his heart was not wholly righteous with the Lord his God" (1 Kings 11:4); "you did well that it was in your heart" (1 Kings 11:18); "but the Lord looks on the heart" (1 Samuel 16:7).

We also find the opposite [of a good and pure heart] in Scripture. Thus, the book of Proverbs reads, "A heart that devises wicked thoughts" (Proverbs 6:18). It states elsewhere, "[Do not eat the bread of someone who has an evil eye for] ... his heart is not with you" (Proverbs 23:6–7), because an evil eye is contingent on the wickedness of the heart. The latter is verified [lit., "known"] by the natural sciences. Therefore, the burnt offering (olah) that was totally consumed was brought unto the Lord for inappropriate thoughts arising in one's mind.[23] On the other hand, the sin offering [hattat, Leviticus 4:2] and the guilt offering [asham, brought for swearing falsely Leviticus, 4:4–26] were brought for verbal trespasses and for sinful acts. This [i.e., the perfection of the heart] is the meaning of "Circumcise therefore the foreskin [orlat] of your heart" (Deuteronomy 10:16).

---

22. The nation receives its reward in this world. The soul, however, receives its reward after death.

23. Hebrew *oleh*. There is a play on words here. The *olah* was brought for thoughts that arise (*oleh*) in the mind. See *Vayikra Rabbah* 7:3: "The burnt-offering atones solely for sinful thoughts."

The definition of *orlah* [foreskin] is "heaviness." Thus, *erel lev* ["uncircumcised in heart"] (Ezekiel 44:9) is synonymous with *kaved lev* [lit., "heavy heart"] in "Pharaoh's heart is heavy" (Exodus 7:14). Also, *va-ani aral sefatayim* ["and I who am of uncircumcised lips"] (Exodus 6:12) means the same as *ki khevad peh u-khevad lashon anokhi* [lit., "for I am of heavy mouth, and of heavy tongue"] (Exodus 4:10). And *arelah oznam* [lit., "their ear is uncircumcised"] (Jeremiah 6:10) is similar in meaning to *ve-oznav hakhbed* [and make their ears heavy] (Isaiah 6:10).

The excision of the foreskin of the flesh is a sign of the covenant between man and his Creator not to defile one's soul by engaging in an act of sexual intercourse that is not in accordance with the way of truth [God's way or God's natural law]. One who refrains from prohibited sexual activity has his reward with him. He will be fruitful and flourish.[24] We thus read, "And I will make My covenant between Me and you, and will multiply you exceedingly" (Genesis 17:2). Scripture also states, *va-araltem orlato et piryo* [lit., "and you shall count the fruit thereof as heavy"] (Leviticus 19:23). The latter also speaks of heaviness. [*Va-araltem orlato*, like the words quoted above, also refers to heaviness.] It refers to a heaviness caused by an excess of moisture. This [fact], too, is known from the natural sciences [that there is an excess of moisture in the fruit produced by a tree in the first three years of growth].

The commandment ["Circumcise therefore the foreskin of your heart" (Deuteronomy 10:16)] means [lit., "includes"] the following: Humble yourselves before the Lord and recognize the truth by submitting to God when He chastises you; remove the foreskin of your heart, and do not harden it as Pharaoh (Exodus 7:14) or Ahaz did, for Scripture tells us, "And in the time of his distress he acted more treacherously against the Lord, this same king Ahaz" (2 Chronicles 28:22). However, King Ahab eventually submitted to God. This pleased the Lord (1 Kings 21:27–29). It is similarly written, "if then by chance they humble their uncircumcised hearts" (Leviticus 26:41). The latter

---

24. Other texts read, "and multiply."

is similar to "In your distress . . . you will return to the Lord your God" (Deuteronomy 4:30).

Scripture also speaks of stiff-neckedness. A stiff-necked person is an individual who, as it were, turns [the back of] his neck toward his master. He stiffens his neck and refuses to turn his face to his master when he calls out to him. Such an individual angers his master. Thus, after stating that a person should circumcise his heart and not be stiff-necked (Deuteronomy 10:16), Scripture states, "For the Lord your God, He is God of gods [*Elohei ha-elohim*] and the Lord of lords [*Adonei ha-adonim*]" (Deuteronomy 10:17). [*Elohim*] refers to the angels in heaven.[25] [*Adonim*] refers to the kings who are lords over the various lands. They are all under God's dominion [as stated in the conclusion of the verse] "He is the great God, the mighty, and the awful." How then can you save yourself [if you are stiff-necked and turn away from him]? He will refuse to accept bribes no matter how valuable.

Scripture concludes with "and be no more stiff-necked" (Deuteronomy 10:16) because earlier in the chapter it states, "for you are a stiff-necked people" (Deuteronomy 9:6). The latter proves that our interpretation [that "stiff-necked" means turning away from God] is correct.[26]

---

25. See Ibn Ezra on Genesis 1:1: "God is called Elohim because His actions are executed via angels who do His work and are called Elohim."

26. Deuteronomy 9:6–7 reads: "Know therefore that it is not for your righteousness that the Lord your God gives you this good land to possess it; for you are a stiff-necked people." It then lists Israel's sins: "Remember, do not forget, how you did make the Lord your God wroth in the wilderness; from the day that you went forth out of the land of Egypt, until you came to this place, you have been rebellious against the Lord. . . ." Thus being stiff-necked means turning away from God and the command to "be no more stiff-necked" means "do not turn aside from God."

9. Positive and Negative Commandments Directed to the Heart

The commandments directed to the heart [i.e., mind] begin with "I am the Lord your God" (Exodus 20:2).[27] This precept directs us to believe wholeheartedly that the Lord who took us out of Egypt is our God. It is thus a positive commandment. The same is the case with "And you shall love the Lord your God" (Deuteronomy 6:5) and "and to stay close to Him" (Deuteronomy 11:22) [i.e., they are all commandments directed to the heart]. It is also true with "but you shall love your neighbor as yourself" (Leviticus 19:18; see chapter 1).

The negative commandments directed to the heart include "You shall have no other gods before Me" (Exodus 20:2), which means you shall not believe in any other gods, and "You shall not hate your brother in your heart" (Leviticus 19:18), (Exodus 20:14).

"Know this day, and take it to heart, that the Lord, He is God in heaven above and upon the earth beneath; there is no one else" (Deuteronomy 4:39) is a positive commandment. So is, "Hear O Israel the Lord our God the Lord is One" (Deuteronomy 6:4).[28]

10. Commandments That Are Observed Verbally

The commandments that are observed with one's mouth are the high priest's confession [on the Day of Atonement; see Leviticus 16:21; it also includes the confession made by the Israelite upon bringing the first fruits, namely,] "you shall speak and say" (Deuteronomy 26:5); [keeping vows, namely,] "That which is gone out of your lips you shall observe" (Deuteronomy 23:24); the recitation of grace after meals; reciting the *Hallel*; praying (see chapter 6); [and teaching God's word to our children and meditating upon God's word, namely,] "you shall teach them diligently unto your children, and shall talk of them" (Deuteronomy 6:7). Observe that the aforementioned are positive

---

27. According to Ibn Ezra, Exodus 20:2 commands us to believe in God. This is also the opinion of Maimonides. See *Mishneh Torah, Hilkhot Yesodei Ha-Torah* 1:6.
28. It commands us to believe that the Lord alone is our God and He is one.

commandments. There are many other similar commandments [that are observed with the mouth].

The negative commandments pertaining to one's lips are "You shall not take the name of the Lord your God in vain" (Exodus 20:7); "You shall not bear false witness against your neighbor" (Exodus 20:13); "You shall not revile God, nor curse a ruler of your people" (Exodus 22:27); "neither let it be heard out of your mouth" (Exodus 23:13); "You shall not make a covenant with them nor with their gods" (Exodus 23:32); and "neither shall you bear witness by going along with the crowd to pervert justice" (Exodus 23:2). There are many other similar negative commandments [that are connected to speech].

11. The Purpose of the Commandments

The commandments that are observed by deeds are numerous. There is no need to mention them.

I found one verse that embodies all the commandments. The verse is "You shall fear the Lord your God; and Him shall you serve" (Deuteronomy 6:13). Now, "You shall fear" encapsulates all negative commandments pertaining to the heart, lips, and deeds. It is the first step that one takes in one's ascent in the service of the glorious God [i.e., "You shall fear" ultimately leads to "Him shall you serve"].

The service of God takes in all positive commandments. These precepts [i.e., the positive commandments] train the heart and lead a person to cleave to God's glorious name. This [i.e., cleaving to God] is what man was created for. Human beings were not created to acquire wealth to bequeath to others or to erect buildings for others to inhabit while they dwell below the earth. Neither was a person brought into being to enjoy a variety of dishes,[29] for the pleasure of eating lasts but for a few moments, whereas much effort is expended in attaining the delicacies, most of which are unhealthy.

Likewise, sleeping with women causes one's strength and body to

---

29. Ibn Ezra takes issue with hedonism in all of its manifestations.

decline.[30] The same is the case with jest and drunkenness, folly, and madness (see Ecclesiastes 1:17).

The intelligent person will understand that the days of one's life are few, that the soul is in the hand of its Creator, and that one does not know when God will reclaim it. He will therefore seek after all things that lead a person to the love of God. The wise person will study the sciences. He will investigate belief [i.e., study metaphysics], so that he recognizes and understands the work of God. The intelligent man will not occupy himself with the vanities of the world. On the contrary, he will isolate himself to study and meditate upon God's law and observing the Lord's precepts. God will then open the eyes of his heart and will create a new and different spirit in him. He will be beloved of his Creator while he is yet alive. His soul will cleave to God and enjoy the fullness of the joy of God's presence [in this world; cf. Psalm 16:11]. Furthermore, God's right hand of bliss will be eternally upon his soul when it separates from the body. This is what the poet Asaf spoke of when he said, "My flesh and my heart fail; but God is the rock of my heart and my portion forever" (Psalm 73:26). The intelligent person will act as did our father Jacob when he vowed, "then shall the Lord be my God" (Genesis 28:21), for when Jacob came to Beth-El, he said, "Put away the strange gods that are among you" (Genesis 35:2). He left the sheep and separated himself to serve God. He never again slept with a woman, for Rachel was dead[31] and [her handmaid] Bilhah was defiled (Genesis 35:22). It was for this reason that he despised [i.e., was no longer intimate] Reuben's mother [Leah] and her handmaid [Zilpah]. Scripture therefore states elsewhere: "Now the sons of Jacob

---

30. Ibn Ezra is saying God did not create man to pursue women. Medieval science taught that emission of semen weakened the body and hastened its decline. See Ibn Ezra on Genesis 3:8. See also Maimonides, *Hilkhot De'ot* 4:19.

31. The woman he truly loved and for whom he served Laban. See Ibn Ezra on Genesis 48:14: "Jacob considered Rachel to be his true wife." Hence Scripture states, "the sons of Rachel, Jacob's wife" (ibid. 46:19 and the notes thereto).

were twelve" (Genesis 35:23). It states this to tell us that after Bilhah was defiled, Jacob never again had sexual relations with a woman and therefore did not sire any additional children.

Now one who reaches the level where he is always conscious of God and His deeds and wonders, and informs people of God's glory by not saying anything with his mouth, without mentioning the Lord's name [with his mouth], is one of those who "turn the many to righteousness" (Daniel 12:3). This is the reason that the prophets swore by God's name in most of their utterances. This is the meaning of "and you shall swear by His name" (Deuteronomy 6:13).

Note that the Torah was given only to the intelligent. We are therefore to explain rationally what is written in Scripture.[32] An example is, "and how I bore you on eagles' wings" (Exodus 19:4). Other examples are "Circumcise therefore the foreskin of your heart" (Deuteronomy 10:16) and "but you shall surely open your hand unto him" (Deuteronomy 15:8). The ancients said that the same is the case with "And they shall spread the garment" (Deuteronomy 22:17). [None of these verses are to be taken literally.]

There are other things that are to be taken literally but also have an esoteric meaning. The account of the Garden of Eden, the tree of knowledge, and the tree of life, the meaning of cherubim, and other similar things are examples. ["For this (i.e., the meaning of the Garden of Eden, the tree of knowledge, and the cherubim) is the whole man" (Ecclesiastes 12:13)].[33]

---

32. When a verse contradicts logic or the physical sciences, we are not to interpret that verse literally. Saadiah Gaon makes the same point in Chapter 7 of his *Sefer Ha-Emunot Ve-Ha-De'ot*. Maimonides does likewise in his introduction to *The Guide for the Perplexed*.

33. According to Ibn Ezra, the story of the Garden of Eden alludes to immortality and the type of life one must lead to attain it. See Ibn Ezra on Genesis 3:24 and the notes thereto. The sentence in brackets is not found in the Waxman, Stern, or Baer editions. It is found in the Levin edition.

Chapter VIII
REASONS FOR THE COMMANDMENTS

1. All Commandments Have a Reason

If a person is intelligent and consistently studies God's law, the Torah will instruct him and edify his soul much more than his teachers instructed and edified him. This is what Scripture means by "I have more understanding than all my teachers" (Psalm 119:99).

How precious are the words of the ancients who said that we are obligated to observe all the commandments and all the enactments of the Sages [*avot*, lit., "fathers"] without seeking a reason why they commanded us to observe these precepts.[1] The ancients spoke the truth [when they told us to observe the commandments without knowing the reason]. For there are many precepts whose reasons are hidden and concealed. Now, if a person will not observe these laws until he knows the reason for their observance, he will remain without guidance. He will be like a child who refuses to eat bread until he first knows how the ground was plowed and the grain planted, harvested, threshed, winnowed, cleansed, ground, sifted, kneaded, and baked. If a child acts thusly, he will surely die of starvation. On the contrary, the correct way for the child to act is to eat normally [lit., constantly] and, as he grows, to ask a little at a time until all of his questions are

---

1. See *Yoma* 67b: "These are the things which I ordained for you; and you dare not question them."

answered. Similarly, an intelligent person may ultimately learn the very many clearly stated reasons that the Torah itself offers for the precepts. However, there are other explanations [for the commandments] that only one man in a thousand knows [for those reasons are not stated in Scripture].

Our master Moses said concerning the commandments, "Surely this great nation is a wise and understanding people [For... what great nation is there, that has... statutes and ordinances so righteous as all this law]" (Deuteronomy 4:6–8). Now, if there is no discernible reason for the commandments, how could the nations say that the statutes are righteous and we who observe them wise?[2]

2. Reasons Given by the Torah for Some of the Commandments

I will now mention a number of the reasons given by the Torah for some of the commandments.

Scripture states, "Sanctify to me all the firstborn" (Exodus 13:2). This is followed by "[And it came to pass, when Pharaoh would not let us go that the Lord slew all firstborn in the land of Egypt (i.e., but spared those of Israel)]. Therefore I sacrifice to the Lord [all that open the womb, being males; but all the firstborn of my sons I redeem]" (Exodus 13:15).[3]

Concerning the Sabbath, Scripture states [the reason], "For in six days [the Lord made heaven and earth... and rested on the seventh day] (Exodus 20:11). The same applies to the Sabbatical year [which also commemorates creation of the world in six days].

Scripture also explains that our slaves are to rest on the Sabbath so that we recall that we were slaves in the land of Egypt (Deuteronomy 5:14). The same reason applies to the eating of unleavened bread and bitter herbs [on Passover, Exodus 12:8].

---

2. Ibn Ezra believes that there are reasons for each and every commandment. He, like Maimonides, takes issue with those who believe that there are no reasons for the commandments. See *The Guide for the Perplexed* 3:26.

3. In other words, we sanctify the firstborn to recall that God spared the firstborn of Israel.

There are three [pilgrimage] festivals, one at the time when the barley ripens [Passover], one when the wheat first appears [Shavuot], and one at the time of the ingathering [Sukkot]. On these festivals, the people of Israel offer thanks to God the Blessed [for providing the season's harvest].

Scripture states, "Every man shall give as he is able, according to the blessing the Lord your God which He has given you" (Deuteronomy 16:17). The meaning of the latter is, give to God from what is His. The concept conveyed by the verse is, "for all things come from You, and we have given You of Your own" (1 Chronicles 29:14).

The Torah states, "They [i.e., the Canaanites] shall not dwell in your land" (Exodus 23:33). It then gives the reason for this commandment, namely, "lest they make you sin against me" (Exodus 23:33).

It states elsewhere, "You shall not spare anything that breathes" (Deuteronomy 20:16). It then gives the reason for this command, namely, "so that they [i.e., the inhabitants of Canaan] will not teach you to do all their abominations" (Deuteronomy 20:18).

Likewise with regard to the prohibition of intermarriage, Scripture states, "and you [shall not] take of their daughters to marry your sons" (Exodus 34:16). It then explains that [their daughters] "will make your sons go astray after their gods" (Exodus 34:16) and "For he will turn away your son from following Me" (Deuteronomy 7:4).

The Torah says, "that your ox and your ass may have rest" (Exodus 23:12) on the Sabbath because you plow with them.[4]

The reason for "Whoso sheds man's blood, by man shall his blood be shed" (Genesis 9:6) is, "for in the image of God He made man" (Genesis 9:6).

The reason "No man shall take the mill or the upper millstone to pledge" (Deuteronomy 24:6) is "for he takes a man's life to pledge"

---

4. The reason that follows is not stated in the Torah. It is Ibn Ezra's interpretation of what Scripture means by "that your ox and your ass may have rest." God does not direct commands to beasts. They are to rest on the Sabbath only because it is prohibited to plow on the Sabbath.

(Deuteronomy 24:6) [i.e., these utensils are vital for the sustenance of life].

Scripture mentions "has no child" [i.e., that a widowed daughter of a priest who is married to an Israelite who is not a priest may eat from the heave offering] because "she returns to her father's house, as in her youth" (Leviticus 22:13).

Scripture tells us that the reason for dwelling in booths on the festival of Sukkot is "that your generations may know that I made the children of Israel dwell in booths, when I brought them out of the land of Egypt" (Leviticus 23:43).

The reason why the land shall not be sold in perpetuity (Leviticus 25:23) is "for the land is Mine" (Leviticus 25:23) [i.e., the land belongs to God].

Also, the reason why Israelites shall not be sold as bond-men is "For they [the Israelites] are My servants" (Leviticus 25:42).

Scripture commanded that trumpets be sounded over burnt offerings as a memorial (Numbers 10:10), so that they would serve as a memorial in time of war.[5] We thus read, "Over Philistia do I sound the trumpets" (Psalms 108:10)

The reason that Scripture gives for the fringes is that "you may remember and do all My commandments" (Numbers 15:40) when you constantly look upon the fringes (Numbers 15:39). The same applies to "And you shall bind them [the *tefillin*] ... and you shall write them [the *mezuzah*]" (Deuteronomy 5:8–9).

Scripture offers two reasons to "Harass the Midianites" (Numbers 25:17). The first is the matter of Peor.[6] The second is the desire of the Midianites to do further harm to the Israelites [besides the incident of Peor], because the daughter of their prince [Cozbi] was slain [by Phinehas; see Numbers 25:1–15].

---

5. When Israel goes to war, the trumpets, as it were, serve to "remind" God that Israel offered burnt offerings in the temple.

6. The Midianites enticed the Israelites to participate in the licentious and idolatrous worship of Baal-Peor (Numbers 25:1–9 and Numbers 31).

The reason for "You shall not abhor an Edomite" (Deuteronomy 23:8) is, "for he is your brother" (Deuteronomy 23:8).

The reason why "you shall not abhor an Egyptian" (Deuteronomy 23:8) is because "you were a stranger in his land" (Deuteronomy 23:8).

The reason why "an Ammonite or a Moabite shall not enter into the assembly of the Lord" (Deuteronomy 23:4) is "because they did not meet you with bread and with water in the way" (Deuteronomy 23:5), and "they did not remember the ancient brotherhood."[7] Furthermore, he [i.e., the Moabites] hired Balaam to harm you (Numbers 23:5).

Scripture also mentions the reason why the king of Israel "shall not multiply to himself" women and horses (Deuteronomy 17:16;17).[8] The reason given is "that his heart not turn away" (Deuteronomy 17:17) and so "that he does not cause the people to return to Egypt" (Deuteronomy 17:16).

The reason why women must marry men from their father's tribe is "that the children of Israel may possess every man the inheritance of his fathers" (Numbers 36:8).

The answer given by Scripture to "What mean the testimonies, and the statutes, and the ordinances, which the Lord our God has commanded?" (Deuteronomy 6:20) is, "We were Pharaoh's bondmen in Egypt; and the Lord brought us out of Egypt with a mighty hand" (Deuteronomy 6:21), and we are obligated to obey the voice of the One who did all this good for us. In addition, "it will be [counted as] righteousness unto us, if we observe to do all this commandment before the Lord our God, as He has commanded us" (Deuteronomy 6:25).

The reason for the Sabbatical year is that the poor of your people may eat (Exodus 23:11).[9]

The reason for "Wherewith Levi has no portion nor inheritance

---

7. Abraham the father of Israel was the uncle of Lot, the father of the Moabites and the Ammonites. Indeed, Abraham told Lot, "for we are brethren" (Genesis 13:8). Amos said something very similar concerning Edom. See Amos 1:9.
8. The Levin edition adds, "and gold and silver" (Deuteronomy 17:16).
9. The earlier mentioned reason given by Ibn Ezra for the sabbatical year

with his brethren" (Deuteronomy 10:9) is that he serves God the Revered.

"The first fruits of your corn, of your wine, and your oil" is to be given to the priest (Deuteronomy 18:4) because the priest is our superior and God has chosen him to pray on our behalf. This is the meaning of "the Lord separated the tribe of Levi…to bless in His name" (Deuteronomy 10:8). We thus read, "And Aaron lifted up his hands toward the people, and blessed them" (Leviticus 9:22).

The reason for "You shall separate three cities [of refuge] for yourselves" (Deuteronomy 19:2) is "lest the avenger of blood pursue the manslayer" (v. 6) and "that innocent blood be not shed in your midst" (v. 10).

The reason for the execution of false witnesses is that "those that remain shall hear, and fear, and shall henceforth commit no more evil" (Deuteronomy 19:20).

The reason for "[When you shall besiege a city…] you shall not destroy the trees thereof [i.e., of the city that is being besieged]" is "for is the tree of the field man, that it should be besieged of you?" (Deuteronomy 20:19).

The reason [for the command to build] a parapet [on the roof of one's house] is "that you bring not blood upon your house" (Deuteronomy 22:8) [i.e., to prevent someone from falling off the roof].

The reason why Scripture prohibits sowing a mixture of seeds is *pen tikdash ha-mele'ah ha-zera* ["lest the fulness of the seed which you have sown be forfeited"] (Deuteronomy 22:9). This, as Rabbi Menahem the Spaniard explains, means, "that all of it shall become holy."[10]

---

refers to the prohibition of working the ground. He now offers a reason for the prohibition of the ingathering in the produce of the soil.

10. And thus cannot be put to profane use. See Ibn Ezra on Deuteronomy 22:9: "The word *tikdash* is related to the word *kodesh*. [The product of two seeds sown together becomes holy] because one type of seed mixes with the other type [and one cannot properly separate the produce and properly tithe it]." According to Rabbi Menahem, *pen tikdash ha-mele'ah ha-zera* should be rendered "lest the fulness of the seed which you have sown be sanctified" (Cohen and Simon).

The girl who did not cry out in the city [when sexually assaulted] (Deuteronomy 22:4) is put to death because "she willingly submitted" [to her assailant]. However, if the incident took place outside the city in a place where no one saw the perpetrator, then it is similar to "when a man rises against his neighbor, and slays him" (Deuteronomy 22:26) [in other words, the woman was overpowered and raped].

The reason for lending to the poor (Deuteronomy 15:8) is "lest he cry unto the Lord against you, and it be a sin in you" (Deuteronomy 15:9).

The reason for "Love you therefore the stranger" is "for you were strangers in the land of Egypt" (Deuteronomy 10:19).

The reason for justice for the stranger, the orphan, and the widow and the taking of a pledge (see Deuteronomy 24:17) is "you shall remember that you were a bondman in Egypt...therefore I command you to do this thing" (Deuteronomy 24:18).

The reason for "When you reap your harvest in your field, and have forgotten a sheaf in the field, you shall not go back to fetch it" (Deuteronomy 24:20) and for "When you gather the grapes of your vineyard, you shall not glean it after yourself, it shall be for the stranger, for the fatherless; and the widow" (Deuteronomy 24:21) is similar. Scripture states, "And you shall remember that you were a bondman in the land of Egypt; therefore I command you to do this thing" (Deuteronomy 24:22).

The purpose of teaching Israel the "song" (Deuteronomy 32:1–43) was so that it would serve them as a witness.[11]

Scripture prohibited the eating of blood because one "should not eat the life with the flesh" (Deuteronomy 12:23).

Scripture commanded that the blood of a sacrifice be offered on the altar life for life, "for it is the blood that makes atonement by reason of the life" (Leviticus 17:11).[12]

---

11. See Ibn Ezra on Deuteronomy 31:19: "The song...will testify before those who ask, Why did all this happen to us?" That is: The song will bear witness that God predicted what will befall Israel because of their sins.
12. The sacrificial blood substitutes for the life of the celebrant that was

The Torah commands that all sacrifices are to be brought to the Tabernacle (Leviticus 5:5) so that Israel "no more sacrifices in the open field to the demons" (Leviticus 5:5), as they were in the habit of doing in Egypt (see Leviticus 17:7 and Rashi thereon).

Scripture clearly states that the reason why the blood of the Paschal Lamb was placed on the lintel and the two side posts was "so that the Lord will not suffer the destroyer to come in unto your houses to smite you" (Exodus 12:23).

When Moses first came to speak to Pharaoh, he already explained to him why Israel was required to offer sacrifices to the Lord. Moses told Pharaoh, "lest He fall upon us with the pestilence, or with the sword" (Exodus 5:3).[13] This secret is clearly explained in the account of Hezekiah.[14] The intelligent will understand.[15]

---

forfeited through sin. The blood embodies the life of the animal. The animal's life thus takes the place of the life of the worshiper. See Ibn Ezra on Leviticus 17:11: "The blood makes atonement by the life which is in it [ba-nefesh she-yesh bo yekhapper]."

13. The meaning of this verse is, lest He fall upon us with the pestilence, or with the sword if we do not offer sacrifices.

14. King Hezekiah told the priests and the Levites, "Our fathers have acted treacherously... they did not offer burnt offerings in the holy place unto the God of Israel. Therefore, the wrath of the Lord was upon Judah and Jerusalem. Hence, he ordered that the Temple be purified and sacrifices brought to make atonement for all of Israel" (2 Chronicles 29:6–24).

15. The secret refers to how sacrifices actually prevent disasters.

Chapter IX

REASONS FOR COMMANDMENTS NOT EXPLAINED IN SCRIPTURE

1. New Month of Nisan, Date of Yom Kippur, Date of Sukkot Festival, Date of Second Passover, Cooking a Kid in Its Mother's Milk, etc.

The poet said, "Open You my eyes, that I may behold wondrous things out of Your law" (Psalm 119:18).[1]

[Scripture states:] "This month [i.e., Nisan] shall be for you the beginning of months" (Exodus 12:2). The first day of Nisan [Hebrew, *yom ha-molad*] is truly the beginning of the year.[2] The Tabernacle

---

1. Ibn Ezra opens chapter 9 with this quote from Psalms because this chapter, unlike the previous one, offers reasons for the commandments not explained in Scripture. Many of the explanations offered are of an esoteric nature.

2. Heb. *ha-rosh be-emet*. Ibn Ezra plays with the word *emet*. Earlier he refers to the season of spring as *tekufat ha-emet* (see Chapter 6). See Mishnah, *Rosh Hashanah* 1:1, which lists four new year days in the year. Ibn Ezra is of the opinion that the first of Nisan is the "real" Rosh Hashanah (new year).

was erected on this day (see Exodus 40:17). Furthermore, "the three-stranded cord"[3] predominates [i.e., Cancer] on the tenth day of Nisan [which is the day that Israel set aside the Paschal lamb in Egypt; see Exodus 12:3]. The sun is then in its glory and the moon is then in its "house."[4] The heavenly bodies are similarly propitiously aligned on the tenth day of the seventh month (Leviticus 23:27).

I have already explained the significance of the Day of Memorial [i.e., Rosh Hashanah].

Passover and Sukkot fall when the moon is full and half full.[5] The Eighth Day of Assembly [the day after Sukkot] is observed because the moon tarries in its journey [in the month of Tishri].[6]

---

3. The sun and moon are then favorably aligned. They are arranged in the "third alignment" or the "third aspect" (the three-stranded cord) also known as the alignment of love (*mabbat ahavah*). See J.L.X. Krinsky, *Chumash, Mehokekei Yehudah*, Exodus 12:13. For a description of the aspects or alignments, see p. 47 of Stern's edition of the *Yesod Mora*. Creizenach explains the three-stranded cord to mean that the moon has traveled a third of its course around the earth.

4. The sky is divided into twelve "houses." They roughly correspond to the twelve divisions of the zodiac. "The sun is then in its glory" is a reference to Aries, which is the sun's "house." A person is in his glory when he is in his house. The moon's house is cancer. I have followed the Stern and Levin editions, which read, lit., "this one in its glory and this one in its house." This is also the reading of Tuv Elem. On the tenth of Nisan, the sun is in Aries which is its place of glory and the moon is in Cancer which is its "house." When they are in the third aspect, the earth is showered with beneficence. The Waxman and Baer editions read, This one in its glory and this one in its house of shame. Creizenach explains this to mean the moon is then in its glory, and Mars is in its house of shame.

5. Both Passover and Sukkot are observed for seven days. The first day of Passover falls on Nisan 15, and the first day of Sukkot falls on Tishri 15. The last day of Passover falls on Nisan 21 and that of Sukkot on Tishri 21. The moon is full on the fifteenth and half full on the twenty-first of the month.

6. And does not enter a favorable alignment until Tishri 22. Hence, an additional day was appended to Sukkot. However, the moon moves faster in Nisan and enters a favorable alignment on the twenty-first day. Hence, Passover is celebrated for seven days.

Circumcision is performed close to seven full days after birth, for according to the Torah's way of counting, even a moment remaining on the day of birth is reckoned as a full day.[7] Likewise, the last day of the year is considered a full year.[8] The importance of the seventh day is well known.[9] The same is the case with the seventh year,[10] and the seven "weeks of years" [i.e., the Jubilee; see Leviticus 25:8] The Jubilee year, when all slaves are freed (Leviticus 25:10), corresponds to [the working life of Levite]. We thus read, "and from the age of fifty years they [i.e., the Levites] shall return from the service of the work" (Numbers 8:25).[11]

---

7. Although Scripture commands that circumcision be performed on the eighth day (Genesis 17:12; Leviticus 12:3), in practice it is performed after about seven full days have passed. Thus, neither the first nor the last day of the eight days before circumcision is a full day, and, in actuality, approximately seven full days pass before the act is performed.

8. Lit. "one day of the year is considered a year." This rule applies to a king. See *Rosh Hashanah* 2b: "When a king is appointed on the 29th of Adar, that day counts as the first year of his reign and the next day the first day of Nisan as the start of his second year."

    According to the teaching of astrology, the seventh day is significant because there is a change in nature and fate on this day. See Ibn Ezra on Genesis 8:5: "Noah observed the quarterly watch." The month is divided into four watches. The watches fall on the seventh day which is a quarter of the month. That is why Noah waited seven days before sending out the dove from the ark after sending out the raven. Also see Ibn Ezra to Leviticus 12:2: "The reason that a woman who gives birth to a child is unclean for seven days is that she must wait until she completes a quarter of days.... A change is seen at the end of seven days." The seventh day is significant with regard to the leper, the Nazirite, the menstruous woman, and one who becomes unclean by touching a dead body and in other rituals. See Leviticus 13:5–6,32–35, 51; 14:9, 32; 15:19; Numbers 6:9; 19:12, 19. Earlier (chapter 8:2), Ibn Ezra noted the reason for the Sabbath. He now notes the importance of the number seven aside from its significance as a Sabbath, a holy day. It serves as reminder that God created the wold in six days and rested on the seventh.

10. The Sabbatical year. See Leviticus 25:4. According to Ibn Ezra, the seventh year, like the seventh day, has astrological significance.

11. That is, after seven weeks of years the Levites are released from Temple

IBN EZRA'S YESOD MORA

The second Passover [observed a month after Passover; see Numbers 9:13] corresponds to the [time when Passover is observed in an] intercalated year.[12]

"You shall not seethe a kid in its mother's milk" (Exodus 23:19) is similar to "You shall not kill it [a female animal from the herd or flock] and its young both in one day" (Leviticus 22:28), "you shall not take the mother with the young" (Deuteronomy 22:6), and "You shall not plow with an ox and an ass together" (Deuteronomy 22:6).[13]

The reason for the prohibition of bestiality, "for neither shall you do thus [i.e., injure the sexual organs of an animal] in your land" (Leviticus 22:24), and for "A woman shall not wear that which pertains unto a man, neither shall a man put on a woman's garment" (Deuteronomy 22:5) is that these actions contradict God's work.[14] Scripture similarly states, "You shall keep my statutes" (Leviticus 19:19). It therefore forbids the wearing of a garment made out of linen and wool.[15]

The reason [why a person suspected of being plagued by certain skin eruptions][16] is quarantined for seven days is well known. The same applies to a menstruous woman (Leviticus 15:25–28) and a woman who gives birth (Leviticus 12:2).

---

service. Similarly, after seven weeks of years pass, all slaves go free.

12. Scripture permits those unable to observe the eating of the Paschal Lamb in its proper time to observe a compensatory ritual a month later, when the holiday falls in an intercalated year.

13. According to Ibn Ezra, the purpose of these laws is to prevent cruelty to animals. See Ibn Ezra on Exodus 23:19: "It is possible that it is prohibited to seethe a kid in its mother's milk because to do so is very cruel." Also see Deuteronomy 22:10: "God had mercy on His creatures."

14. They are unnatural acts. For God wanted the sexes to be distinct. He also did not want man and beast to copulate.

15. Leviticus 19:19. According to Ibn Ezra, the prohibition of wearing linen and wool symbolizes the prohibition of mixing what God wanted to keep apart.

16. By certain skin eruptions. See Leviticus chs. 13–14.

100

Valuation[17] begins at the age of one month [when the moon] returns to the place [where it was at a person's birth].[18] Up to age five, one's valuation is five *shekalim*. These five shekalim correspond to age five [lit., "in keeping with the aforementioned number"]. From age five to age twenty, one's valuation is twenty shekalim. From age twenty to age sixty, when one is in the prime of one's intellectual and physical strength, one's valuation is fifty shekalim.[19] These fifty shekalim correspond to the age of five [when one's value begins to increase]. From the age of sixty and on, the amount declines by five.[20]

The valuations of females are about half that of males. They are three [shekalim from a month until the age of five]; ten [shekalim from the age of five to the age of twenty] and thirty [shekalim from the age of twenty to the age of sixty].

The sending of the male goat to Azazel (Leviticus 16:17–22) is similar to the purification ritual of a leper.[21] Its esoteric meaning is explained in the writings of the holy Sages.[22] The same is true con-

---

17. A person may vow to donate to the Temple his own or someone else's worth. The valuation is fixed by the Torah in Leviticus 27:1–9.

18. Lit. "until it returns to the place." When the moon completes a cycle, i.e., when the child is a month old. Komtiyano; Cohen and Simon. "Until the return to the place" might also mean until the person dies. *Ad shuv el ha-makom* seems to me to be a reference to "till you return to the ground" (Gen. 3:1). In other words valuation lasts from a month for as long as a person lives.

19. Ten times as much as at the earliest period of life. It is for this reason that the maximum never exceeds fifty shekalim even after person has passed the age of fifty.

20. Lit. "and from there minus five." The text is vague. From the age of sixty and on, a man's valuation is fifteen shekalim, five less than that given at the ages of five and twenty. See Leviticus 27:7.

21. Wherein a bird is "let go...into the open field." Cf. Leviticus 14:1–7. The he-goat carried away the sins of Israel while the bird carried away the uncleanliness of the leper.

22. It isn't clear what Ibn Ezra is referring to. According to *Pirkei de-Rabbi Eliezer*, the male goat was sent to Samael (Satan) to bribe him not to accuse Israel of any sins on Yom Kippur. Ibn Ezra on Leviticus 16:8 hints that the

cerning the heifer whose neck was broken in the valley (Deuteronomy 21:6).[23] The one who understands the secret of Hebrew grammar will understand the meaning of *lo ye'aved bo* (Deuteronomy 21:4).[24]

2. Reasons for Commandments
Not Explained in Scripture (Continued)

Rabbi Saadiah Gaon says that there is no reason for a person to wonder why the red heifer purified the unclean but rendered those clean unclean [until evening, Numbers 19:6–10], for behold, honey aids or harms according to the composition of the one who eats it.[25]

The reason why unclean cattle, unclean fowl, and things that creep in the water are prohibited (Leviticus 34, Deuteronomy 14) is well known.[26]

It is an affront to donate a harlot's fee or the price of a dog [to God's Temple, which is why such an act is prohibited; see Deuteronomy 23:19]. The same principle applies to the offering of a blemished animal as a sacrifice (Leviticus 22:2–25), to a priest who is blemished

---

male goat carried Israel's sins to a place where demons dwell, that is, to a place where no humans live. Cf. "You will hurl our sins into the depths of the sea" (Micah 7:19). Thus Israel was purged of all sin on Yom Kippur. The bird in the purification ritual of the leper served the same purpose.

23. The heifer was decapitated in a valley that was a wilderness. According to Ibn Ezra, it bore the sin of murder.

24. Deuteronomy 21:4 reads, *asher lo ye'aved bo*, which can a be rendered in two ways: (1) "which is not worked (plowed)" or (2) "which will not be worked with." According to the first interpretation *ya'aved* is a present form. According to the second interpretation it is a future form.

25. A person who comes into contact with a corpse is rendered unclean for seven days. He becomes clean only upon being sprinkled with the ashes of a red heifer. See Numbers 19.

26. Ibn Ezra writes, "It is well known that the food which one eats turns into one's own very flesh" (on Leviticus 11:43). Therefore, one who eats unclean things becomes unclean. Thus, the reason for the prohibition of eating unclean creatures is the preservation of Israel's sanctity. Hence, Scripture states, "sanctify yourselves therefore, and be ye holy; for I am holy" (Leviticus 11:44).

(v. 20), or a bald Kohen offering sacrifices.[27] For this is the opposite of God's work.[28]

Scripture explains the law, "you shall furnish him liberally [i.e., you shall give a freed slave what he needs]" (Deuteronomy 15:14), with the statement, "and you shall remember that you were a bondman in the land of Egypt" (Deuteronomy 15:15), and the Lord brought you out from there with a vast amount of wealth.[29]

Length of days was promised for sending away a mother bird (see Deuteronomy 22:6–7). It was not promised for taking away the mother bird's offspring, for taking the chicks is optional. We find the same reward [i.e., length of days] promised for honoring our parents, who brought us into this world and will lengthen our days (Exodus 20:12).[30] The aforementioned [i.e., the same reward is given for sending away the mother bird and honoring parents] is so because *ve-ha'arakhta* ["that you may prolong"] in "that you may prolong your days" [concerning the mother bird, Deuteronomy 22:7] is a transitive verb.[31]

"But you shall fear your God" follows "you shall not put a stumbling

---

27. Ibn Ezra on Leviticus 21:5: "The reason why Scripture warns the *kohanim* not to 'make baldness upon their head, or to shave off the corners of their beard, nor make any cuttings in their flesh' when mourning a death is that one who has a bald head, or whose beard has been shorn or whose flesh has cuttings is prohibited to serve before the Lord."

28. This is not the state that God intended for people or animals. God does not want people to blemish themselves or rip out their hair. Hence, a blemished or bald priest may not officiate in the Temple.

29. Ibn Ezra's interpretation of "and you shall remember that you were a bondman in the land of Egypt."

30. Exodus 20:12 reads "Honor your father and your mother, so that they may prolong your days upon the land that the Lord your God gives you." Ibn Ezra explains this as follows: "Your parents will be the cause of your days being long. God will reward you with a long life for honoring them." Thus, one's parents will be the cause of a long life.

31. *Ve-ha'arakhta* is a transitive verb meaning "you will prolong," that is, by observing the precept "of sending away the mother" you will prolong your days. We thus see that the same reward is given for sending away the mother bird and honoring parents.

block before the blind nor curse the deaf" (Leviticus 19:14), lest God take away the sight of a person who puts a stumbling block before the blind, and He take away the hearing of an individual who curses the deaf. The law commanding one to respect the aged is similar (Leviticus 18:32).[32] Scripture teaches, if you fear not the old, fear God who will judge you when you become old.[33]

Scripture tells us regarding idolatry, "[You shall have no other gods] before Me" (Exodus 20:3). This is to be interpreted in the sense of [the gods] that have not made the heavens and the earth (Jeremiah 10:10).[34] Scripture also states, "You shall not make with Me [gods of silver, or gods of gold, you shall not make unto you]" (Exodus 20:20) because "You yourselves have seen that I have talked to you from heaven" (Exodus 20:19), and as Moses explained, "you saw no form" (Deuteronomy 4:12) [when God revealed Himself to you, hence do not make an image of God].

It is also possible that the meaning of "You shall not make with Me gods of silver, or gods of gold, you shall not make unto you" is: you have no need to make an image to worship when you serve Me.[35] I have already explained that the incident of the golden calf did not entail idolatry.[36] "Tomorrow shall be a feast to the Lord" (Exodus

---

32. In that Scripture states, "but you shall fear the Lord" with regard to the law commanding us to fear the aged.
33. That is why "and you shall fear the Lord" (Leviticus 19:31) follows "You shall rise up before the hoary head, and honor the face of the old man" (Leviticus 19:31).
34. In other words, Exodus 20:3 does not refer to real gods but to gods invented by men (Creizenach).
35. According to the first interpretation, the meaning of "You shall not make with Me gods of silver, or gods of gold, you shall not make for yourself" is, you have seen that I have no image, therefore make no image of Me. According to the second interpretation, its meaning is, I do not require you to make any image for use in My worship. Therefore, do not employ an image when you worship Me.
36. See Ibn Ezra's introduction to his comments on Exodus 32. Ibn Ezra notes this here because he has just explained the meaning of Exodus 22:20,

32:5) clearly shows this to be the case [i.e., that the golden calf was not idolatry but rather directed towards God]. This [verse] is precisely what Aaron commanded the people to do. The Israelites acted in accordance with Aaron's command. We thus read, "And they rose up early on the morrow, and offered burnt offerings" (Exodus 32:6). The Tetragrammaton [YHVH used in this verse], unlike the term *Elohim*, refers only to the Lord.[37]

3. Reasons for the Way Tabernacle Was Constructed

The intelligent [person] will understand the secret of the Tabernacle[38] and of the ark of the covenant from the voice that went forth from between the two cherubim (Exodus 25:22; Numbers 7:89).[39]

The ark was two and a half cubits long [and a cubit and a half wide; Exodus 25:10] because each one of the tablets [upon which the ten commandments were inscribed] was square shaped. Its length the same size as its width. They filled the inside of the ark [i.e., the tablets

---

which prohibits the use of an image in the worship of the Lord. It was this prohibition that Israel violated when they made the golden calf.

37. Hence, it was the Lord whom the people worshiped. They did not worship the golden calf.

38. The Tabernacle served as a place for God's presence. See Exodus 25:12: "And let them make Me a sanctuary, that I may dwell among them." Also see Exodus 25:40: "There are places where God's power is more manifest than in other places." Rabbi Joseph ben Eliezer (the *Tzafenat Pane'ach*) explains that Ibn Ezra believed that the Tabernacle and its vessels corresponded to the upper world. He is quoted by Y.L. Fleisher in his edition of Ibn Ezra's short commentary to Exodus. Vienna 1926, p. 235. Rabbi Joseph ben Eliezer quotes the following Midrash to support Ibn Ezra's interpretation off the Tabernacle: "God raised Moses up [to heaven] and showed him [the upper world]. God then said to Moses make a copy [on earth] of what you see here." *Midrash Shir Ha-Shirim* to Song of Songs 3:11.

39. The ark served as symbol of God's throne, the *kissei ha-kavod*. God communicated to Moses via the ark. See Exodus 5:22: "And there I will meet with you, and I will speak with you from above the ark-cover, from between the two cherubim which are upon the ark of the testimony, of all things which I will give you in commandment unto the children of Israel."

were the exact size as the inside of the ark]. The walls of the ark were a half a cubit wide.[40] The ark was a cubit and a half in height.[41] This measurement, like that of the table of shewbread (Exodus 25:23–30), included its legs,[42] for Scripture clearly states, "upon its [the ark's] four feet [pa'amotav]" (Exodus 25:12). The term pa'am is often employed in Hebrew.[43] It does not mean "corners,"[44] as the phrase "and two rings" (Exodus 25:12) clearly shows.[45] For according to the exegetes [who maintain that pa'amotav means "its corners"], the text should have read, "two of the rings" [rather than "and two rings"].

The altar of incense (Exodus 30:1–20) was placed between the *menorah* and the table of shewbread outside the curtain [which

---

40. This accounts for the extra half cubit in width and in length. Thus, the inside of the ark was a cubit in width and two cubits in length. However, measured from the outside the ark was two and a half cubits long and a cubit and a half wide because its walls were a half cubit in thickness. See Ibn Ezra on Exodus 25:10.

41. According to Creizenach and Levin. Exodus 25:10.

42. We do not know the actual height of that part of the ark where the tablets were placed. According to Ibn Ezra to Exodus 25:12, each tablet was a half a cubit in thickness. Ibn Ezra interprets in this way because it would be impossible under normal conditions for Moses to carry two tablets, each of which was the size of a square cubit.

43. The word is found in Isaiah 26:6, Psalm 85:14, and Song of Songs 7:2.

44. See Onkelos and Rashi on Exodus 25:12.

45. Lit. "the two rings." Exodus 25:12 reads, "And you shall cast four rings of gold for it, and put them in its four pa'amot; and two rings shall be on its one corner [tzalo], and two rings on the other side corner [tzalo]." The clause "and two rings shall be on its one corner [tzalo], and two rings on its other side corner [tzalo]" implies that the rings mentioned in the second part of the verse are not the same as those in the first part. If they were, the verse would have read, "And you shall cast four rings of gold for it, and put them in its four pa'amot; two of the rings shall be on its one side corner, and two of the rings on its other side corner." Now, being that the rings mentioned in the second part of the verse were placed on the side corners of the ark, the rings mentioned in the first part were placed elsewhere. Hence, the term pa'am cannot mean "corner."

separated the holy from the holy of holies].[46] The altar [of incense, which was two cubits tall; see Exodus 20:2] was taller than the *menorah* and the table of shewbread.[47]

The secret of the ten curtains (Exodus 26:1) and also that of the eleven curtains (Exodus 26:7) [placed over the ten curtains] is also known.[48] The same applies[49] to the reason why [the first set of curtains was] twenty-eight cubits long (Exodus 26:2) and [the second set of curtains was] thirty cubits long (Exodus 26:8).[50]

The copper altar [to serve as the base for sacrifices] (Exodus 27:1–8) had a net beneath its ledge that reached from the bottom halfway up the altar. This was the actual way it was constructed.

The secret of the *ephod* (Exodus 28:6–12) is extremely precious, for six names were inscribed on each one of the two sapphire stones

---

46. In other words, the altar of incense, the *menorah*, and the table of shewbread were placed in the section of the Tabernacle known as the *kodesh* (the holy) (Exodus 40:26).

47. The table of shewbread was a cubit and a half in height. The Torah does not mention the height of the *menorah*. Ibn Ezra assumes that it was lower than that of the altar. According to the Sages, however, the *menorah* was eighteen handbreadths, that is, that is, three cubits in height. See Rashi on Exodus 25:35.

48. They were made according to the specifications given in Exodus 26:11–16 so that they would properly cover the wooden frame of the Tabernacle. The curtains represent the heavens. See Psalms 104:2: "He stretches out the heavens *like a curtain*."

49. That is, we also know the reason why one set of curtains was twenty-eight cubits long and the second set thirty cubits long.

50. The Tabernacle was ten cubits wide and ten cubits high. The bottom cubit of the Tabernacle's sideboards fit into sockets. The first set of curtains covered the top of the Tabernacle plus the nine exposed cubits of the sideboards. The second set of curtains covered all that the first did, plus the sockets. This is the reason why the first set of curtains was twenty-eight cubits long, and the second set thirty cubits long.

that were on the *ephod*.[51] One stone was on its right, and another one was on its left.[52]

Observe: There was no image on the stones [of the *ephod*]. This corresponds [to the twelve sections of the sky]. These sections can be perceived only by the mind.[53] They correspond to the number of the tribes of Israel.

The breastplate was "like the work of the *ephod*" (Exodus 28:15).[54] It was square (v. 16), corresponding to the four compass points. Each one of its stones (vv. 17–20) was therefore unlike the other.[55] The boxes and the rings that were permanently set in the breastplate (Exodus 28:23–25) allude to the celestial equator. The *urim* (Exodus 28:30) are to be taken at face value.[56] So too the *tummim* [also allude to heavenly

---

51. According to Ibn Ezra, the *ephod* was an astrological instrument that the high priest used to predict the future. See Ibn Ezra and Nahmanides on Exodus 28:6.

52. The twelve names on the two stones of the *ephod* correspond to the twelve constellations, six of which are found in the northern part of the sky and six in the southern part of the sky. The twelve names on the *ephod* are also divided into two groups.

53. Lit. "to thought." The sky is divided into twelve sections containing the twelve constellations. The lines marking off these sections cannot be seen by the eye. They can be conceived only by the mind.

54. It had similar astrological significance. Its function, however, was not identical to that of the *ephod*. For heavenly beneficence descended upon Israel through the breastplate and not through the *ephod*. See Ibn Ezra on Exodus 28:6

55. Each stone was unlike any other, showing that each one of the twelve tribes was unique. Each stone symbolized the heavenly beneficence that descended upon Israel through the breastplate.

56. The word *urim* means "lights." Ibn Ezra probably means that these "lights" correspond to the sun and moon (Simon and Levin), though he does not explicitly say so. However, since the Tabernacle corresponds to heaven and *urim* means "lights," Ibn Ezra assumes it is a reference to the lights in heaven – i.e., the sun and moon. Josephus also sees the Tabernacle as a representation of heaven.

bodies]. The *tummim* correspond to the number five.[57] Moses first placed them [the *urim* and *tummim*] on the breastplate, in accordance with the position of the heavenly bodies [i.e., the constellations], on the day that he erected the Tabernacle. The wise will understand.

---

57. Literally, the circular number. The *tummim* correspond to the number five which is a whole or complete number and allude to the five moving stars (planets). It should be noted that the ancients were aware of only the five visible planets, namely, Venus, Mars, Jupiter, Saturn, and Mercury.

Five is called the circular number because it which turns back to itself, that is, it is present in its sums, when multiplied by 5. For example $5 \times 5 = 25$; $25 \times 5 = 125$; $125 \times 5 = 625$ and so forth. We do not find this in any other number with the exception of 6. Cohen and Simon, p. 171, 187.

Chapter x

THE RELIGIOUS LIFE

1. The *Shema*

How precious is the Torah of our God. How true are His testimonies. How beautiful are His words. For Scripture speaks of the four shifting positions of the human body: sitting, walking, lying down, and rising (see Deuteronomy 6:4–7).[1] All of the aforementioned are intransitive verbs [sitting, walking, lying down, and rising].

Do not be troubled by the verb *yishkavennah* (Deuteronomy 28:30), for its meaning is "shall lie down with her."[2] *Yishkavennah* is similar

---

1. The Torah states: "Hear O Israel, the Lord our God, the Lord is one.... And these words which I command you this day, shall be upon your heart; and you ... shall talk of them when you sit in your house, and when you walk by the way, and when you lie down, and when you rise up" (Deuteronomy 6:4–7).

    In other words, the *Shema* contains these four positions of sitting, walking, lying down, and rising. Prima facie, "and when you lie down" presents a problem. The verse seems to imply that one should rehearse God's word while asleep. Hence, "and when you lie down" does not mean "when you sleep," but is to be taken literally. We thus see that God's words are precious, true, and beautiful; that is, they are carefully chosen.

2. *Yishkavennah* usually refers to the act of intercourse. It thus appears to be transitive. However, since its literal meaning is "to lie down," it is actually intransitive. Ibn Ezra insists that all of the verbs in Deuteronomy 6:6–7 that deal with the shifting position of the human body – including

111

to the word *yegurekha* ("shall sojourn with you") in "Evil shall not sojourn with You" (Psalm 5:5).[3]

Our Sages employing talmudic terminology distinguished between the active form *shokhev* ("lies") and the passive form *nishkav* ("lain with").[4] However, in scriptural usage, both of them mean "lying down" [both forms are intransitive] as *shakhavti* in "Behold I lay [*shakhavti*] yesterday with my father" (Genesis 19:34) proves.[5]

Note that when a person lies down, he is awake.[6] However, Scripture states, "and lay down [*va-yishkav*] in that place" (Genesis 28:11) and does not say "and he slept [in that place]" because most people are prone when asleep [hence *shakhav* sometimes is used in the sense "to sleep"]. Scripture reads, "And David slept [*va-yishkav*] with his fathers" (1 Kings 2:10) because a sleeping person is similar to a corpse.[7]

When a person rests in one place, he is sitting. Sitting is, at it were, half the state of rising. "Rising" [*kimah*] is defined as standing, as "in the house shall stand [*ve-kam*]" (Leviticus 25:30) [thus *u-ve-kumekha* ("and when you rise up") means "when you stand up")].

"Walking" is defined as moving from place to place. It is the opposite of sitting.

---

be-shokhbekha ("when you lie down"), which comes from the same root as *yishkavvenah* – are intransitive.

3. The point being that the suffix does not indicate that the verb is transitive. *Yegurekha* does not mean "sojourn you" but "sojourn with you." Similarly, *yishkavennah* does not mean "lie her" but "lie down with her."

4. According to the Rabbis, *shokhev*, is a transitive verb, and the active form of the root *shin, caf, bet*, refers to the male who penetrates the female, while the passive form of the verb applies to the one who is penetrated during intercourse.

5. This was said by one of Lot's daughters. We thus see that the active form *shakhav* is intransitive.

6. In other words, and when thou lie down does not mean when you sleep. Ibn Ezra interprets thusly because the Torah would not obligate us to do anything when we sleep.

7. Ibn Ezra's point is that *shokhav* means "lying down." However, its meaning was extended to include sleeping and death. Cohen and Simon, p. 174.

When a person is lying down, a [horizontal] line can be drawn from his head to his toe.[8] Thus, standing [i.e., rising] is the opposite of lying down. Psalm 1:1 reads, "that has not walked... Nor stood... Nor sat." It does not read "nor lain" because a person is usually asleep when lying.

The Torah reads, "and shall talk of them" (Deuteronomy 6:7). Its meaning is, "and shall talk of them" in your heart as in, "I spoke with my own heart" (Ecclesiastes 1:16). "And shall talk of them" is also to be taken literally, that is, it refers to speaking with one's mouth.

God thus commanded us to meditate upon His law during all activities and in all bodily states (see Deuteronomy 6:6). Scripture clearly states this in "And in His law does he meditate day and night" (Psalm 1:2). Solomon similarly advised people to seek wisdom in all states, namely, "When you walk, it shall lead you; when you lie down, it shall watch over you, and when you wake [that is, when you stand or sit] it shall talk with you" (Proverbs 6:22).

2. The *Shema* (Continued)

[Scripture states:] "And these words [shall be upon your heart]" (Deuteronomy 6:6). This means that a person must know that the Lord is One and that there is no existence to anything that exists unless it cleaves to God.[9] Scripture therefore says, "And you shall love the Lord your God with all your heart" (Deuteronomy 6:5). The meaning of the latter is, "if you desire to exist in this world and also in the world to come, then love God." I will allude to this secret at the end of the book. It [i.e., knowledge and love of God] is the foundation of all wisdom.[10] God alone is the Creator of all. God knows the particulars by His knowledge of the whole, for the particulars are in flux.[11]

---

8. Lit. "lying is like a line from head to feet."
9. Ibn Ezra's paraphrase of "Hear O Israel, the Lord our God, the Lord is one. And these words... shall be upon your heart."
10. Maimonides employs practically the same language in his *Mishneh Torah*. See *Hilkhot Yesodei Ha-Torah* 1:1: "The foundation of foundations and the pillar of all wisdom is, To know that there is a first cause."
11. According to Ibn Ezra, God's knowledge extends only to the general and

Man's soul is unique.[12] When given by God, it is like a tablet set before a scribe. When God's writing, which consists of the categorical knowledge of the things made [lit., "born"] out of the four elements,[13] the knowledge of the spheres, the throne of glory, the secret of the chariot (see Ezekiel 1), and the knowledge of the Most High, is inscribed on this tablet [of man's soul], the soul cleaves to God the Glorious while it is yet in man and also afterward when its power is removed from the body which is its place [lit., "palace" here on Earth].[14]

It is thus wrong for an intelligent person to seek anything in this world except that which will benefit him in the world to come. Do you not see that with regard to the prohibited sexual relationships, Scripture states "I am the Lord" (Leviticus 18:6) [meaning that one who desires to cleave to God should stay away from unseemly things]. For the person who abstains from having sexual relations with those whom Scripture has prohibited sexual contact with is holy. He is in the company of those who are close to God the Glorious. Thus Asaf [one of the Psalmists] states, "But as for me, the nearness of God is my good" (Psalm 73:28). The latter is preceded by "For, lo, they who

---

the eternal. Ibn Ezra believes that God knows the particular only to the extent that it is involved in the general and permanent. See Ibn Ezra on Genesis 18:21. Maimonides is also of the opinion that Divine providence is proportional to a person's intellectual development. See *The Guide for the Perplexed* 3:18. This idea was strongly attacked by Don Isaac Abarbanel (comment on Genesis 18:20) and Rabbi Hasdai Crescas (*Sefer Or Ha-Shem* 2:1). See Chapter 10:4 of this work, God "is far and close."

12. Man is created in God's image. According to Ibn Ezra, this refers to man's soul. See Ibn Ezra on Genesis 1:26. Ibn Ezra thus points out that man's soul, like that of its Creator, is unique.

13. Lit. "the four roots." See chapter 1. Like God, man must attain eternal knowledge. Hence, Ibn Ezra speaks of knowledge of the categories rather than knowledge of the particulars.

14. According to Ibn Ezra, man must master the physical and the metaphysical sciences in order to attain immortality. In his introduction to *The Guide for the Perplexed*, Maimonides refers to the former as *ma'aseh bereshit* and to the latter as *ma'aseh merkavah*.

go far from You shall perish."[15] David, likewise, says: "For you will not abandon my soul to *she'ol*" (Psalm 17: 10) when my flesh [i.e., body] is there [in the grave]. For *she'ol* refers to the grave, which is below the surface of the earth. Compare, "If I make my bed in *she'ol*, behold You are there" (Psalm 139:8).

Scripture also says, "You make me to know the path of life" (Psalm 16:11). The poet also says, "But God will redeem my soul from the power of *she'ol*; For He will receive me [*yikaheni*]. Selah" (Psalm 49:16). The word *yikaheni* ["He will receive me"] refers to an exalted state.[16] It is like "and he [Enoch] was not; for God took him" (Genesis 5:24)[17] and "And afterward receive me with glory" (Psalm 73:24) is similar [in that it also refers to immortality].

3. Holiness Requires Abstention from Sexual Relations

[In preparation to God's revelation at Mount Sinai] Scripture states, "sanctify them today and tomorrow" (Exodus 19:10). The Torah then goes on to say "come not near a woman" (Exodus 19:15).[18] It is for this reason that a man who has relations with his wife is unclean (Leviticus 15:18) and is prohibited from praying until he washes.[19] The Sages of

---

15. Ibn Ezra understands "shall perish" to mean "shall perish in this and in the next world."

16. It refers to immortality, being with God. See *Mishneh Torah, Hilkhot Teshuvah 8:2.*

17. God granted Enoch immortality.

18. Do not have sexual relations with a woman. In other words, "sanctify them" means "instruct them not to have sexual relations."

19. See *Berakhot* 20b–21a. Ibn Ezra believed that the Torah declared a man who had a seminal emission, a menstruant, or a woman who gave birth unclean because the aforementioned relate to sexual activity or sexual organs. He believed that a person should abstain from sexual intercourse as much as possible. See his earlier comment:

   The intelligent person will act as did our father Jacob when he vowed, "then shall the Lord be my God" (Genesis 28:21), for when Jacob came to Beth-El, he said "Put away the strange gods that are among you" (Genesis 35:2). He left the sheep and separated himself to serve

the Mishnah similarly noted that it was customary during the period of the Second Temple for a skin to be washed [i.e., immersed in a *mikveh*] even if one drop of semen fell upon it (Leviticus 15:17, *Kelim* 15:17). Furthermore, a person who experiences a seminal emission is prohibited to eat sanctified flesh [i.e., flesh from an offering, Leviticus 7:20, 15:16]. Scripture was likewise very stringent with regard to a menstruous woman and a woman who gave birth.[20]

The Nazirite is a holy person (Numbers ch. 6).[21] When the Nazirite completes his term and wants to go back to drinking wine, he must bring a burnt offering, a sin offering, and a peace offering. He also must shave his head at the entrance of the Tent of Meeting. He is treated disrespectfully [by having his head shaved] because he is distancing himself from his holiness and is descending in state.[22]

God. He never again slept with a woman, for Rachel was dead and Bilhah was defiled.... Scripture therefore states elsewhere. 'Now the sons of Jacob were twelve' (Genesis 35:21). It states this to tell us that after Bilhah was defiled, Jacob never again had sexual relations with a woman and therefore did not sire any additional children" (*Yesod Mora*, Chapter 7 section 11).

Ibn Ezra did not believe that there is a biblical precept to marry. See chapter 2:12 of the *Yesod Mora*.

20. The laws dealing with the "uncleanliness" of a menstruous woman and a woman who gave birth are very strict with regard to both the time that the uncleanliness lasts and how the uncleanliness is transmitted to another person or object. For the menstruous woman, see Leviticus 15:19–24. For the woman who gave birth, see Leviticus 12:1–5. Ibn Ezra believed that the Torah declared a person who had a seminal emission or a menstruating woman or a woman who gave birth unclean because the aforementioned relate to sexual activity or sexual organs.

21. The Nazirite is holy because he separates himself from wine. See Maimonides' *The Guide for the Perplexed* 3:33: "But abstinence from drinking wine is also called holiness; in reference to the Nazirite, it is therefore said, 'He shall be holy' (Numbers 6:5)."

22. By ceasing to be a Nazirite. This is also the opinion of Nahmanides. See Nahmanides on Numbers 6:11: "A Nazirite must bring a sin-offering when the days of his Naziritehood are fulfilled ... for until now he was separated

Also [like the Nazirite,] a woman who gives birth to a child [and resumes relations with her husband after a prescribed period of time] brings a lamb in its first year (Leviticus 12:1–8).[23]

The owner of a field must give the heave offering [i.e., *terumah*, Numbers 15:19–21], the first of his corn and oil (Deuteronomy 18:4), tithes (Leviticus 23:10; Deuteronomy 18:4; 26:1–11), and a portion of his dough to the priest (Numbers 15:20). He must also leave that which he forgets in the field (Deuteronomy 24:19), the corner of his field [i.e., *pe'ah*], and "the gleanings" [i.e., *leket* for the poor, the widow, and the fatherless; see Leviticus 19:9, 23:22].

The owner of a vineyard cannot use the fruit of his vines for the first three years. He must bring his grapes to Jerusalem in the fourth year and praise God there (Leviticus 19:23). He must give the first fruits (Numbers 18:12–13), the first of the wine (Deuteronomy 18:4), and the various tithes (Deuteronomy 12:17) to the priest. He must leave the tender fruit and the fallen fruit [for the poor] (Leviticus 19:10).

The laws pertaining to the Sabbatical and Jubilee years (Leviticus ch. 25) apply to the owners of fields and vineyards.

The shepherd must give the first of the fleece (Deuteronomy 18:4), the firstborn (Exodus 13:2), and the tenth born [to the priest] (Leviticus 27:32).

One who partakes of peace offerings [*shelamim*] must, aside from the designated parts [which are burned on the altar: Leviticus 3:1–5], give the thigh (Leviticus 7:32), the breast (Leviticus 7:31), the cheeks (Deuteronomy 18:3), and the maw (ibid.) [to the priest].

Scripture states, "every man according to the gift of his hand" (Deuteronomy 16:17). This teaches that one should give [to God]

---

in sanctity and the service of God, and he should...have remained separated forever" (Chavel's translation).

23. It appears that Ibn Ezra believes that the woman has to bring a sacrifice because she is going to resume having sexual relations. However on Leviticus 12:6, Ibn Ezra says that the sacrifice is to atone for any evil thoughts that entered her mind due to the pain that she experienced while giving birth.

"in accordance with what God has given him."[24] This is how the commandment of appearing at the sanctuary is observed (see Numbers 16:16).

The end of the matter is: Elijah the man of God and Elisha the prophet show the way.[25] [They forsook the world and served God alone.][26]

---

24. This explains why all the above have to be given to the poor and to the priest. According to Ibn Ezra, giving a gift to a deserving person out of respect to God is tantamount to giving the gift to God.
25. Elijah's and Elisha's lives show that separation from the pleasures of this world and cleaving to God is the goal of human existence. Elijah is described in Scripture as an ascetic personality. See 2 Kings, chapter 17. Since Elisha was Elijah's disciple, Ibn Ezra believes that he, too, must have lived an ascetic life.
26. Some editions omit this line.

Chapter XI

THE SECRET OF
THE DIVINE NAME

1. The Hebrew Alphabet

I am unable to discuss the secret of God's glorious name without first mentioning some of the meanings of the letters of the Hebrew alphabet.[1]

All the letters that human beings enunciate have their origin in one of the five following places: the throat comes first, the palate second, the tongue third, the teeth fourth, the lips last. The throat produces the *ayin, het, heh,* and *alef.* The palate produces the *gimmel, yod, caf,* and *kof.* The tongue produces the *dalet, tet, lamed, nun,* and *tav.* The teeth produce *the zayin, samekh, shin, resh,* and *tzadi.* The lips produce the *bet, vav, mem,* and *peh.*

The Hebrew alphabet contains twenty-two letters. Five of these letters come in two forms [*mem, nun, tzadi, peh,* and *caf*]. [Four of the latter, namely, *the nun, caf, peh,* and *tzadi*] have an extended vertical

---

1. Lit. "the holy tongue." According to the *Sefer Yetzirah* 1:1, God created the
    world utilizing thirty-two ways of wisdom. In the *Kuzari,* Rabbi Judah
    Ha-Levi explains that the aforementioned refers to the twenty-two letters
    of the Hebrew alphabet (God spoke and the world came into being) and
    the first ten numbers (all created things are based on measure and weight).
    Ibn Ezra accepted this theory and believes that God's name alludes to
    important aspects of the alphabet and mathematics. See *Kuzari* ch. 4.

line, in place of their usual horizontal line at their base, to indicate the end of a word.[2] One of them [the *mem*] is closed when it comes at the end of a word.

2. Letters that Serve as Root Letters and Letters that Serve as Both Prefixes and Suffixes

Half of the letters [*gimmel, dalet, zayin, het, tet, samekh, ayin, peh, tzadi, kof,* and *resh*] of the Hebrew alphabet serve only as root letters. They are never dropped.[3] They never serve as prefixes or suffixes. However, they may be doubled, as in the words *yerakrak*[4] [greenish] *adamdam*[5] [reddish] (Leviticus 13:49), and *sheharhoret*[6] [swarthy] (Song of Songs 1:6). Now when the second and third root letters are doubled, we have a diminutive [thus *adamdam* means "reddish" and not "redder"].[7] However, when the first and second root letters are doubled, we have a superlative [Heb., *le-yitron*]. Compare, *yofyafita* ["fairer"][8] (Psalm 45:3) and *tisagsegi* [you made it to grow] (Isaiah 17:11).[9]

The other half of the alphabet [*alef, bet, heh, vav, yod, caf, lamed, mem, nun, shin, tav*] consists of letters that are at times root letters and at other times serve as prefixes and suffixes.[10] *Kastil av hamon* – which

---

2. Lit. "to indicate that the word is not connected (to another word)." In other words, the *nun, kof, peh,* and *tzadi* are drawn straight down at the end of a word, while in their usual form, they are bent round toward the left.
3. Certain root letters, such as the *heh* or *nun,* are dropped in a number of conjugational forms.
4. From the root *yod, resh, kof.* The *resh* and *kof* are doubled in *yerakrak.*
5. From the root *alef, dalet, mem.* The *dalet* and *mem* are doubled in *adamdam.*
6. From the root *shin, het, resh.* The *het* and *resh* are doubled in *sheharhoret.*
7. It should be noted that not everyone agrees with this interpretation. According to Rashi, *yerakrak* means "very green," *adamdam* "very red," *sheharhoret* "very dark."
8. From the root *yod, peh, heh. Yofyafita* literally means "you became beautiful."
9. From the root *sin, gimel, heh.*
10. Lit. "ministering letters." Ibn Ezra can make this point because in medieval Hebrew, such letters were called *mesharetim,* ministers or servants. Any

is similar to my name[11] – or *ot mevin haskel*[12] – are their mnemonic signs. It is only right to choose letters that are easily pronounced to serve as prefixes and suffixes. For these letters are often sounded.

3. The Letters That Serve as Suffixes and Prefixes

The gutturals are the letters which are first sounded.[13] They begin with the *ayin*.[14] Next comes the *het*. Both of these letters are hard to pronounce. Hence, they are not found in the alphabet employed by the uncircumcised [i.e., the Christians, but they are pronounced by the Arabs]. Likewise, one who did not sound these letters as a matter of course when growing up cannot enunciate them [as an adult]. Hence, the Hebrews chose [only] the *alef* and the *heh* [from among the gutturals] to serve as prefixes and suffixes. Thus, half of the gutturals serve as root letters and half serve as suffixes and prefixes.

The Hebrews chose the first palatals, namely the *yod* and the *caf*,[15] for the distinction [of serving as root letters and prefixes and suffixes] because the palate is next to the throat and the *yod* and the *caf* are close to the *alef* and *heh* [which serve as root letters, prefixes, and suffixes].

The Hebrews chose about half of the linguals, namely, two letters,

---

letter that, in addition to being a root letter, also "serves" a word is called a ministering letter.

11. Ibn Ezra's first name was Abraham. *Av hamon* (father of a multitude) alludes to Abraham, who was the father of multitude of nations (Genesis 17:5). *Kastil* is the Hebrew form of Castille. Thus, *kastil av hamon* alludes to Abraham of Castille or Abraham ibn Ezra of Castille.

12. "A sign helps [or causes] an intelligent person to understand." Or "An intelligent person understands a sign."

13. The letters are sounded by the throat, palate, tongue, teeth and lips. The throat is the deepest part of thee body which produces sounds. Hence it is referred to as the first place where sound is produced.

14. The *ayin* is produced in the deepest part of the throat. Hence it is said to be the first letter to be sounded.

15. Actually, the fist palatals are *gimel* and *yod*. Rabbi Komtiyano explains that Ibn Ezra ignores the *gimel* because it is difficult to sound.

the *nun* and the *tav* [to serve as prefixes and suffixes].[16] Now, there are five linguals [*dalet, tet, lamed, nun,* and *tav*]. Hence, an additional lingual, the *lamed,* was also set aside to serve as a prefix. The *lamed* was so chosen because it is easily pronounced. The *lamed* was placed in the center of the alphabet because it is produced by the tongue, which lies in the middle of the other sound-producing organs [i.e., between the throat in back and lips and teeth in front]. The *lamed* was placed above the other letters because the tongue is raised when the *lamed* is sounded. It was given the name *lamed,* which comes from the same root as the word *limmud* [learning], because its main function [as a preposition] is to explain why something occurred. The aforementioned is the important secret [of the *lamed*]. We, therefore, read, *imri li* [say of me] (Genesis 20:13).[17] There are many similar instances.

Four of the dentals [*zayin, samekh, resh,* and *tzadi*] were set aside as root letters, leaving only the [remaining dental] *shin* to serve as a prefix. Only one dental was chosen to serve as a prefix because it is very difficult to pronounce the dentals individually or in combination with each other. It should be noted that the *shin* is sparingly employed as a prefix. It takes the place of the word *asher* [that], as in *she-kakhah lo* [that is in such a case] (Psalm 144:15), *sha-lamah eheyeh* [for why should I be] (Song of Songs 1:7), and *be-sha-gam* [for that he is also] in "for that he is also flesh" (Genesis 6:3).

The *zayin, tzadi,* and *samekh* have a whistling sound and are very difficult to pronounce [which is why they were not chosen to serve as prefixes or suffixes]. The same also applies to the *resh.* The fact that small children cannot pronounce it until they mature and the cords of their brains grow strong is proof of this. It is for this reason [i.e., the difficulty in pronouncing dentals] that they [i.e., the Hebrews] found it necessary to assign three labials [*bet, vav,* and *mem,* rather than two] to serve as prefixes and suffixes, with one of the labials, the *peh,* serving [only] as a root letter.

---

16. Ibn Ezra does not explain why these two letters were so chosen.
17. Lit. "say to me" and idiomatically "say of me," the reason being that the *lamed* hints at information. Hence, *imri li* means "inform them about me."

4. The Reason for the Order of the Hebrew Alphabet

The *alef* was placed at the head of the alphabet because it is the easiest guttural[18] to pronounce, and it is sounded before the *heh*.[19] A labial [i.e., the letter *bet*] that is furthest [from the spot in the throat where the *alef* is sounded] was placed next to the *alef*. In the same way, the *vav* [a labial] follows the *heh* [a guttural], and the *peh* [a labial] the *ayin* [a guttural]. Now the *alef* and the *bet* serve as prefixes. The *gimmel* and *dalet* (which follow) stand in contrast [to the *alef* and the *bet*], for the *gimmel* and *dalet* are [only] root letters formed by the tongue and palate.[20] Next come the *heh* and the *vav* that serve as suffixes and prefixes. In contrast, the *zayin* and *het* that follow, serve [only] as root letters. The *tet* [that comes next] is considered a letter that serves as both a prefix and a suffix because it interchanges with the *tav* [in certain *hitpa'el* forms]. [After *tet*] follow the *yod, caf, lamed, mem,* and *nun*; we thus have [here] six letters that serve as both prefixes and suffixes. They are followed by six root letters, namely, the *samekh, ayin, peh, tzadi, kof,* and *resh*.

The *alef* serves as a prefix and not as a suffix because the *alef* is the first letter of the alphabet. The *tav* [the last letter of the alphabet] serves both as a prefix and as a suffix. The *tav* is used as the sign of the feminine because its written form [but not spoken sound] resembles a *heh*.[21] The *tav* indicates the feminine when the silent *heh* turns into a *tav* [lit., "into a sounded letter in the third person perfect or in the

---

18. According to Ibn Ezra, the alphabet opens with a guttural because the throat is the first of the sound-producing organs. Next come the palate, tongue, teeth, and lips. Ibn Ezra views the body from the standpoint of the inner organs.
19. The *alef* sound is produced deeper in the throat than is the *heh* sound.
20. Whereas the *alef* is a guttural and the *bet* a labial. Furthermore, the *alef* and the *bet* serve both as root letters and as prefixes.
21. In roots ending in a *heh* when in the third person perfect, in the construct, and in the plural. Compare *hayetah*, the third person perfect form of the root *heh, yod, heh*, and *parot, parat*, the plural and construct forms of *parah*. See Ibn Ezra's long commentary on Exodus 1:16.

construct form"].[22] Thus, *hokhmah* [wisdom] turns into *hokhmat* [wisdom of] in "wisdom of heart" (Exodus 35:35). Similarly, the silent *heh* in the verb *asah* [from the root *ayin, sin, heh,* "he made"] turns into a *tav* in *asetah* ["she made"]. We find the same in *banetah* ["she built," from *bet, nun, heh*] and *kanetah* ["she bought," from *kof, nun, heh*]. We are also amazed that the *heh* in the word *amah* ["bondwoman," from *alef, mem, heh*] in "Cast out this maid-servant bondwoman" (Genesis 21:10) is sounded in the word *amahot* ["maidservants"] in "the two maid-servants" (Genesis 31:33).[23] The *tav* [which means "mark"] is so called [because it is formed] by adding a line [i.e., mark] to the *heh* [the "mark" (*tav*) changes the *heh* into a *tav*].

5. The Vowel Letters

I will now speak about the vowel letters [*alef, heh, vav,* and *yod*].[24] These letters are the foundation of God's revered Name.

The *alef* is fit to be a first person [singular] masculine and feminine prefix.[25] When the *heh* comes at the end of a noun, it indicates [lit., is a sign of] the feminine, both when silent and when dotted [Heb. *mappik*; a *heh* with a *mappik* is sounded]. A *vav* vocalized with a *holam* or a *shuruk* at the end of a word indicates the masculine, as in *yado* [his hand], *raglo* [his foot], and *yesovavenhu, yevonenehu, yitzerenhu* ["He compassed him about, He cared for him, He kept

---

22. Lit. into a sounded letter in the third person perfect or in the construct form.

23. We are "amazed" because the word should have been pronounced *amot*, that is, the silent *heh* should have changed into a single *tav*, as in most other nouns ending in a *heh*. Compare *mittah* (bed) with *mittot* (beds) and *parah* (cow) with *parot* (cows).

24. Heb. *otiyot ha-meshekh*, lit., "the elongated letters." These letters also serve as vowels, that is, the *alef* and *heh* indicate the "ah" sound, the *vav* the "oh" and "ooh" sounds, and the *yod* the "iy" and "ei" sounds.

25. For it is the easiest guttural to pronounce. Lit. "The *alef* is fit to be a first-person prefix that takes in both the masculine and the feminine." It serves as such in the imperfect. Compare *eshmor* (I will keep) and *ekhtov* (I will write).

him"] (Deuteronomy 32:10). The *yod* indicates the masculine when a prefix, as in *ya'aseh* ["he will do"], and the feminine when a suffix, as in *u-de'i u-re'i* ["know and see"] (Jeremiah 2:19).

6. The Vowel Letters (Continued)

Note that the *alef* is always silent when it comes at the end of a word. This is not the case with the other vowel letters, namely, the *heh*, *vav*, and *yod*. There is no need to mention that the *alef*, *heh*, *vav*, and *yod* interchange [lit., "switch and change"] and are sometimes added or dropped [from a word]. We thus find *Ishai* [with an *alef*] used for *Yishai* [where the *alef* is replaced with a *yod*] (1 Chronicles 2:13–14) and *he-amon* [with an *alef*, "the multitude"] (Jeremiah 52:15) used in place of *he-hamon* [with a *heh*, lit., "the great multitude"] (2 Samuel 18:29). We similarly find "Marah" [which usually end in a *heh*] spelled with an *alef* in "call me Marah" (Ruth 1:20) and *tomeru*[26] ["say you," which is usually spelled with an *alef*, but as an exception it is not] in "And say you to Amasa" (2 Samuel 19:14).

There are times when the *alef* comes in the middle or end of a word and is silent, as is the case with the word *tzavvere* ["neck," which has a silent *alef*] in "and he fell upon his brother's neck" (Genesis 45:14). We also find the *alef* to be silent at the end of a word, as in the word *het* ["sin"] in "and it shall be sin in you" (Deuteronomy 15:9). Sometimes the silent *alef* at the end of a word is a root letter, as in the word *bari* ["fat," from *bet*, *resh*, *alef*]. At other times it is superfluous, as in the words *naki* [innocent] (Joel 4:19), *he-halekhu* [that went] (Joshua 10:14), and *eifo* ["where is"] (Judges 9:38). Sometimes the *alef*, like the *yod* of *etzarekha* ["I formed you," from the root *yod*, *tzadi*, *resh*] in "Before I formed you" (Jeremiah 1:5) and the *yod* in *etzak* ["I will pour," from *yod*, *tzadi*, *kof*] in "For I will pour" (Isaiah 44:3), is replaced by

---

26. *Tomeru* (in 2 Samuel 19:14) is vocalized with a *holam*. Ibn Ezra considers every *holam* a *vav*. It is also possible that in Ibn Ezra's version of Scripture, *tomeru* was spelled with a *vav*. Be that as it may, the point is that the *alef* and *vav* interchange.

a *dagesh*. The *alef* of the word *yashim*[27] ["appalled"] in "Surely their habitation shall be appalled at them" (Jeremiah 49:20) is an example of the aforementioned.

We also find the *dagesh* taking the place of a *heh*. We find this to be the case in the word *genavattu*[28] ["steals away"] in "And as chaff that the storm steals away" (Job 21:18) and *yeladattu*[29] ["has borne him"] in "who loves you has borne him" (Ruth 4: 15). The same is the case with the word *yishmerennu* ["kept it in"] in "and its owner has not kept it in" (Exodus 21:36), wherein the *dagesh* compensates for the *heh* of *yishmerenhu*. There is no reason to elaborate.

7. The Letters that Make Up the Personal Name of God

I have already noted that these letters [*alef, heh, vav,* and *yod*] were chosen to be in the count of the letters [that make up God's name].[30] One [represented by *alef*] is the cause of all numbers. However, it is not itself a number.[31] Ten [represented by *yod*] is similar to the number one, for it includes all the ones and is the first of the tens. Five [*heh*] and six [*vav*] are round numbers because both of them are middle numbers.[32]

---

27. According to Ibn Ezra, the root of *yashim* is *alef, shin, mem*. There is no *alef* in *yashim*. However, there is *dagesh* in the *shin* of *yashim*.

28. A variant of *genavathu*.

29. A variant of *yeladathu*.

30. These letters make up God's *nomem propium*, that is, YHVH and its variant EHYH. See Ibn Ezra on Exodus 3:15 and his *Sefer Hashem*, part three.

31. Ibn Ezra makes the same point in his Long Commentary on Exodus 3:15. The Pythagoreans did not consider one to be a number. See Aristotle's *Metaphysics* 14a.

32. They are always found in their squared and cubed forms. Thus, $5 \times 5 = 25$ and $6 \times 6 = 36$. However, $3 \times 3 = 9$ and $4 \times 4 = 16$. The 5 and 6 are present in 25 and 36, as opposed to 3 and 4, that are "lost" in 9 and 16. See end of chapter 9. Ibn Ezra elaborates on this theme in his long commentary on Exodus 3:15.

8. The Shape and Name of the Vowel
Letters and their Function as Prefixes and Suffixes

Note that the length [of a body] consists of a line drawn between two points [from top to bottom]. If we add "width," we have another line [from one side to the other]. These two lines form the area. Now a body has six sides [because it also has depth, hence it has up, down, east, west, front, and back]. The same is the case with [the *alef*] the first letter.[33] A body bears the "accidents."[34] The statement, "I am" (Exodus 20:2) [which begins with *alef*] similarly carries the nine statements that follow.[35] A body may be divided into an infinite number of parts, hence it is called *alef*.[36]

Heh relates to form.[37] It means "behold" (e.g., Genesis 47:23). It indicates the definite article. Two lines of the *heh* form a right angle [where the right leg and top line meet]. Another is close by [the left leg, which is unconnected to the top]. The *heh* is therefore the sign of the feminine when placed at the end of word.[38] Compare the words

---

33. The *alef* consists of three lines, a diagonal line with one line above the diagonal and one below it. These three lines allude the three lines of a body; a line going from up to down; a line going east to west, and a line going from front to back.

34. According to Aristotle, there are ten categories: substance, quantity, quality, relation, place, time, posture, state, action, and passion. See *The Encyclopedia of Philosophy* (New York and London: Macmillan, 1967), vol. 1, p. 47, s.v., "categories." Quantity, quality, relation, place, time, posture, state, action, and passion describe the state of a given substance (body). Hence substance is said to bear them.

35. The first commandment, which opens with an *alef* (*anokhi*, "I am"), commands us to believe in God. All nine commandments that follow are based on that belief. Thus, the first commandment carries the nine that follow. See Ibn Ezra's long commentary on Exodus 19:1.

36. The word *alef* means "a thousand." According to Ibn Ezra, the word *alef* alludes to the thousands upon thousands of parts into which a substance (body) may be divided.

37. All things consist of matter and form. *Heh* teaches that God created form. *Alef* alludes to God's creation of bodies.

38. The physical world consists of form and matter. It also consists of male

na'arah [girl], *almanah* [widow], and *averah* [passes] [in *ve-ruah averah*, "but the wind passes"] (Job. 37:21) [which are all feminine and end in *heh*].

The *vav* is shaped like a hook. Compare, *vavei* ["hooks of"] in "the hooks of the pillars" (Exodus 27: 10). The [word] *vav* has a double sound[39] because it is produced by the joining of the lips. The *vav* is a masculine suffix because the *heh* is the sign of the feminine. Compare *yishmerehu vi-hayyehu* ["preserve him, and keep him alive"] (Psalm 41:3) and *yirdefehu* ["shall pursue him"] [all of which end in *vav*]. The *vav* is also used as a feminine plural in such forms as *asu* [they made] and *tavvu* [they spun] because it is produced by the coming together of the lips.[40] [This is the reason why the *vav* is also employed] as a [connective] prefix [in such forms], as in *Re'uven ve-Shimon* [Reuben and Simeon].[41] The *vav*'s vowels change when the *vav* is prefixed to any of the other labials.[42]

9. The Emphatic *Heh* and the Interrogative *Heh*

Note that there are two types of *heh* prefixes, the emphatic *heh*, which indicates the definite article, and the interrogative *heh*, which introduces a question. Each one of these *heh*'s possesses its own vocalization [lit., "there is a difference in their vocalizations"].[43]

---

and female. The *heh* alludes to the feminine aspect of the world. Hence it is used as feminine form. See Cohen and Simon. p. 188.

39. The *vav* has two "v" sounds. It is the only letter that is doubly sounded.

40. These are third-person-perfect plurals. These forms are used for both the masculine and the feminine. Hence, the *vav* serves a double purpose, that is, in certain forms it is both a masculine and a feminine suffix.

41. The *vav* is employed as a connective because it itself is formed by the joining of the lips.

42. Lit. "with its comrades," that is, other labials. A connective *vav* is ordinarily vocalized with a *sheva*. However, when a connective *vav* precedes a labial, it is vocalized with a *shuruk*.

43. The *heh*, which indicates the definite article, is usually vocalized with a *pattah*. The interrogative *heh* is usually vocalized with a *hataf pattah*.

10. The *Yod*

The *yod* is employed both as a prefix and as a suffix. Note that when a *yod* is prefixed to a word, it indicates the third-person masculine both in the singular and in the plural [as in *yikhtov*, "he will write" and *yikhtevu*, "they will write"].

When the *yod* is employed as a third-person prefix,[44] its grammatical function is the opposite of that of the *alef*.[45] However, its function is similar to that of the *alef*'[46] when it is employed as a suffix, for it then indicates both the first-person masculine and the first-person feminine. Compare *yadi* [my hand] and *ragli* [my foot]. The *yod* is sounded when it indicates the plural.[47] It is silent in the construct. Compare *yedei*[48] *nashim* [the hands of women] (Lamentations 4:10).

11. The Significance of the Number Ten (*Yod*)

Ten is the foundation of all sums [i.e., the numbers one through ten are the foundation of all sums] for all sums that follow ten are made up of a part or parts of ten, or come into being by doubling ten, multiplying ten,[49] or by a combination of the two. Furthermore, it is well known that wind and fire form one sphere, and water and earth a second sphere.[50] There is indisputable proof that these spheres are circled by eight other spheres.[51] All of this clearly adds up to ten. The

---

44. Lit. "When it is in mind," that is, when in the third person. The person is not usually present when he is spoken of. Rather he is "in mind."

45. Lit. "one" (*alef* = 1). The *alef* is a first-person prefix. Thus, the subject is present. This is not usually the case when one employs the third person.

46. Which is a first-person prefix. Here too Ibn Ezra literally reads "one."

47. As in the word *yadai* (my hands) (Creizenach).

48. *Yedei* ends in a *yod*. However, the *yod* is silent because it is swallowed up by the *tzere*.

49. According to Creizenach.

50. According to Aristotle, the sublunar world consists of four elements: earth, water, wind (air), and fire. See ch. 1.

51. The sphere of the moon, the sphere of the sun, the spheres of each of the five planets, and the sphere of the constellations. Ibn Ezra omits the

yod [which is numerically equivalent to ten] therefore has the shape of the periphery of a circle that encompasses everything in it.[52]

The word *yod* means a "gathering." It comes from the same root as the words *todah* ["company"] and *todot* ["companies"] [i.e., the root *yod, dalet, heh*] in, "And the other company" (Nehemiah 12:38) and "two great companies" (Nehemiah 12:31).

Now if one starts counting the spheres from the first sphere[53] then the first sphere is the holy sphere. On the other hand, if one starts the count of the spheres from its counterpart [i.e., the lunar sphere], then the tenth sphere is the holy sphere. Therefore, both the firstborn and the tenth (Leviticus 27:33) are holy.[54]

12. Additional Aspects of the Vowel Letters

However, from another point of view, the integers end with nine [rather than ten; lit., "there are nine ones"]. For ten is the first of the tens, and one is not considered a number. There are thus only eight numbers. Four of them – namely, two, three, five, and seven – are prime numbers.[55]

When we add one, which is a root, and a square, a foundation,[56]

---

diurnal sphere and the sphere of the active intellect because they do not contain any body.

52. According to the Pythagoreans, the number ten was sacred. It was symbolized by the dotted triangle, the *tatractys*, "source and root of everlasting nature." See *Encyclopedia of Philosophy*, vols. 7 and 8, p. 38.

53. There are ten spheres surrounding the earth, namely, the lunar sphere, the solar sphere, the five spheres of the planets, the sphere of the constellations, the ninth sphere – which moves all of the above-mentioned spheres – and the tenth sphere which Ibn Ezra identifies with the *kissei ha-Kavod*; Ibn Ezra identifies the tenth sphere with *kissei ha-Kavod* at Psalm 8:4.

54. They allude to the sphere of the *kissei ha-Kavod*, which is both the first and the tenth sphere.

55. A prime number is a number that can be evenly divided only by itself and by one.

56. Another word for "root." One is the root and square of one and the root and cube of one.

and a cube, to the square of the first of the even numbers [i.e., two], we get five [i.e., $1 + 2^2 = 5$]. If we add one to the square of the first of the odd numbers [i.e., three], we get ten [$1 + 3^2 = 10$]. We thus have the revered name of God [$(1 + 2^2) + (1 + 3^2) = 15$, which represents *Yah*]. If we add one to the square of five, we get the sum of God's entire name [$1 + 5^5 = 26$, which represents *YHVH*]. The same is also the case if we add up the letters that spell out *yod, heh*.[57] If we add one to the square of seven, we get fifty [$1 + 7^7 = 50$], [which alludes to] the holy jubilee year (Leviticus 25:10–12) and the day when the festival of Shavuot is observed [i.e., fifty days after Passover; see Leviticus 23:15–17].

I will now reveal a secret [concerning the number five]. The number five contains all the [prime] numbers that precede it [i.e., $2 + 3 = 5$].

The unique name of God [i.e., *Yah*] is numerically equivalent to [any of] the three numbers [of the magic box].[58]

If one adds half of the name [i.e., *Yah*, which is the first two letters of *YHVH*] to the numerical equivalent of *Yah*, we get 120.[59] The same is the case if we add the sum of the square of all of the even numbers that precede the number nine.[60]

---

57. The same is also the case if we add the sum of the letters that spell out the divine name *Yah* (the letters *yod heh*). *Yod* is *yod vav dalet*, $10 + 6 + 4 = 20$. *Heh* is *heh alef*, $5 + 1 = 6$, for a total of 26.

58. Also known as Al Gahzali's square. This is a box whose numbers equal fifteen whether added vertically, horizontally, or diagonally. The box is arranged as follows:

4	9	2
3	5	7
8	1	6

59. If we add up all the numbers between one and fourteen and add fifteen, the numerical equivalent of *Yah*, to this number we get 120. $1 + 2 + 3 + 4 \ldots + 15 = 120 \ldots$

60. $2^2 + 4^2 + 6^2 + 8^2 = 120$.

These numbers always add up to nine when they are multiplied by nine and their integers are added to each other.[61]

When the ones [i.e., the numbers one through nine] are added [to 120] we get 165.[62] The same is the case when we multiply one half of God's name by its other half [i.e., YH is 15 and VH is 11, and 15 × 11 = 165].

When the square of the first letter making up God's name [yod represents 10, and $10^2 = 100$] is subtracted from the sum of the square of the first and second letters of God's name [i.e., yod, heh: yod stands for 10 and heh represents 5. 10 + 5 = 15, and $15^2 = 225$], we get the cube of the second letter of the Lord's name [heh represents five, and $5^3 = 125$.

When the sum of the square of the first two letters of God's name [yod heh is 10 + 5 = 15, and $15^2 = 225$] is subtracted from the sum of the square of the three letters of the Lord's name [yod, heh, vav is 10 + 5 + 6 = 21, and $21^2 = 441$], we get the cube of the third letter [vav is 6, and $6^3 = 216$] of the Divine name.

13. The Number Ten (Continued)

I continue to explain [the secret of the number ten, represented by yod, which is one of the letters of the Divine name]:

It is known that the square of the side of an equilateral triangle inscribed [lit., "drawn"] in a circle is equal to the square of the height of an equilateral triangle whose sides are equal to the diameter of the circle. When the height of an equilateral triangle is squared, it equals three quarters of the square of any of its sides [as stated in the Pythagorean theorem].

When a cord is drawn across a third of the circle's diameter, then the square of the cord plus the square of the segment [of the line between the point of intersection] equals the square of the circle's diameter. The results will differ [that is, the square of the cord plus the

---

61. $9 \times 2 = 18$; $8 + 1 = 9$; $9 \times 4 = 36$, $6 + 3 = 9$; $9 \times 5 = 45$, $4 + 5 = 9$; $8 \times 9 = 72$, $7 + 2 = 9$.

62. For $1 + 2 + 3 + 4 + 5 + 6 + 7 + 8 + 9 = 45$. $120 + 45 = 165$.

square of the segment will either] be greater or lesser [than the square of the diameter] if other measurements are employed [i.e., depending on whether the cord is drawn higher or lower across the circle].

If the diameter of the circle measures ten [units] and a cord is drawn across the top third of its diameter, and a second cord is drawn across the bottom third of its diameter, then the area of the triangle or parallelogram that is formed will equal the circumference of the circle. Therefore, the square of the area of an equilateral triangle in a circle whose diameter is fifteen [units] is exactly five thousand [units].

The square of [the circumference of] a circle whose diameter is ten [units] is 987 and five-ninths plus eight-ninths of a ninth, the square root of which is thirty-one degrees plus 25′ 36″ and 50‴.[63]

When all the letters of God's name are added, we get seventy-two.[64] The Sages therefore said that it [i.e., the seventy-two letter name] is the Lord's explicit name [Hebrew, *Shem Ha-Meforash*].

The area of equilateral triangles in all circles whose diameter is less than ten will relate to the circumference in accordance with the diameter's relation to ten. The reverse will be the case if the diameter is more than ten.[65]

---

63. According to Creizenach.
64. The letters of the Divine name are *YHVH*.

  - *Yod* is spelled *yod* (10), *vav* (6), *dalet* (4) = 20
  - *Heh* is spelled *heh* (5), *yod* (10) = 15
  - *Vav* is spelled *vav* (6), *yod* (10), *vav* (6) = 22
  - *Heh* is spelled *heh* (5), *yod* (10) = 15

  The sum of these is 20 + 15 + 22 + 15 = 72.
65. If the diameter of the circle is greater than ten (in reality 9.6735966), then the relation of the area of the triangle to the circumference of the circle will be greater than one. If the diameter of the circle is less than ten, then the relation of the area of the triangle to the circumference of the circle will be less than one.

Chapter XII

THE PURPOSE OF
HUMAN EXISTENCE

1. God Is Eternal and Unchanging

Blessed be the Lord who alone is exalted (cf. Isaiah 2:17). He is the everlasting God (cf. Isaiah 40:28). The Lord inhabits eternity (cf. Isaiah 57:15). He is enthroned from of old. Selah (cf. Psalm 55:20).

God is unaffected by those who exist for His sake and are close to Him [the angels] or by those who were created by the glorious for His glory (cf. Isaiah 43:7).[1] The Psalmist similarly said, "For He commanded, and they were created" (Psalm 148:5) [God alone is everlasting; everything else is created].

I offer you a parable utilizing the upper [i.e., heavenly] bodies.[2] The stars of the great circling sphere [i.e., the sphere of constellations] have one motion. The arrangement of their distances from each other [i.e., their alignment] is eternally fixed. The motion of the seven ministers [i.e., the five planets plus sun and moon], each one in its respective sphere, is also permanently fixed. However [in contrast to the stars],

---

1. God's existence is independent of creation. The heavenly hosts and earthly beings do not affect God's essence. See Maimonides, *Yesodei Ha-Torah* 1:12: "Behold it states: 'I, God, have not changed' (Malachi 3:6)."
2. Of permanence. Ibn Ezra's point is that the heavenly bodies effect what happens on earth. However, they remain unchanged. So too with God. He brings about change but remains unchanged.

their motion facing the center [i.e., as viewed from Earth], changes
[appears to change]. For some of them move in a straight line. At times,
they run and at other times they tarry. Sometimes they stand still [i.e.,
does not appear to move at all] and at other times they go backward.
The position of one body to the other changes ad infinitum. At times
they are in conjunction, and at times they separate. Sometimes they
are aligned in [one of] the seven aspects, and sometimes they are not.
They at times ascend [towards their apogee] in their large sphere, and
at other times in their small sphere.[3]

They sometimes move in the ecliptic. At other times they are
found either to the right or to the left of the ecliptic. They do not fall
ill or expire [i.e., they are eternal and unchanging]. Their light neither
increases nor decreases. It only appears so to the eye.

Now, the moon is of inferior status [to the other heavenly bodies],
for its light changes in accordance with its distance from the sun.
Whatever befalls the planets [with regard to motion and luminosity],
befalls the moon and then some.

It is because of the above-noted heavenly motions and some
additional occurrences that change comes to all things born of the
earth be they metal, plants, or living beings,[4] for no two arrangements
[of the heavenly bodies] will be found to be the same in myriads of
millions of years. It is therefore written in the *Sefer Yetzirah* (3:4) that
the possible combination of words that can be formed from [the first]
eleven letters[5] [of the Hebrew alphabet]is such that it is impossible

---

3. The planets were believed to move in two spheres: a large sphere, and
a small sphere called an epicycle. The center of the epicycle lay on the
periphery of the large sphere. The motion of the planet in these two
spheres accounts for its apparent movements. See Judah Landa, *Torah
and Science* (Hoboken, NJ: KTAV, 1991), Chapter 4.
4. The beings found on Earth are divided into mineral (metal), vegetable,
and animal.
5. Lit. "until eleven." Actually our editions of the *Sefer Yetzirah* (3:4) speak
of seven letters. It reads:

   Two stones build two houses, Three stones build six houses, Four
   stones build twenty-four houses, Five stones build 120 houses, Six

for the mouth to enunciate them or for the ear to hear them.[6] If this
is the case with such a small number [of letters], how much more
so is it true [for the combinations possible] for an amount of [stars]
exceeding the sand upon the shore of the sea.

2. The Divine Names YHVH and Elohim

It is because there is nothing on the earth, aside from man's soul, that is
everlasting, that God's glorious name is not mentioned in the account
of creation. Only the name Elohim ["angels"] is employed,[7] for God
is also called by their [the angels'] name. Speech is similarly called
safah [lip] and *lashon* [tongue].[8] The Sages therefore said, "God's
complete name [YHVH] was called over a complete world" (*Bereshit
Rabbah* 13:3).[9]

The name [YHVH] is attached to Elohim until the birth of Cain.[10]
When Eve gave birth to Cain, she realized that the human race would
continue to exist. She therefore said, "I have gotten a man with the
help of YHVH" (Genesis 4:1).[11] It was for this reason that Moses men-

---

stones build 720 houses, Seven stones build 5040 houses. From there
on, go forth and compute what the mouth cannot speak and the ear
cannot hear.

The stones refer to letters and the houses to words. With two letters you can
make two words, i.e., from *alef* and *bet* you can make the words *av* (father)
and *ba* (come). From *alef*, *bet*, and *gimel* you can make six words, *ab"g*,
ag"b, *ba"g*, *bg"a*, *ga"b*, *gb"a*, and so forth (Komtiyano, Simon and Cohen).

6. The number is 39, 916, 800 (Komtiyano, Levin, Simon and Cohen).
7. Which according to Ibn Ezra means "angels." "God is called Elohim
   because His actions are executed via angels who do His will and who are
   referred to as Elohim" (Ibn Ezra on Genesis 1:1).
8. According to Ibn Ezra, speech is called *safah* or *lashon* because "it is seen
   to come from the lips [or tongue]." See Ibn Ezra on Genesis 1:1.
9. Which, according to Ibn Ezra, shows that God is termed by that through
   which He is manifest.
10. That is, from Genesis 2:4 to 3:22 God is referred to as YHVH Elohim (the
    Lord God). From the birth of Cain (Genesis 4:1), the name YHVH stands
    by itself.
11. "Eve used the Tetragrammaton, and not the term Elohim, because the

tioned only God's glorious name [YHVH] to Pharaoh (see Exodus 5:1). This name [YHVH] refers only to the God of the Hebrews.[12] Anyone who receives its power [i.e., the power of the Divine Name] can create wonders.[13] This name is therefore not found in the Book of Kohelet because it speaks of God's wisdom and the Divine power that is upon everything. It does not speak of the Divine power that is upon an individual, such as Moses.[14]

Jethro therefore said, "Now I know that the Lord [YHVH] is greater than all gods [Elohim; angels through whom God rules]" (Exodus 18:11)[15] that the Lord [YHVH] is God of gods [Elohim].[16]

The name YHVH is sometimes used as a proper noun and sometimes as an adjective.[17] The phrase YHVH Tzeva'ot [Lord of Hosts] (e.g., 1 Samuel 15:2) is proof of this.[18]

God's throne, that is the ark,[19] is called Name. It is so called in

---

Lord's spirit now rested upon the earth via the human race even as it does on the heavenly bodies" (Ibn Ezra on Genesis 4:1).

12. The other names for the Deity found in Scripture may or may not refer to the Lord. YHVH always refers only to the Lord.

13. One who knows the secret of this name can interfere with the laws of nature. See Ibn Ezra on Numbers 20:8.

14. According to Ibn Ezra, Elohim represents the power of God as it is revealed in natural law. YHVH represents God as revealed in the supernatural. Rabbi Judah Ha-Levi, an older contemporary of Ibn Ezra, made a similar distinction in *Kuzari* book 5.

15. Now that Jethro saw the laws of nature suspended, he saw the power of YHVH.

16. According to Creizenach.

17. See Ibn Ezra on Exodus 3:15: "The Lord's personal name is sometimes used as an adjective," that is with the meaning of "maintainer of the universe" (Yehaveh) or "Lord of Hosts" (YHVH Tzeva'ot) (Lord who work via the angels). See Simon and Cohen.

18. YHVH is in the construct with Tzeva'ot. Proper nouns do not come in the construct. Hence, the term YHVH in YHVH Tzeva'ot is an adjective.

19. Lit. "after the manner of the ark." According to Levin. Baer and the other editions read "after the manner of the world."

the book of Chronicles.[20] The book of Samuel explains that the ark is called "Name" because "the name of the Lord of hosts who sits upon the cherubim is upon it" (2 Samuel 6:2, as Ibn Ezra understood it). It is similar to "I Am That I Am" (Exodus 3:14).[21] "As the light of the seven days" (Isaiah 30:26), wherein each day the light increased and ceased doing so on the seventh day, likewise explains [the term] "sevenfold" [which precedes it]. Similarly, "And shall come forth and fight with him, even with the king of the north" (Daniel 11:11)[22] and "and out of the midst thereof as the color of eluctrum, out of the midst of the fire" (Ezekiel 1:4).[23]

3. Knowing God

Now carefully note that the number one [which alludes to one God] is the secret of all sums.[24] However, it itself is not a sum,[25] for [like God] it stands by itself and has no need for the numbers that follow it.[26] Furthermore, all numbers are made up of one.[27] All numbers do

---

20. We thus see that God's name is used as an adjective. See 1 Chronicles 13:6: "To bring up from thence the ark of God, the Lord who sits upon the cherubim, called the Name" (translated by Ibn Ezra).
21. According to Ibn Ezra, "That I Am" explains "I Am." See Ibn Ezra on Exodus 3:14. Similarly, "[because] the name of the Lord of hosts who sits upon the cherubim is upon it" (2 Samuel 6:2) explains "the ark of God called the name" that precedes it. Ibn Ezra's point is that biblical verses often explain the terms that they employ.
22. "Even with the king of the north" explains "with him."
23. "Out of the midst of the fire" explains "and out of the midst thereof."
24. It is the foundation of all numbers. It is the first of the numbers and is found in all numbers.
25. It is not considered to be a number. This is the opinion of Pythagoreans. Cf. Aristotle, *Metaphysics*, 14a, 1087b. See Chapter 11 in this work. See also Ibn Ezra on Exodus 3:15, *Sefer Ha-Ehad* 1, and *Sefer Ha-Shem* 3.
26. God's existence is similarly independent of His creation. See also Maimonides, *Hilkhot Yesodei Ha-Torah* 1:2–3.
27. Similarly, God permeates all of creation. See Ibn Ezra on Genesis 1:26: "God is one. He is the Creator of all. He is all."

on two sides what one does on one of the sides that exist because of it.[28]

The philosophers therefore called man a microcosm.[29] This is the secret of Metatron [God's highest angel], the inner prince.[30] This is the secret of the five things of which the Sages spoke [the five ways in which man's soul is similar to God (*Berakhot* 10a)]. The *Shi'ur Komah* therefore states, "Rabbi Ishmael said, whoever knows this dimension of the Creator of the world, is assured of a place in the world to come. I and Akiva guarantee this."[31]

An intelligent person can know the One in the following way. He can know the One because everything is connected to God [hence man can discover certain aspects of God by learning how God works in the world.]. However, a created being cannot know Him from the aspect of His entire goodness [i.e., a person can never completely know God]. This may be compared to the sunlight that passes over someone whose eyes are closed. He cannot see the face of the brightness of the sun until it passes.[32] Scripture therefore states, "I will make all My goodness pass before you" (Exodus 33:19). Now, cleaving unto God's total goodness is metaphorically called cleaving to God's face.[33]

---

28. All numbers are half the sum of the numbers that immediately precede and follow, for example, 2 is half of 1 + 3; 3 is half of 2 + 4; 4 is half of 3 + 5; 5 is half of 4 + 6, and so on. However, one by itself is half of two. Ibn Ezra's point is that God is the cause of all things. He is in all things. He is independent of everything that He created.

29. Man has a soul, which comes from God. This soul fills the body in the same way that God fills the universe.

30. Metatron is the name of the angel closest to God. Man's body is a microcosm and his soul is its Metatron. See the third way of interpreting Scripture in Ibn Ezra's introduction to his commentary on Pentateuch: "Man's intelligence is the angel which mediates between him and his God."

31. Ibn Ezra did not take the *Shi'ur Komah* literally. He interprets "whoever knows the dimensions of the Creator of the world," to mean whoever knows how God works in the world (Simon and Cohen, I. Levin).

32. A person cannot look directly at the sun. He can only enjoy the sunlight when not facing the sun.

33. Or seeing God's face. See Exodus 33:19. This is beyond human understanding.

The cleaving of created beings to God is called [seeing God's] back (see *Yesod Mora* 10:2). This is what Scripture means by "and you shall see My back" (Exodus 33:19). Scripture metaphorically speaks of a human body. For the one who speaks is human. Likewise, the one who hears is human.[34]

4. Connecting to God

The one who has learned the science of the soul is able to understand these things [i.e., the spiritual or metaphysical world]. For they[35] are not bodies, nor are they similar to bodies.

Now because the Cause [God, the First Cause of all existence] is far and close,[36] the Hebrews said, "For the portion of the Lord is His people" (Deuteronomy 32:9); "O Lord, the portion of my inheritance and of my cup" (Psalm 16:5); "The Lord is my portion, says my soul" (Lamentations 3:24). It is furthermore written, "Yet they are Your people and Your inheritance" (Deuteronomy 10:29). Scripture also states, "the Lord is his inheritance" (Deuteronomy 10:9).[37] Employing other terms[38] which are also true, Scripture writes, "Blessed be the Lord my Rock" (Psalm 144:1). Another verse states, "My God, my rock, in Him

---

34. The Torah was given to human beings who speak and hear. It therefore had to employ human terminology. On the other hand, "For the one who speaks [or spoke] is human. Likewise, the one who hears [or heard] is human" might refer to Moses who received the Torah (Levin, Yalkut; Ibn Ezra, p. 374). It is also possible that "For the one who speaks [or spoke] is human" refers to Moses who gave the Torah to Israel, and that "Likewise the one who hears [or heard] is human" refers to Israel, who heard the words of Moses. Be the aforementioned as it may, Ibn Ezra's point is that the Torah employed anthropomorphic language. Maimonides makes an identical point in *The Guide for the Perplexed* 1:26.
35. The beings that make up the spiritual world. The spiritual world, like the soul, does not consist of bodies.
36. God is both far and close to the individual. He is far off because a person can never fully know God. However, He is close because God's presence permeates all being.
37. These verses speak of God being close to His people.
38. Verses which speak of God's closeness to the individual.

I take refuge" (Psalm 18:3). Scripture similarly states, "He is your glory" (Deuteronomy 10:21); "O God of my praise" (Psalm 109:1); "My high tower, and my deliverer" (Psalm 144:2). Another verse states, "The God of my mercy" (Psalm 59:11). Therefore, the secret of the prayers is [contained in] the statement, "I will extol You, my God, O King" (Psalm 145:1); "Bless the Lord, you angels of His" (Psalm 103:20); "O magnify the Lord with me" (Psalm 34:4).[39] This secret [i.e., that a person should always be conscious of God and praise and extol Him and cleave to Him] is the principle of this chapter. "This is the gate of the Lord; The righteous shall enter into it" (Psalm 118:20).

---

39. The main reason for praying is to extol God and thereby cleave to Him.

CONCLUSION

I, Abraham the son of Meir the Spaniard, who is called Ibn Ezra, commenced to compose this book in the city of London on the Isle of England. I began in the month of Tammuz and completed the manuscript four weeks later in the month of Av, in the year four thousand, nine hundred and nineteen (1159).[1]

This book is concluded.

Praise is due to God Alone.
For His wonderful deeds of
Loving-kindness, which He showed
To Abraham His servant.[2]

---

1. A variant manuscript reads: Four thousand, nine hundred and eighteen (1158).
2. Cohen and Simon, pp. 211–212. Some editions omit or have a variant. See the aforementioned.

BIBLIOGRAPHY

Abraham ibn Ezra. *Sefer Yesod Mora Ve-Sod Ha-Torah*. With the commentary *Livyat Chen*. Ed. Zalmen Stern. Prague: Landau, 1833.

———. *Sefer Yesod Mora*. Trans. M. Creizenach. Frankfurt am Main and Leipzig: J. Baer, 1840.

———. *Sefer Yesod Mora Ve-Sod Ha-Torah*. Ed. Shemu'el Waxman. Jerusalem: Chokhmat Yisra'el, 1931.

———. "*Sefer Yesod Mora Ve-Sod Ha-Torah*." In *Yalkut Avraham ibn Ezra*, ed. Israel Levin. New York and Tel Aviv: Israel Matz Hebrew Classics and I. Edward Kiev Library Foundation, 1985.

Baer, J. and Creizenach. M., *Sefer Yesod Mora*. Frankfurt am Main and Leipzig: 1840.

Bernfeld, Shimon. *Da'at Elohim*. Warsaw, 1922.

Cohen, Joseph and Uriel Simon. *Rabbi Abraham ibn Ezra, Yesod Mora Ve-Sod Torah: Israel*, 2007.

Cohon, Samuel S. *Jewish Theology*. Assen, the Netherlands: Royal Vangorcum, Ltd., 1971.

Encyclopaedia Judaica. Jerusalem: Keter, 1972.

Feldman, W.M. *Rabbinical Mathematics and Astronomy*. New York: 1978.

Friedlander, Michael. *The Commentary of Ibn Ezra on Isaiah*. New York: Feldheim, 1961.

Graetz, Henrich. *Divre Yeme Yisrael*. Trans. J.P. Rabinowitz. Vol. 4, Warsaw: Alapin, 1916.

Guttmann, Julius. *The Philosophy of Judaism*. Trans. David W. Silverman. Northvale, NJ: Jason Aronson, 1988.

Husik, Isaac. *A History of Mediaeval Jewish Philosophy.* Philadelphia: Jewish Publication Society, 1916.

Kahana, David. *Rabbi Abraham ibn Ezra.* Warsaw: Ahiasaf, 1922.

Karpeles, Gustav. *Geshichte Der Judischen Literatur.* Vol. 1. Berlin: Poppelauer, 1909.

Kellner, Menachem. *Dogma in Medieval Jewish Thought.* Oxford: Oxford University Press, 1986.

Klatzin, Jacob. *Otzar Ha-Munahim Ha-filosofiyim.* Berling: Eshkol, 1928.

Komtiyano, Rabbi Mordekhai ben Eliezer. *Commentary on Yesod Mora.* Edited and Annotated by Dov Schwartz. Bar Ilan University, Israel, 2010.

Krochmal, Nachman. *Moreh Nevukhe Ha-Zeman.* Ed. Simon Rawidowicz. Waltham, MA: Ararat, 1961.

Kurzweil, Zevi. *The Modern Impulse of Traditional Judaism.* Hoboken, NJ: Ktav, 1985.

Levine, Etan. *Abraham ibn Ezra's Commentary to the Pentateuch.* Vatican manuscript 38. Jerusalem: Makor, 1974.

Levin, Israel. *Sefer Yesod Mora Ve-Sod Torah. Yalkut Avraham ibn Ezra.* New York and Tel Aviv: Israel, 1985.

Melamed, Ezra Tzion. *Mefareshe Ha-Mikra.* Jerusalem: Magnes Press, 1978.

Schwartz, Dov. *Pirush Kadmon Al Sefer Yesod Mora: Bi'ur Yesod Mora Le-Rabbi Morddekhai ben Eliezer Komtiyano.* Israel, 2010.

Sela, Shlomo. *Astrology and Biblical Exegesis in Abraham ibn Ezra's Thought.* Israel, 1999.

Simon, Uriel. *Four Approaches to the Book of Psalms from Saadiah Gaon to Abraham Ibn Ezra.* New York: State University of New York Press, 1991.

Sirat, C. *Hagut Filosofit Be-Yeme Ha-Benayim.* Jersualem: Keter, 1975.

Stern, Zalmen. *Abraham ibn Ezra. Sefer Yesod Mora Ve-Sod Torah.* With the commentary *Livyat Chen.* Prague: 1833.

Stitskin, Leon. *Eight Jewish Philosophers.* Jerusalem and New York: Feldheim, 1979.

Strickman, H. Norman, and Silver, Arthur. *Ibn Ezra's Commentary on the Pentateuch, Genesis*. Translated and annotated. New York: Menorah Press, 1988.

Waxman, M. *A History of Jewish Literature*. Cranbury, NJ: Yoseloff, 1960.

Waxman, Shemu'el. *Sefer Yesod Mora Ve-Sod Torah*. Jerusalem: Chokhmat Yisra'el, 1931.

ע"כ אמר יתרו (שמות י"ח:י"א) עתה ידעתי כי גדול ה' מכל הא·להים והשם.
הוא א·להי א·להים ופעם שהוא שם עצם ופעם שם תואר והעד ה' צבאות
וכסאו נקרא שם כדרך הארץ כתכתב בדברי הימים ומפורש בספר שמואל למה
נקרא שם כי (שמואל ב ו':ב') שם ה' צבאות יושב הכרובים עליו כמו (שמות
ג':י"ד) אהיה אשר אהיה וככה (ישעיהו ל':כ"ו) כאור שבעת הימים פי' שבעתים
שכל יום הוסיף האור ובשביעי עמד וככה (דניאל י"א:י"א) ונלחם עמו עם מלך
הצפון (יחזקאל א':ד') ומתוכה כעין החשמל מתוך האש.

ועתה שים לבך כי האחד סוד כל חשבון והנה חשבון כי הוא עומד
בעצמו ואין צורך לו לאשר הם אחריו גם כל חשבון הוא מחובר מאחדים וכל
חשבון יעשה משתי פאותיו מה שיעשה האחד בפאה אחת מפאת הנמצאים
בעבורו ע"כ קראו חכמי התושיה האדם עולם קטן וזה סוד מטטרון שר הפנים
וזה סוד שאמרו חז"ל בחמשה דברים ע"כ כתוב בשיעור קומה אמר רבי
ישמעאל כל היודע שיעורו של יוצר בראשית מובטח לו שהוא בן העולם הבא
ואני ועקיבא ערבים בדבר ומזה הדרך יוכל המשכיל לדעת לדעת האחד מפאת שהכל
בו הוא דבק רק מפאת הטוב כולו אין כח לדעתו לדעתו והמשל כאור השמש
שעוברת על פני שתום העין ולא יוכל לראות פני השמש רק עד שיעבור ע"כ
כתיב (שמות ל"ג:י"ט) אני אעביר כל טובי על פניך והנה הדבקו בטוב כלו
כדמות הפנים והדבק הנבראים בו כדמות אחורים וזה (שמות ל"ג:כ"ג) וראית
את אחורי וזה המשל באדם כי המדבר אדם והשומע אדם ואשר למד חכמת
הנפש יוכל להבין אלה הדברים. כי אינם גופות ולא כגופות ובעבור היות הסבה
רחוקה וקרובה. ע"כ אמרו העברים (דברים ל"ב:ט') כי חלק ה' עמו (תהלים
ט"ז:ה') ה' מנת חלקי וכוסי (איכה ג':כ"ד) חלקי ה' אמרה נפשי וכתיב (דברים
ט':כ"ט) והם עמך ונחלתך וכתיב (דברים יח) ה' הוא נחלתו ודרך אחרת גם
היא אמת כתיב (תהלים קמ"ד:א') ברוך ה' צורי וכתוב אחר (שמואל ב כ"ג:ג')
א·להי צורי אחסה בו וכן (דברים י) הוא תהלתך (תהלים ק"ט:כ"ו) א·לקי
תהלתי וכתיב (תהלים קמ"ד:ב') חסדי ומצודתי וכתיב (תהלים נ"ט:י"א) א·להי
חסדי ע"כ סוד התפלות לומר (תהלים קמ"ה:א') ארוממך א·להי המלך (תהלים
ק"ג:ג') ברכו ה' מלאכיו (תהלים ל"ד:ד') גדלו לה' אתי והסוד הזה עקר כל זה
השער (תהלים קי"ח:כ') זה השער לה' צדיקים יבאו בו:

האלכסון אז תמצא שברי המשולש או שברי הצלע המרובע כקו העגול על כן מרובע קו משולש שוה בעגול אלכסונו חמשה עשר אלפים בלי תוספות או מגרעת ומרובע עגול שאלכסונו עשרה הם תשע מאות ושמונים ושבעה וחמש תשיעיות ושמונה תשיעיות התשיעית והשרש אחד ושלשים מעלות וחמשה ועשרים ראשונים וחמשה ושלשים שניים גם חמשה שלישיים וכאשר תחבר מספר כל השם יעלה שנים ושבעים ע"כ אמרו הקדמונים כי הוא השם המפורש וכל עגול שאלכסונו פחות מעשרה יהיו שברי המשולש השוה לקו העגול כערך העגול אל עשרה והפך זה בהיותו יתר מעשרה:

שער י"ב

ברוך השם הנשגב לבדו א־לחי עולם שוכן עד ויושב קדם סלה ולא ישתנה בעבור העומדים למענהו הקרובים אליו או בעבור הנבראים לכבודו ביד הנכבדים וככה אמר המשורר (תהלים קמ"ח:ה') כי הוא צוה ונבראו ואתן לך משל בגופות העליונים כי כוכבי הגלגל הגדול המקיף תנועתה אחת וערך מרחקם זה אל זה אחת שוה לעולם ותנועת השבעה משרתים עומדת גם היא על דרך אחת כל אחד מהם בגלגלו רק תנועתם כנגד מוצק הארץ משתנה כי יש מהם ישרים בהליכתם פעם במרוצה פעם בהתמהמה ופעם עומדים ופעם שבים אחורנית ומערכת זה אל זה משתנה עד אין קץ. פעם מתחברים ופעם מתפרדים ופעם בלי מבט ופעם בשבעה מבטים ופעם עולים ויורדים בגדול ובקטן ופעם בקו (המזלות) ופעם שמאליים או ימיניים והם בעצמם לא יחלו ולא יכלו ולא יוסיף אורם ולא יחסר רק כנגד מראה העין והלבנה במדרגה השפלה כי ישתנה אורה כפי מרחקה מהשמש ויקרה לתנועותיה כל מה שיקרה למשרתים ויותר ובעבור כל אלה הדברים הנזכרים גם אחרים ישתנו כל הנולדים בארץ מהמקורות והצמחים והחיים כי לא יתכן שתמצא מערכת שוה לאחת ברבבות אלף אלפי שנים ע"כ כתוב בספר יצירה עד אחד עשר אין הפה יכול לדבר ולא האוזן יכולה לשמוע אם כן זה במספר רב מחול ימים ובעבור שאין בארץ דבר עומד רק נשמת האדם לבדו על כן לא תמצא השם הנכבד נזכר במעשה בראשית רק מלת אלהים שגם השם נקרא על שמם כדמות הדבורים שיקראו שפה ולשון ע"כ אמרו חכמינו ז"ל (בראשית רבה יג:ג) נקרא שם מלא על עולם מלא ונקרא עם א־להים עד שנולד קין וברואות חוה כי מין האדם עומד בהוליד קין ע"כ אמרה (בראשית ד':א') קניתי איש את ה' ובעבור זה לא הזכיר משה לפרעה רק השם הנכבד שהוא א־להי העברים שיוכל המקבל כחו לחדש מופתים בארץ ע"כ לא תמצאו זה השם בספר קהלת כי הוא דבר על חכמת הא־להים והכח שקבל הכל לא היה במשה

אחר קרוב אליו עמו ע"כ הי' הה"א סי' הנקבה באחרונה (איוב לז) ורוח עברה
נערה אלמנה והוי"ו כדמות ווי העמודים ונכפל להדביק השפתים ובעבור היות
הה"א לנקבה הי' זה סימן לזכרים ישמרנהו ויחייהו ירדפהו ובעבור הדבק היה
לשון רבים באחרונה גם נקבות עשו טוו ובראשונה ראובן ושמעון והשתנה
הוי"ו בהתחברו עם חבריו ודע כי הה"א הנוסף בראשונה על שני דרכים דבר
נמצא כה"א הדעת או שאלה אם הוא נמצא כה"א חתימא ויש ביניהם הפרש
בנקוד והיו"ד ישרת בראשונה ובאחרונה והנה בראשיתו סי' לשון זכר יחיד
ורבים שאינם עם המדבר והוא כמחשבה ע"כ הוא הפך אחד ובאחרונה
דומה לאחד כי היו"ד סי' המדבר זכר או נקבה ידי רגלי ונראית היו"ד לשון רבים
ובסמוך היו"ד הנעלם (איכה ד) ידי נשים:

והחשבון יסודו עשרה כי כל חשבון שהוא אחריו הוא חלק או חלקים ממנו
או מתחדש בעבור כפלו או בעבור מחברתו אל אחריו או בהתחבר השנים
דרכים ועוד ידוע כי גלגל הרוח והאש אחד וכן גם גלגל המים והארץ ומקיפים
אותה ח' גלגלים בראיות גמורות והנה הכל עשרה ע"כ צורות יו"ד כדמות קו
עגול שהוא מקיף כל אשר בתוכו ופירוש קהלה מגזרת והתודה השנית שתי
תודות והנה המחל מלמעלה האחד קדש ואם יחל מלמטה מהעומד כנגדו
הנה העשירי קדש ע"כ הי' הבכור והעשירי קדש והנה מפאה אחרת האחרים
תשעה כי עשרה תחלת כלל והאחד אינו מספר והנה השמנה הם המספרים
הארבעה ראשונים והם שנים ושלשה וחמשה ושבעה וכאשר תחבר האחד
שהוא שרש ומרובע ויסוד ומעוקב אל מרובע ראש חשבון הזוגות הנה יעלה
ה"א ואם תחברנו אל מרובע ראש חשבון שאינו זוג הנה יו"ד והנה השם הנכבד
כאשר תחברנו אל מרובע ה"א הנה חשבון כל השם וככה חשבון שתי האותיות
במבטא וכאשר תחברנו אל מרובע ז' הנה חמשים שנת היובל קדש וככה יום חג
שבועות והנה סוד חמשה כולל כל המספרים אשר לפניו והשם היחיד כמספר
השלשה אותיות. והנה חצי כל השם בחברך כל המספרים אשר לפניו ויעלה
מאה ועשרים וככה מספר המרובעים בזוגות בתשעת המספרים שהם כחשבון
עגול בכפלו וכאשר תחבר האחדים מאה וששים וחמש וככה יעלה כפל החצי
הראשון על החצי וכאשר תחסר מרובע האות הראשון ממרובע השנים נחברים
אז תמצא מעקב האות השני וכאשר תחסר מרובע השנים נחברים ממרובע
השלשה נחברים אז תמצא מעוקב האות השלישי. וסוד העשרה עוד אפרש
הנה ידוע כי מרובע צלע המשולש השוה בתוך העגול כמרובע עמוד המשולש
השוה בכל צלע אלכסון העגול כאשר הוא מרובע עמוד המשולש השוה שלשת
רביעיות מרובע הצלע וכאשר נוציא יתר בשלישית האלכסון יהי' מרובע היתר
עם מרובע החצי כמו מרובע אלכסון העגול ובחשבון אחר לא יעלה ככה רק
פחות או יתר ובעגול שהוא אלכסונו עשרה בהוציאך החצי של שתי שלישיות

ובעבור היות אותיות השינים קשים גם התחברם קשה ע"כ שמו הד' שרשים
ושמו השי"ן לבדו משרת ושרותו מעט תחת אשר (תהלים קמד) שככה לו
(שיר השירים א) שלמה אהיה (בראשית א) בשגם הוא כי זי"ן וצ' וסמ"ך שהם
אותיות השריקה קשים מאד ג"כ אות הרי"ש והעד הנערים הקטנים שלא יוכלו
לבטא בו עד שיתגדלו ויתחזקו חבלי המוח ע"כ הוצרכו לשום השלשה אותיות
השפה משרתים והניחו אחד שרש והוא הפ"א ובעבור היות האל"ף הקל הגרון
והוא לפני ההה"א ע"כ שמוהו בראש ושמו אחריו אות מהשפה שהוא הרחוק
וככה אחר ההה"א ואחר העי"ן פ"א והנה א"ב שנים משרתים וכנגדם ג"ד
שרשים מהחיך והלשון ואחר כן ה'ו' משרתים וכנגדם ז"ח שרשים ובעבור כי
אות ט' מתחלף תחת ת' חשבוהו כמו משרת ואחריו י' כ' ל' מ' נ' והנה ששה
משרתים ואחריהם ששה שרשים ס' ע' פ' צ' ק' ר' ובעבור כי האל"ף תחלת
כל אותיות לא ישית באחרונה רק בראשונה ואות תי"ו ישרת בראשית המלה
ובאחריתו ובעבור כי זה האות דומה לה"א במכתב היה הסימן לשון נקבה ושב
ההי"א הנעלם אות נראה חכמה (שמות לה) חכמת לב וה"א עשה שגם היא נעלם
שבתי"ו עשתה בנתה גם יש לתמוה מן ה"א (בראשית כא) גרש האמה הזאת
ששב ה' נראה שתי האמהות ונקרא תי"ו בעבור הקו הנוסף על הה"א ועתה
אדבר על האותיות המשך שהם יסוד השם הנכבד ואומר כי האל"ף ראויה להיות
סימן המדבר המחל והיא כוללת זכר ונקבה וההי"א באחרונה נח גם במפיק
סימן לשון נקבה והוי"ו באחרונה עם חולם לזכר ידו רגלו או שורק (דברים לב)
יסובבנהו יכוננהו ינצרנהו והיוד תחלתו זכר יעשה וסופו לשון נקבה ודעי וראי
ודע כי האל"ף באחרונה לעולם נח נעלם ולא כן חבריו שהם הו"י ואין צורך
להזכיר כי אותיות אהו"י מתחלפים ומתהפכים ופעם נוספים ופעם נגרעים
(דברי הימים א ב) ישי ואישי (ירמיהו נב) האמן (שמואל ב יח) ההמון יקראון
לימרא (שמואל ב יט) ולעמשא תמרו ויש נכתב ולא נקרא כמו בריא רק האלף
עקר שנוסף כמו נקיא (יהושע י) ההלכוא אפוא ויש מובלע בדגש כמו (ירמיהו
מט) אם לא ישים עליהם כהתבלע יו"ד (ירמיהו א) בטרם אצרך (ישעיהו מד)
כי אצק מים גם ה"א מתבלע כה"א (איוב כא) גנבתו סופה (רות ד) אשר
אהבתך ילדתו וככה (שמות כא) ישמרנו בעליו הדגש להחסרון ה"א ישמרנהו
ואין צורך להאריך וכבר הזכרתי למה נבחרו להיותם במספר ראשון כי האחד
סבת המספר ואיננו מספר והעשרה דומה לאחד כי הוא כולל האחדים והוא
ראש העשרות וחמשה וששה חשבון עגול כי שניהם אמצעים ודע כי האורך קו
בין שתי נקודות והרוחב שני קוים והנה זה שטח והנה בגוף יש לו שני פאות
וככה הקוים בראשית ר"ל הא"לף והוא נושא את המקרים כדבור (שמות כ)
אנכי שהוא נושא כל התשעה והגוף מתחלק לחלקים רבים אין קץ לו ע"כ קראו
שמו אל"ף ופירוש ה"א הצורה כמו הנה והיא שני קוים יש לה מקצוע ויש קו

והוא אל תגשו אל אשה. ע"כ הוא טמא השוכב עם אשתו. ואסור שיתפלל עד
שירחץ. וככה הזכירו אנשי המשנה ע"ה שהי' מנהג ישראל בבית שני לרחוץ
הבגד או העור שנפלה עליו אפילו טפה אחת. ולא יאכל בשר קודש. והחמיר
הכתוב על הנדה והיולדת והנזיר קדוש ובהשלימו ימי נזרו וירצה לשוב לשתות
יין יביא עולה וחטאת ושלמים וגילוח שערו פתח אהל מועד דרך בזיון לו
בעבור שירחק מקדושתו וירד ממעלתו גם היולדת תביא כבש בן שנתו. ובעל
השדה יתן תרומה וראשית ומעשרות ושכחה ופאה וחלה (ותרומה) ובעל הכרם
ערלה והלולים ובכורים. גם ראשית תירוש ומעשרות ועוללות ופרט. והשנה
השביעית. והיובל כוללת בעל השדה והכרם ובעל הצאן יתן ראשית הגז ובכור
ועשירי. ואוכל שלמים. שוק וחזה וזרוע ולחיים וקיבה לבד האמורים. כתוב
(דברים טז) איש כמתנת ידו והטעם שראוי שיתן כפי מה שנתן לו השם וזהו
הראיון. וסוף דבר אליהו איש א־להים גם אלישע יוכיחו:

שער י"א

לא אוכל לדבר על סוד השם הנכבד עד שאזכיר קצת טעמי אותיות לשון
הקודש כל האותיות שהאדם יבטא בהם מוצאיהם חמש המקומות הראשון
אותיות הגרון והם אחה"ע והשני החיך והם גיכ"ק והשלישי הלשון והם
דטלנ"ת והרביעי השנים והם זסשר"ץ. החמישי השפה והם בומ"ף ואותיות
לשון הקדש כ"ב ונכפלו החמשה בעבור שאחזה הקו שיהי' ברוחב והוסיפו
על האורך להורות שאין המלה סמוכה והשני כפולים סגרוהו בסוף והנה חצי
אותיותיהם שרשים לעולם לא נגרעים ולא נוספים אע"פ שיכפלו כמו (ויקרא
יג) ירקרק (שיר השירים א) שחרחורת (ויקרא יג) אדמדם וזה הכפל לחסרון
אם העי"ן והלמ"ד כפולים ואם נכפלו הפ"א והעי"ן יהי' הכפל ליתרון כמו
(תהלים מה) יפיפית וככה (ישעיהו יז) תשגשגי וחצי אותיות פעם שרשים
ופעם משרתים בראשית חמלה או בסופה וסימנים כשתו"ל א"ב המו"ן כאש"ר
הו"א שמ"י או"ת מבי"ן השכ"ל והנכון לבחור הקלים במוצא להיותם משרתים
בעבור שיבטאו בהם הרבה והנה תחלת האותיות ע' ואחריו ח' ושניהם כבדים
על כן לא ימצאו במכתב נכרים ולא יוכל לבטא בהם מי שאינו רגיל בנעוריו
על כן בחרו העברים האל"ף והה"א. חצי זה המוצא שרש וחציו משרת ובחרו
מאותיות החי"ך הראשונים והם יו"ד גם כ"ף להיות סמוכים אל הראשונים
הנבחרים ובחרו מאותיות הלשון שנים קרובים מחצים והם נו"ן וגם תי"ו
ובעבור שהם חמשה והלמ"ד קל על הלשון שמוהו מהמשרתים ובעבור היותו
אמצעי שמוהו למעלה על כל האותיות למ"ד מגזרת לימוד כי עקרו
לדעת למה הי' הדבר והוא הסוד הנכבד ע"כ (בראשית כ) אמרי לי וחבריו

שער י

מה יקרה תורת א-להינו ומה נאמנו עדותיו ומה נמלצו אמרותיו כי הזכיר
הכתוב דרכי האדם ארבעה שהם משתנים שבת ולכת ומשכב וקימה וכלם
פעלים עומדים ואל יקשה עליך ישכבנה כי הטעם ישכב אתה כמו (תהלים ה)
לא יגורך רע וחכמינו בלשון התלמוד הפרישו בין שוכב לנשכב ובדרך המקרא
שניהם שוכבים והעד (בראשית יט) הן שכבתי אמש את אבי. והנה השכיבה
בהקיץ ובעבור שברוב השינה האדם שוכב אמר הכתוב (בראשית כח) וישכב
במקום ההוא ולא הזכיר וייששן גם הישן דומה למת על כן כתיב (מלכים א ב)
וישכב דוד. והנה הישיבה מנוחת האדם במקום אחד וכאלו היא חצי קימה
והקימה היא העמידה כמו (ויקרא כה) וקם הבית. והנה ההליכה תנועה ממקום
למקום והוא הפך הישיבה והשכיבה כמו נטוי מראשו לרגליו והנה הקימה שהיא
העמידה להפך ובספר תהלות לא הלך לא עמד לא ישב ולא הזכיר לא שכב כי
ברוב שכיבה האדם ישן ובתורה כתוב (דברים ו) ודברת בם בלב כמו (קהלת
לו) דברתי אני אל לבי גם בפה. והנה כל עסקיו על איזה דרך שיתהפך צוה
להגות בתורתו וככה כתוב ובתורתו יהגה יומם ולילה. ואמר שלמה ע״ה בקש
החכמה (משלי ו) בהתהלכך תנחה אותך בשכבך תשמור עליך והקיצות היא
תשיחך ואתה עומד או יושב והדברים האלה שידע שהשם אחד ואין היות להווה
רק שידבק בו על כן (דברים ו) ואהבת את ה׳ א-להיך בכל לבבך. אם תאהב
שתעמוד בחיי העולם הזה גם בעולם הבא אהוב את השם ובסוף הספר ארמוז
לך זה הסוד כי הוא יסוד כל חכמה כי השם לבדו בורא הכל ויודע חלקי הכל
בדרך כל כי החלקים משתנים ונשמת האדם לבדו כאשר נתנה ה׳ היא כלוח
מוכן לכתוב עליו ובהכתב על זה הלוח מכתב א-להים שהוא דעת הנכללים
בנולדים מהארבע השרשים ודעת הגלגלים וכסא הכבוד וסוד המרכבה ודעת
עליון אז תהיה הנשמה דבקה בה׳ הנכבד בעודה באדם וככה בהפרד כחה מעל
גויתה שהוא הארמון שלה. והנה אין נכון למשכיל שיבקש לעולם הזה רק מה
שיהיה לו לעולם הבא הלא תראה כתוב בדברי העריות אני ה׳ כי הקדוש
המרחיק מעריות אז יהיה מן הדבקים אל השם הנכבד כדברי אסף (תהלים עג)
ואני קרבת א-להים לי טוב ולמעלה כי הנה רחקיך יאבדו ואמר דוד (תהלים
טז) כי לא תעזוב נפשי לשאול לרדת בשרי שם כי השאול הוא הקבר שהוא
בתחתיות הארץ. כמו (תהלים קלט) ואציעה שאול הנך ואמר (תהלים טז)
תודיעני אורח חיים וככה אמר המשורר (תהלים מט) אך א-להים יפדה נפשי
מיד שאול ומלת יקחני מעלה גדולה כמו (בראשית ה) ואיננו כי לקח אותו א-
להים וככה (תהלים עג) ואחר כבוד תקחני וכתוב (שמות יט) וקדשתם היום

כמספר הזה ומן ה' עד כ' ככה עשרים ומבן ד' ועד ס' אז ככה נפשו וגופו הוא
חמשים כנגד ה' שנים ומשם חסר ה' ולנקבה קרוב מחצי והנה הוא שלשה
ועשרים ושלשים. ודבר עזאזל כמעשה הצרעת ומפורש סודו בדברי חכמינו
הקדושים וככה דבר הערפה בנחל והמבין סוד דיקות הלשון יבין טעם אשר לא
יעבד בו. אמר הגאון ר' סעדיה אין לתמוה מדבר פרה אדומה שהיא מטמאה
הטהורים ומטהרת הטמאים כי הנה הדבש מועיל ומזיק כפי השתנות מזג גוף
האוכל. וטעם הבהמה הטמאה והעוף הטמא ושרץ המים ידוע. ואתנן זונה
ומחיר כלב למען הבזיון וכן להקריב קרבן אשר בו מום או יקריבנו כהן אשר
בו מום או ראשו מוקרח כי הוא הפך מעשה ה'. וכמצות (דברים ט"ו:י"ד-ט"ו)
הענק תעניק לו וזכרת כי עבד היית וה' הוציאך ברכוש גדול. ואריכות ימים
למשלוח הקן לא בעבור לקיחת הבנים כי היא רשות וככה בכבוד אב ואם
שהוציאו לעולם הזה והם יאריכו ימיך כי (דברים כ"ב:ז) והארכת ימים פועל
יוצא הוא. ואמר (ויקרא י"ט:י"ד) ויראת מא·להיך במצות לפני עור ודבר החרש
פן ישמיך כמוהם וככה להדר פני זקן ואם לא תירא ממנו ירא מה' שיביאך
במשפט בימי זקנותך. וכתוב על פני בע"ז על דרך (ירמיהו י'י"א) די שמיא
וארקא לא עבדו וככה (שמות כ':כ') אתם ראיתם כי מן השמים דברתי עמכם
ולא ראיתם כל תמונה כאשר פירש משה ע"ה (שמות כ) על כן לא תעשון
אתי או טעמו אין לכם צורך עמי לעשות תמונה לעבדה וכבר פרשתי מעשה
העגל כי לא היה ע"ז והעד (שמות ל"ב:ה') כי חג לה' מחר שאהרן צוה כן
וככה עשו ויהי ממחרת ויעלו עולות וזה ה' הוא לבדו ואינו כמלת אלהים.
וסוד הארון ידעהו המשכיל מהקול היוצא מבין שני הכרובים ואמתים וחצי
ארכו להיות הלוח רבוע ארכו כרחבו כמלא הארון והחצי בעובי הקורה והנה
החצי בקומה עם הרגלים כדרך השולחן כי כן כתוב על ארבע פעמותיו וזאת
המלה במקומות רבים בלשון הקודש ואיננה זוית והעד הנאמן ושתי הטבעות
כי על דרך המפרשים היה ראוי להיות שתי הטבעות. ומזבח הקטורת נתון בין
המנורה ובין השלחן מחוץ לפרוכת והמזבח גבוה משניהם וככה הוא ועשר
יריעות. גם עשתי עשרה ידוע סודם וככה כ"ח גם שלשים ומזבח הנחושת
תחת כרכובו ומלמטה עד חציו וככה הוא באמת. וסוד האפוד נכבד מאד
כי היה בשתי האבנים שהם באפוד ושהם שמאליים גם ימנים ששה שמות
בכל אבן והנה שתיהן אבן שהם והנה אין בה צורה וזה כנגד המחשבה ואלה
החלקים בישראל. והחשן כמעשה אפוד והיה רבוע כנגד נקודות הארבע על
כן לא תדמה אבן אל אבן. ודבר המשבצות והטבעות שיהיה בכל זמן החשן
על חשב האפוד שהוא הקו הגדול התיכון שאיננו נוטה. והאורים כמשמען גם
התומים כחשבון העגול ומשה נתנם בתחלה על החשן כאשר היו ביום הקים
את המשכן והמשכילים יבינו:

כה

להתפלל בעדך וזהו ולברך בשמו כמו (ויקרא כב) וישא אהרן את ידיו. וטעם
(דברים יט) שלש ערים פן ירדוף גואל הדם ולא ישפך דם נקי וטעם ההריגה
והנשארים (דברים יז) ישמעו וייראו ולא יוסיפו לעשות עוד וטעם (דברים כ)
לא תשחית את עצה כי האדם עץ השדה. וטעם מעקה (שמות כב) ולא תשים
דמים בביתך (דברים כב) ופן תקדש המלאה הזרע טעם כלאים כי הכל ישוב
קדש כאשר פירש ר' מנחם ספרדי וטעם להמית (דברים כב) את הנערה אשר
לא צעקה בעיר והנה ברצונה היה וחוץ לעיר (דברים כב) כאשר יקום איש על
רעהו במקום אין רואהו. וטעם עבוט (דברים טו) וקרא עליך אל ה'. (דברים י)
ואהבתם את הגר כי גרים הייתם. וטעם משפט גר יתום ואלמנה ולחבול בגדה
(דברים טו) וזכרת כי עבד היית על כן אנכי מצוך וככה (דברים כד) לא תשוב
לקחתו כי תבצור וזכרת על כן אנכי מצוך ולמד השירה להם שתהיה בהם
לעד. ואסר הדם והטעם (דברים יב) ולא תאכל הנפש עם הבשר וצוה להיותו
קרב על המזבח להיות נפש תחת נפש כי הדם הוא בנפש יכפר וצוה להביא כל
זבח אל אהל מועד והטעם שלא יזבחו על פני השדה כמנהגם במצרים לזבוח
לשעירים ולתת מן הדם על המשקוף ועל שתי המזוזות הטעם מפורש (שמות
יב) ולא יתן המשחית וכבר הזכיר זה מרע"ה בתחלת ביאתו לדבר אל פרעה
פירש טעם למה נזבח (שמות ה) פן יפגענו בדבר או בחרב. גם זה הסוד מבואר
היטב בדברי יחזקיהו והמשכיל יבין:

שער ט

אמר המשורר (תהלים קי"ט:י"ח) גל עיני ואביטה נפלאות מתורתיך. (שמות
י"ב:ב') החדש הזה לכם ראש חדשים יום המולד הוא הראש באמת ובו הוקם
המשכן ובעשור ובעשור דבר החוט המשולש זה נכבד וזה בבית קלון וככה (שמות
י"ב:ג') בעשור לחדש הזה ויום הזכרון פירשתיו ובחג המצות ובחג הסוכות
בשלם וחציו ובעבור התמהמה במהלך על כן יום שמיני עצרת והמילה קרוב
מז' ימים שלמים כי רגע שנשאר בו חשוב יום בחשבון התורה וככה יום בשנה
חשוב שנה. ודבר השביעי ידוע גם ככה השנה השביעית ושבע שבועות השנים
יובל לקרוא דרור כנגד (במדבר ח':כ"ה) מבן חמשים שנה ישוב מצבא העבודה.
ופסח שני כנגד שנת העבור. (שמות כ':י"ט-כ':י"ג:י"ט) ולא תבשל גדי כמו
(ויקרא כ"ב:כ"ח) לא תשחטו ביום אחד (דברים כ"ב:ו'-ז') לא תקח האם על
הבנים (ויקרא כ"ב:כ"ח) ולא תחרוש. ודבר הרובע ובארצכם לא תעשו (ויקרא
כ"ב:כ"ד) לא יהיה כלי גבר ולא ילבש גבר הפך מעשה ה'. וככה (ויקרא י"ח:ד')
ואת חקותי תשמרו על כן בגד כלאים. וסגירת שבעת ימים הטעם ידוע וככה
הנדה והיולדת והערך מבן חדש עד שוב אל המקום ועד ה' שנים ה' שקלים

נחרש ונזרע ונקצר ונברר והובדר ונטחן ונופה ונילש ונאפה והנה אם עושה כן ימות ברעב. רק הנכון שיאכל תמיד וכאשר יגדל ישאל מעט עד שידע כל השאלות וככה המשכיל יוכל לדעת טעמים רבים בתורה אשר הם מבוארים באר היטב ויש שהם מבוארים לאדם אחד מאלף. ומשה אדוננו ע"ה אמר על כל המצות (דברים ד':ו') רק עם חכם ונבון הגוי הגדול הזה ואם אין להם טעמים שנוכל לדעת מה טיבם איך יאמרו העמים שהם חקים צדיקים ואנחנו השומרים אותם חכמים ואזכיר קצת הטעמים הנזכרים בתורה.

כתוב (שמות יג) קדש לי כל בכור וכתוב (שמות יג) על כן אני זובח ודבר השבת (שמות כ) כי ששת ימים וככה שנת השמיטה ושביתת העבד (דברים טז) למען תזכור. וככה מצות ומרורים והמועדים שלשה באביב השעורים ובכורי חטים והאסיף להודות לפני השם יתברך. וכתיב (דברים טז) איש כמתנת ידו כברכת ה' א-להיך אשר נתן לך תן לו משלו כדרך (דברי הימים א כט) כי ממך הכל ומידך נתנו לך. וצוה (שמות כג) לא ישבו בארצך והטעם פן יחטיאו אותך לי. וכתיב במקום אחר (דברים כ) לא תחיה כל נשמה למען אשר לא ילמדו אתכם וככה להתחתן בגוים ולקח מבנותיו והטעם (שמות לד) והזנו את בניך וכן כי יסיר את בנך מאחרי ואמר בשבת (שמות כג) למען ינוח שורך וחמורך שתחרוש בהם. וטעם (בראשית ט) שופך דם האדם באדם דמו ישפך כי בצלם א-להים ברא את האדם. (דברים כד) ולא יחבול רחים ורכב כי נפש הוא חובל. והזכיר טעם (ויקרא כד) וזרע אין לה בעבור שתשוב אל בית אביה כנעוריה. ובחג הסוכות + (ויקרא כג) למען ידעו דורותיכם. וטעם (ויקרא כה) לא תמכר לצמיתות כי לי כל הארץ. וככה (ויקרא כה) כי לי בני ישראל עבדים טעם (שמות כה) לא ימכרו ממכרת עבד. וצוה להריע בחצוצרות על העולה להיות לזכרון כהריעם במלחמה כמו (תהלים ס) עלי פלשת אתרועע. והציצית (במדבר טו) למען תזכרו בראותו בכל רגע וככה וקשרתם וכתבתם. והזכיר על (במדבר כה) צרור את המדינים שני טעמים האחד דבר פעור והשני שמחשבתם לעשות לכם עוד רע בעבור הריגת בת נשיאם. וטעם (דברים כג) לא תתעב אדומי כי אחיך הוא ולא תתעב מצרי כי גר היית בארצו וטעם עמוני ומואבי שלא קדמו ולא זכרו האחוה הקדמונית ועוד ששכר בלעם להרע לך. והזכיר טעם (דברים יז) לא ירבה לו נשים וסוסים והזכיר (דברים יז) ולא יסור לבבו ולא ישיב את העם מצרימה. וטעם להבעל הנשים למטה אבותיהן (דברים לו) למען ירשו בני ישראל איש נחלת אבותיו וטעם (דברים ו) מה העדות והחקים עבדים היינו ויוציאנו ואנחנו חייבים לשמוע בקולו שעשה לנו הטובה הזאת ועוד (ברים ו) וצדקה תהיה לנו. וטעם השמיטה (שמות כג) ואכלו אביוני עמך. וטעם (שמות י) על כן לא היה ללוי חלק ונחלה כי הוא עובד ה' הנכבד וטעם (שמות יח) ראשית דגנך כי טוב הוא ממך ובו בחר ה'

המדרגה הראשונה שיעלה ממנה אל עבודת ה' יתעלה והיא כוללת כל מצות עשה. ואלה ירגילו לבו וידריכוהו עד כי ידבק בשם יתברך הנכבד כי בעבור זה נברא האדם כי לא נברא לקנות הון ולא לבנות בנינים יעזבם לזרים והוא ידור תחת הארץ ולא להתענג במיני מאכלים כי רגעים מעטים הם והיגיעה רבה גם יזיקו בודרם. גם משכב הנשים יכלה כחו ובשרו. גם דברי שחוק והשתכר סכלות והוללות כי המשכיל יבין כי ימי חייו מעטים הם וביד בוראו נפשו ולא ידע מתי יפקדנה. על כן יש לו לבקש כל דבר שיביאנו לאהוב אותו ללמוד חכמה ולחפש האמונה עד שיכיר ויתבונן מעשה ה' ולא יתעסק בהבלי העולם רק להתבודד ללמוד ולהגות בתורת ה' ולשמור מצותיו והשם יפקח עיניו ולבו ויחדש בקרבו רוח אחרת אז יהיה בחייו אהוב ליוצרו ונפשו דבקה בו ותשבע שובע שמחות את פניו ובהפרדה מעל הגויה תהיינה נעימות ימין אלהיו עליו נצח וזה שאמר אסף (תהלים עג) כלה שארי ולבבי צור לבבי וחלקי א-להים לעולם כדרך יעקב אבינו שנדר (בראשית כח) והיה ה' לי לא-להים כי כאשר בא אל בית אל אמר (בראשית לה) הסירו את אלהי הנכר והניח הצאן והתבודד לעבוד השם ולא שכב עם אשה כי רחל מתה וחוללה בלהה ובעבור זה מאס באם ראובן ושפחתה על כן כתיב בפסוק אחר (בראשית לה) ויהיו בני יעקב שנים עשר להודיע שלא שכב עם אשה אחר כך על כן לא הוליד עוד. והנה מי שהשיג זאת המעלה שזכר השם ומעשיו ונפלאותיו לא יסורו מלבו גם לא ידבר דבר בפיו שלא יזכיר השם להודיע לבני האדם כבודו על כן נשבעו הנביאים ברוב דבריהם וזהו (דברים ו) ובשמו תשבע ואז יהיה (דניאל יב) ממצדיקי הרבים.

ודע כי התורה לא נתנה רק לאנשי לבב על כן יש לפרש דברים כתובים בדרך שיקול הדעת כמו (שמות י"ט:ד') ואשא אתכם על כנפי נשרים וככה (דברים י':ט"ז) ומלתם את ערלת לבבכם (דברים ט':ו:ח') פתח תפתח את ידך והקדמונים אמרו כי כך (דברים כב) ופרשו את השמלה ויש דברים שהם אמת כמשמעם גם הם בדרך משל כמו גן עדן ועץ הדעת ועץ החיים וטעם הכרובים הדומה להם.

שער ח

ההוגה תמיד בתורת ה' אם יש לו לב היא תורהו ותשכיל נפשו יותר מאשר למדוהו והשכילוהו מלמדיו וזהו (תהלים קי"ט:צ"ט) מכל מלמדי השכלתי. ומה נכבדו דברי הקדמונים שאמרו חייבים הכל לשמור כל המצות וכל התקונים שתקנום האבות ולא יבקש טעם למה צוו אלה המצוות ואמת דברו כי יש מצות רבות נפלאות ונעלמות והנה אם לא ישמרם האדם עד שידע טעמם הנה ישאר בלא תורה ויהיה נמשל לנער שלא ירצה לאכול לחם עד שידע איך בתחלה

שתקנו האבות אף על פי שרובם הם במעשה או בפה הכל הם לתקן הלב (דברי
הימים א כח) כי כל לבבות דורש ה' וכל יצר מחשבות מבין וכתוב (תהלים קכה)
ולישרים בלבותם והפך זה (משלי כג) לב חרש מחשבות און וכתוב אחר (משלי ו)
ולבו בל עמך כי רוע עין תלוי ברוע הלב וזה ידוע מחכמת התולדות. על כן היתה
העולה כליל כולה לשם על דבר העולה על הרוח דבר שאיננו נכון והחטאת
והאשם על חטא בפה או במעשה וזה פירושו (דברים י) ומלתם את ערלת לבבכם.
ודע כי מלת ערלה כבדות והנה ערל לב כמו (שמות ז) כבד לב פרעה. (שמות
ו) ואני ערל שפתים כמו (שמות ד) כי כבד פה. גם (ירמיהו ו) ערלה אזנם כמו
(ישעיהו ו) ואזניו הכבד. ובהכרת ערלת הבשר יהיה לאות ברית בין האדם ובין
בוראו שלא יטנף נפשו במשכב שאיננו על דרך אמת ושכרו אתו שיפרה וירבה
וככה כתיב (בראשית יז) ואתנה בריתי ביני ובינך וארבה אותך. וכתיב (ויקרא
יט) וערלתם ערלתו גם היא כובד ברוב הליחה גם זה מהתולדות. והנה המצוה
היא כוללת שתענו מפני השם ותכנעו כאשר ייסר אתכם ותבינו האמת שתסירו
ערלת לבבכם ולא תכבדו לבבכם כמעשה פרעה או אחז וכעת הצר לו (דברי
הימים ב כח) ויוסף למעול בה' (מלכים א כא) ואחאב נכנע (דברים יב) וישר
בעיני ה' וככה כתיב (ויקרא כו) אז יכנע לבבכם הערל. והנה זאת כמו (דברים ד)
בצר לך ושבת. וקשי עורף משל לאדם יקשה ערפו וישיבנו אל אדוניו וכאשר
יקראנו לא ישיב אליו פניו והנה הוא מקציף. על כך אחרי אלה (יהושע ב) כי
ה' א-להיכם הוא א-להי האלהים הם המלאכים בשמים ואדוני המלכים שהם
האדונים בארץ והכל ברשותו והוא א-ל גדול וגבור ונורא ואיך תוכל להנצל
ולא יאבה כי תרבה שוחד. והעד כי בתחלת הפרשה (דברים ט) כי עם קשה
עורף אתה על כן וערפכם וגו'. ומצות הלב תחלתם (שמות כ) אנכי ה' א-להיך
שיאמין בכל לבו שהשם שהוציאו ממצרים הוא א-להיו והנה היא מצות עשה
וככה (דברים ו) ואהבת את ה' א-להיך (דברים יא) ולדבקה בו וככה (ויקרא יט)
ואהבת לרעך כמוך. ולא תעשה (שמות כ) לא יהיה לך אלהים אחרים באמונת
הלב (ויקרא יט) ולא תשנא את אחיך (שמות כ) לא תחמוד. (דברים ד) וידעת
היום והשבות אל לבבך מצות עשה וככה (דברים ו) שמע ישראל ה' א-להינו ה'
אחד. ומצות הפה וידוי כהן (דברים כו) וענית ואמרת (דברים כג) מוצא שפתיך
וברכת המזון והלל ותפלה (דברים ו) ושננתם לבניך ודברת בם והנה מצות
עשה ורבים ככה. (שמות כ) ולא תעשה (שמות כ) לא תשא את שם ה' א-להיך
(שמות כ) לא תענה ברעך (שמות כב) אלהים לא תקלל ולא תאור (שמות כג) לא
תזכירו (שמות כג) ולא ישמע על פיך (שמות כג) לא תכרות להם ברית (שמות
כג) ולא תענה על ריב ורבים ככה והמצות במעשה הם רבות ואין צורך לזכרם.
ומצאתי פסוק אחד כולל כל המצות והוא (דברים י) את ה' א-להיך תירא ואותו
תעבוד. והנה מלת תירא כוללת כל מצות לא תעשה בלב ובפה ובמעשה וזו היא

ל"ה:ו') אם צדקת מה תתן לו ורבו פשעיך מה תעשה לו. ועתה ארמוז לך סוד
נכבד מצאנו כתוב (ישעיהו ס"ג:י"ז) למה תתענו ה' מדרכך (מלכים א י"ח:ל"ז)
ואתה הסיבות את לבם אחורנית. ומשה אמר (דברים ל':ט"ו) ראה נתתי לפניך
את החיים ואת הטוב ועוד (איכה ג':ל"ח) מפי עליון לא תצא הרעות והטוב.
ואמרו קדמוננו (נדה טז:) הכל בידי שמים חוץ מיראת שמים. ודע כי צמח
האדמה הנעבדת טוב מצמח האדמה שאינה נעבדת ויש שמנה ורזה ובדרך משל
אמת אפרש כי ג' כחות בחיות האדם ואם תחפוץ קרא אותם בג' שמות נשמה
ורוח ונפש והנה הנפש היא הכח הצומח שהיא בכבד וכל חי וצומח משתתף
בכח הזה וזאת הנפש גוף והיא המתאוה לאכול ודבר המשגל. והרוח בלב ובה
חיי האדם שיתנועע והיא כוללת האדם והבהמה גם היא גוף ובצאת זאת הרוח
שהיא דומה לאויר מהגויה אז ימות האדם וזאת הרוח מתגברת והיא הכעסנית.
והנשמה היא העליונה וכחה במוח ותולדות בני אדם ויצריהם משתנים יש מי
ששלשתם חזקות בו ויש נחלשות ויש השתים בתמורה ואין צורך להאריך כי
הנשמה מבקשת מה שיועילנה ממעשי ה' כי הוא מקור חייה והנפש מבקשת
תענוגי הגוף לטוב לה והנה הרוח אמצעית ובעבור שצורך יש למוח אל הכבד
והלב גם שניהם למוח והכלל כל אחד זה לזה על כן קראו העברים הנשמה רוח
ונפש והנה הכל קשורים עם הגוף ואם אדם יאכל מאכלים שיחמם הדם אז ירבה
כעסו והנה מעשה הגוף ברוח ואם הגוף ישר במזגו ואדם אחר הכעיסו בדבריו
או במעשיו תגבר יד הרוח בלב ויוליד חום בגוף והנה תשתנה הגוף בעבור
הרוח וכל משכיל ינחה גופו כפי צורך נשמתו ולא תשתנה היא בהשתנות הגוף
וזאת היא המעלה הגדולה שנתן ה' לישראל כי אם ישמרו מצות ה' אין צורך
לרופאים עם השם כאשר עשה אסא ותפסו הכתוב ואין טענה ממלת (שמות
כ"א:י"ט) ורפא ירפא כי איננו מהבנין הקל רק הוא כמו (מלכים א א) וירפא
את מזבח ה' ואיננו כמו (דברים ל"ב:ל"ט) מחצתי ואני ארפא ובאיוב (איוב
ה':י"ח) ימחץ וידיו תרפנה. וככה צבא השמים חלק ה' לכל העמים וזה פירוש
(ישעיהו כד) יפקוד ה' על צבא המרום. וזה כנגד המקבל בדרך חכמת המזלות
והשם לקח לישראל לנחלה ויוציאם מרשות המזלות כל זמן שהם ברשותו
לעשות אשר צום בתורתו על כן אמרו הקדמונים (שבת קנו:) אין מזל לישראל
ובעבור זה כתוב (שמות ל':ג:ט"ז) ונפלינו אני ועמך. ואין לטעון ואיך ישנה
השם חקות שמים הנה זה יוכיח. והנה היה הטוב כלו בעבור כל הטוב ובעבור
רע מעט אין מדרך החכמה למנוע מה שהוא טוב רובו. על כן יש כח במשכיל
לבחור הטוב והרע כי אין הגזירות רק כפי המקבל על כן כתוב (דברים ט"ו:ד')
אפס כי לא יהיה בך אביון על תנאי אם הכל או הרוב טוב וכן כתוב (דברים
ט"ו:ד') רק אם שמוע תשמע. והיחיד מועיל נפשו באחריתו.

ועתה שים לבך ודע כי כל המצות הכתובות בתורה או המקבלות או התקונים

והטעם לא תעגנו באכילה ושתיה כי העני הפך התענוג וככה (ויקרא כ':ז')
והתקדשתם והייתם קדושים פירושו אל תשקצו את נפשותיכם לאכול כל דבר
נמאס ומשחית בתולדות והנזיר אשר לא ישתה יין הוא קדוש.

והנה כל המצות על שלש דרכים הא' באמונת הלב והשני בפה והשלישי
במעשה וכאשר האחד נמצא בכל חשבון ככה עקר כל מצוה שהיא תלויה בפה
או במעשה צריכה לאמונת הלב ואם לאו הכל שוא ותהו. ורז"ל אמרו (סנהדרין
ק"ו:) רחמנא לבא בעי והוא בוחן לב וחוקר כליות וכתיב (דברים ל':י"ד) בפיך
ובלבבך לעשותו וזה הכתוב כולל השלש דרכים בפיך ידוע ובלבבך אמונת
הלב לעשותו שתעשה המצות שהם במעשה. וככה כתוב (דברים י':י"ב) מה ה'
שואל מעמך כי אם ליראה את ה' א-להיך בכל לבבך ובכל נפשך. ודוד המלך
אמר (תהלים כ"ד:ד') נקי כפים ובר לבב אשר לא נשא לשוא נפשו. וכן (תהלים
ט"ו:ב'-ג') הולך תמים ופועל צדק ודובר אמת בלבבו לא רגל.

ועתה שים לבך כי אין טורח במצות לא תעשה לאשר יש לו לב להבין כי ה'
נטע בלב שכל שיוכל אדם בו להשמר מכל נזק. והמשל ברופא שאמר לאדם
שאינו יודע המאכלים שיזיקו לו כפי תולדתו אל תאכל כל מה שאזהירך שאם
תאכלם תבא לידי חולי ותמות וכל איש דעת לא תאוה נפשו לאכול דבר
שיזיקנו רק יהיה נתעב ונמאס בעיניו אף על פי ששמע שהוא מאכל ערב והנה
ישום עיקר מאכלו לחיות ולא יבקש החיים בעבור שיאכל כי זה דרך הבהמות
כי אין להם נשמה שתתיה אחר הפרדה מעל הגויה הלא תראה כתוב בתורה
(בראשית א':כ"ד) תוצא הארץ נפש חיה ישרצו המים ולא כן האדם רק נעשה
האדם בדמות מלאך ואם המלאך חי לעולם ככה מי שהוא בדמותו על כן אמר
אחד מהמשכילים כי העונש בארבע מיתות בית דין על לא תעשה וככה כרת
ומיתה בידי שמים והשכר על מצות עשה. וקדמונינו הביאו ראיה כי יש שכר
לנשמר ממצות ממצות לא תעשה (דברים י':י"ג:כ"ה) לא תאכלנו למען ייטב לך
ויש אומר כי השכר ישוב לאשר הזכיר באחרונה (דברים י"ב:כ"ה) כי תעשה
הישר ויש אומרים למצות לא תאכלנו הכתוב למעלה (דברים י"ב:ט"ז-י"ז)
על הארץ תשפכנו כמים אשר לא יאספו עד שלא יאכלנו אדם כי הדם הוא
הנפש וזה ידוע מחכמת התולדות. גם נכון הוא שיראת השם שהיא מצות עשה
כוללת כל מצות עשה ומצות לא תעשה כאשר הזכיר משה אחר (דברים י)
ליראה לשמור כל מצותיו וחקותיו לטוב לך שהם עשה ולא תעשה כי המונע
עצמו מעשיית עבירה בעבור יראתו מהשם אז טוב לו ומלת לטוב לך כוללת
טוב העולם הזה והבא ביחד והשכר על מצות עשה כי יש בהם טורח והמשל
כמי שיגע עצמו על פי הרופא לבשל מאכל מה שיאכל שיועילנו והנה שכרו
אתו ופעולתו לפניו והנה לטוב לך שתקבל שכר ותמלט מעונש והנה הטוב הוא
לאדם שומר מצות הרופא כי לא יועיל ולא יזיק הרופא כדברי אליהוא (איוב

י"ב:ג') וביום השמיני ימול בשר ערלתו. וכתוב על דבר (דברים ה':ט"ו) היתום
והאלמנה וזכרת כי עבד היית ואל תתגבר על מעשי ידי השם:

שער ו

יש מצות מבוארות בתורה ויש מצות שלא ידענו פירושם באמת רק מפי
הקדושים המעתיקים שקבלו בן מאביו ותלמיד מרבו ולולי הקבלה יוכל אדם
לפרש אותם פירוש אחר. ויש מצות קבלנום מהם ואין זכר להם בתורה וכלל
אומר לך לולי אנשי כנסת הגדולה ואנשי המשנה והתלמוד כבר אבדה תורת
אלהינו ונשכח זכרה ח"ו כי אלה העמידו כל דבר על בוריו ובארו לנו המצות
באר היטב וכל המשפטים כאשר קבלום. ויש שימצאו עדות ברורה מן התורה
ויש דרך דרש ויש דרך אסמכתא בעלמא ומי שיש לו לב יוכל להכיר מתי
אומרים דרש ומתי אומרים פשט כי אין כל דבריהם על דרך אחד והשם שנתן
להם חכמה הוא יתן משכורתם שלמה: והנה בירמיהו (ירמיהו י"ז:כ"ב) ולא
תוציאו משא מבתיכם ביום השבת ולא נזכר זה בתורה והמצות המקובלות
מהאבות שיש להם זכר בתורה רבות ושאין להם זכר. ואזכיר קצת אלה ואלה
כמה ברכות בכל יום והתפלות וברכת המזון והלל. ואמר רב בחיי כי (דברים
י':כ"א) הוא תהלתך והוא א-להיך. וקריאת שמע ועירוב וקידוש והבדלה ושלש
סעודות ויש אומרים נר שבת. וככה תקיעת שופר ביום הזכרון כי לולי הקבלה
היה נראה כי הוא על דרך ראש חדש ניסן כי הוא העקר לפני שתכנס תקופת
האמת על כן אמרו שהוא יום הדין. וככה הלולב כי אין מפורש בתורה רק
(ויקרא כ"ג:מ"ו) ולקחתם ולולי הקבלה היה לו טעם אחר. וככה ספירת העומר
כי הם הפרישו בין (ויקרא כג) וספרתם לכם ובין (ויקרא טו) וספרה לה. וככה
הטריפה ויש לה טעם נכבד מחכמת תולדות שמים וככה ז' ימי חופה ואבלות
ובקור חולים וקבורת מתים ונר חנוכה ומקרא מגילה וד' כוסות וכבר פרשתי
(במדבר כ"ז:י"א) וירש אותה כי היא אסמכתא בעלמא:

שער ז

שים לבך להתבונן כי כל המצות שהם עקרים או תלויות בדבר או לזכר כתובות
או מקובלות הם מצות עשה או לא תעשה מפורש או עשה שעקרו וסודו לא
תעשה כאשר כתוב (שמות ל"א:ט"ז) ושמרו בני ישראל את השבת לעשות
את השבת. והשביתה איננה מעשה רק כלוי מעשה ומנוחה ממנו. כי כן כתוב
(בראשית ב':ב') וישבות ביום השביעי מכל מלאכתו ופירוש לעשות לפני יום
השבת כדי שלא יעשה בו מלאכה וככה (ויקרא ט"ז:כ"ט) תענו את נפשותיכם

ואשה נרבעת. והעריות הקרובות מאד. על כן נכון הוא להיות פירוש (ויקרא
כא:כ) הקרובה אליו דבק עם אחותו שהיא בת אביו ואמו בדרך (שמות י"ד:ל')
וירא ישראל את מצרים מת על שפת הים. על כן אמר אברהם (בראשית כ) וגם
אמנה אחותי בת אבי היא. והעד שאין עונש בית דין. ואם טען טוען למה האחות
ולא האח אולי יאמר לנו למה הבתולה ולא הבעולה ואין זה המשפט לאח:

ויש מהמצות שהם לזכר למצות העקרים כמו השבת זכר למעשה
בראשית ושביתת העבד זכר ליציאת מצרים וככה פסח ומצות ומרורים וסוכות
והמזוזה ותפלין ביד ובראש והציצית אף על פי שאין התכלת מעכב כמו שמרור
לא יעכב מצות המצות כי התכלת הוא לזכר על כן מעיל האפוד כליל תכלת
וציץ נזר הקדש קשור בפתיל תכלת ואין המתעטף עושה מצוה שלמה כי הוא
חייב כל היום ובהיותו בשוק וראה צורות אז יתור לבו אחרי עיניו יותר מאשר
יתור בשעת התפלה. והזכרתי זה בעבור שראיתי אנשים רבים אינם יראי השם
והם מתעטפים בטלית כבוד דרך כבוד לנפשם. גם האפוד והחשן לזכרון. וככה גיד
הנשה שהוא אסור באכילה לזכר הפך אכילת הפסח. ועתה אפרש כי כאשר קבל
האב עליו ועל זרעו חייב הבן לשמוע בקול אביו כימי הפורים ודברי הצומות
וזעקתם הכתוב במגלה (והם הארבע צומות הכתובים בתרי עשר אשר קבלו
עליהם ועל זרעם נביאים וזקנים שבדור על המאורעות הרעות (אסתר ט':כ"ז)
ותכתוב אסתר המלכה ומרדכי אגרת השנית לקיים עליהם ימי הפורים כאשר
קימו מרדכי ואסתר עליהם וכאשר וקימו על נפשם ועל זרעם נביאים ראשונים
דברי הצומות הארבע) אם אל יעבור על מצות אדני הכל. וטעם זה הדבר שיהיה
נזכר החסד שעשה השם עם יעקב שהוא לבדו אבינו ולא ישתתף בו עמנו אחר
כאברהם ויצחק כי השם בחרו בחרו ולא נתערב עם זרעו מי שלא בחר השם כאברהם
ולא נתגאל במאכלם ויין משתיהם כדרך שהזכיר בתורה (בראשית ט':כ"ה)
ארור כנען שלא יתערב עם בני ישראל שהוא מבני שם שהוא אבי כל בני עבר
שנתיחסו אליו שברכו נח עם זרע מקולל. ואמר הנביא (הושע י"ב:ב:ג') וריב לה'
עם יהודה ולפקוד על יעקב והטעם הבנים (ר"ל ויחרדו בנים מים. עיין שם
בהושע) והעד עם יהודה ואמר אחרי כן בבטן עקב את אחיו שהשם נתן בו כח
שתאחז ידו בעקב עשו לפני צאתו מן הרחם ולא עשה כן לכל נולד והאומרים
כי אחר צאתו היה זה לא יתכן כי כתוב וידו אוחזת ואלו היה כדבריהם היה
כתוב ואחרי כן יצא אחיו ואחזה ידו. ועוד בבטן עקב את אחיו ובאונו שרה
את אלהים שהתאבק עם המלאך ולא יכול לו והנה יש לו מעלה גדולה ועוד
מדרך חכמת הרופאים כי כל אבר מחזיק דמיונו אם הוא בריא והפך הדבר.
ובעבור שכתוב (בראשית ל"ב:ב:כ"ו) ותקע כף ירך יעקב על כן לא יאכל מהיום
ההוא והלאה וחייבים לנהוג כבוד באביהם והוצרכתי להאריך בעבור שהוא על
דרך הפשט כי לא נזכר רק בעבור החוק ואין כמוהו המילה כי כתוב (ויקרא

והמצורע והטמאים. ורוב המצות כולל הזכרים והנקבות. ויש לזכרים לבדם כמו המילה ומקרה לילה ופטר רחם ופדיון בכור ופי שנים. ויש לנקבות לבדן כנדה ויולדת וסוטה ונדר בעולה או קטנה. ויש תלויות בדבר אחר כמו העולות והמוספין במקום הנבחר ושלש פעמים ומצות רבות ככה. ומהתלויות אם היה לנו בן מלנוהו ופדנוהו אם היה בכור ואם נטענו עץ למאכל ערלנוהו וחללנוהו ואם שדה או כרם עשרנוהו ואם הלוינו כסף לא נהיה כנושים ואם קנאנו נשינו נעשה כמשפט ואם היו לנו עבדים או שפחות או מי שיקח אשה נעשה ככתוב עליהן והמצות הדומות לאלה רבות הדינים ורובם דינים ומשפטים. ויש מצות רבות תלויות בזמנים כמילה בן שמונת ימים והערך מבן חדש ועד בן חמש ועד בן עשרים ועד בן ששים. ויש מצות רבות ביום כעולות והמילה ויש בלילה כאכילת פסח וספירת העומר. ויש בין היום ובין הלילה כסוף זמן שחיטת הפסח והדלקת הנרות וביאת הטמאים אל המחנה ויש בצהרים כתפלת המנחה ותחלת שחיטת הפסח. ויש פעם בשבוע בשבת ופעם בשנה כחג השבועות ויום הזכרון וצום כפור וחג שמיני עצרת ויש שבעת ימים כמצות כי על דרך הפשט כי הם חייב כי הכתוב הזכיר הפסח ואמר (דברים ט"ז:ג') שבעת ימים תאכל עליו מצות לחם עני למען תזכר את יום צאתך והנה הזכיר הטעם כי עד שבעת ימים אכלו ישראל המצות כי הענן היה הולך יומם ולילה עד שטבע פרעה אז הסיעם משה עד שנעשה המשכן כאשר פירשתי זה במקומו. וככה שבעת ימי סוכה והדלקת הנר שמונה ימים. וככה מקרא מגילה בזמנה. ולגמור הלל י"ח ימים ולילה אחד ולקרוא בכל ראש חדש וששת ימי הפסח. וספירת העומר שבעה שבועות וקדוש השנה השביעית ושנת החמישים:

ויש מצות רבות שאינן תלויות בדבר ולא בזמן ידוע והם חיוב לכל בני מצות זכרים ונקבות מלך וכהן ועשיר ועני בישראל גם בגר בריא או מנוגע תורה אחת לכל ואלה המצות הם העיקרים:

שער ה

המצות שהם עקרים שאינם תלויות במקום או בזמן או בדבר אחר הם הנטועות בלב הם הפקודים כמו פקדון שהוא נתון ביד אשר הפקד אתו על כן אמר המלך דוד (תהלים י"ט:ט') פקודי ה' ישרים משמחי לב. ואלה היו ידועות בשקול הדעת לפני תת התורה ביד משה והם רבות כעשרת הדברות חוץ מהשבת והם נשנו על יד משה ועל כאלה אמר (בראשית כ':י"ב':י"ב':י':ו:ה') וישמור משמרתי מצותי חקותי ותורותי כי אלו היה יודע כי כל העריות לא היה לוקח יעקב אבינו שתי אחיות יחד על כן נפרש (ויקרא י"ח:כ"ז) כי את כל התועבות האל על רובם כמשכב זכור שהוא הפך חפץ השם ונתעב בתולדה וככה מין אחר

הנזכרות. וככה עשו קדמונינו ביום הכפורים שהוא אסור באכילה וזהו העיקר
כי כל עינוי הדבק עם נפש בכל המקרא הוא צום והיה כן כי הנפש כחה בכבד
שהיא המתאוה (דברים י"ג:כ') כי תאוה נפשך. (איוב ל"ג:כ') ונפשו מאכל
תאוה. (ויקרא ז':י"ח) והנפש האוכלת. והעדים כי כן הוא (ישעיהו נ"ח:ג')
למה צמנו ולא ראית ענינו נפשנו הטעם כפול וככה (ישעיהו נ"ח:ה') הכזה
יהיה צום אבחרהו יום ענות אדם נפשו ועוד (ישעיהו נ"ח:ה') ונפש נענה
תשביע וכבר פירשתי ענין (תהלים ל"ה:י"ג) ענותי בצום נפשי למה נפתח
בי"ת בצום ואמרו כי גם הוא אסור בשתיה כי מצאו (דברים י"ד:כ"ג) ואכלת
לפני ה' א-להיך מעשר דגנך תירושך ויצהרך ובדניאל (דניאל י':י"ב) וסוף לא
סכתי ושם תשוב להבין ולהתענות ואין זכר לנפש והנה גם הוא אסור ברחיצה
והם אמרו שירחץ בעל קרי ומה שמרצו אמרי הקדמונים (אבות ב:א) הוי זהיר
במצוה קלה כבחמורה ועוד (אבות ד:ב) כי שכר מצוה מצוה.

והנה בעשרת הדברים החמשה כנגד השם הם הדבקים בלב והם החמורים
והחל כנגד דבור האדם ששי לא תרצח מהחמור. וכלל אומר כי כל כרת ומיתה
היא על מצות לא תעשה כי הוא מכעיס יותר מהמתעצל לעשות מה שצוה. ולא
מצאתי כרת במצות עשה כי אם במילה כי היא לאות ברית עומדת בגופו כל
ימי חייו. ופעם אחת היא חייב מצוה והחיוב על אבי הנולד או אב בית דין רק
אם גדל ולא ימול יש עליו כרת. וככה כרת על מי שחדל לעשות הפסח כי זכר
יציאת מצרים עקר לכל המצות על כן כתוב אחר (שמות ל"ד:י"ז-י"ח) אלהי
מסכה לא תעשה לך את חג המצות תשמור וכתובה תשובה (דברים ו':כ"א)
מה העדות עבדים היינו לפרעה במצרים.

ועתה ארמוז לך מצוה אחת כוללת כל מצות עשה והיא בכרת באשר תסתכל
טעם כל ארור הוא על סתר כי כן החל וברובם מפורש ודבר חותנת ואחות
כי יתיחד עמם בלי חשד והבהמה אין לה זה פה ובסוף אמר (דברים כז) ארור אשר
לא יקים את דברי התורה להכעיס בסתר. כי בגלוי בית דין יכריחנו או יקח
הדין ממנו על כן נכון הוא להיות פירוש אלה כמו (חגי ב) אם יגע טמא נפש
בכל אלה. וקרבן השוגג יוכיח כי המזיד בכח בגלוי מחלל השם והנה ראינו
שעברו כל ישראל על מצות (דברים כ) לא תחיה כל נשמה מפני שבועתם
שלא יחללו את השם:

שער ד

יש מצות חיוב הצבור כעולות ולחם הפנים ויין לנסך ושמן למאור. ויש
למשפחה ידועה כמו מצות הגדול הכהנים הגדולים וההדיוטים והלוים והם
מצות רבות. ויש לאדם לבדו מאיזה משפחה שיהיה כמצות המלך והנזיר

ולשתות ארבע כוסות רק החיוב הוא לשותה. והזכרתי כל זה בעבור ששמעתי על חכם חסיד שהיה משוטט בחוצות לבקש מי שיש לו עוף שישחטנו ודעתו על הברכה למלאות מאה ברכות בכל יום:

ויש בעלי אזהרות שהכניסו במצות לאוין שפירושם טעם כמו ולא יסור לבבו ולא ישיב את העם ולא יזח את החשן כאשר ירכסוהו או לא יזח וככה ולא ימות במלחמה ולולי הקבלה נכון היה להיות כאלה לא יסור ממנו:

ויש שהכניסו במצות מה שהוא רשות כמו (דברים י"ד:כ"א) לגר אשר בשעריך או מכור לנכרי וככה (שמות כ"ב:ל') לכלב תשליכון אותו כי הטעם דבק עם ואנשי קדש תהיון לי. והנה בשר שנטרף איננו למאכלך רק לכלב השומר צאנך תשליכנו על כן נפתח למד לכלב ולולי הקבלה היה נראה ככה לעולם בהם תעבודו כי כל המצות מיד האבות קבלנום ואין הפרש בדברי המצות בין דבריהם ובין דברי תורה תורה כי גם הם נתונים לנו והם קבלו מאבותם ואבותם מהנביאים והכל מפי השם ביד משה.

והנה אתן לך משל במצוה אחת שחשובה שנים כמו זכור ושמור וקדוש השבת והקריאה לשבת עונג ועשות דרכים ומצוא חפץ ודבר דבר הנם מצות רבות והעיקר (שמות כ':י') לא תעשה כל מלאכה והנה הוא חייב לזכור כל ימי השבוע מתי הוא השביעי ויהיה שמור לו והנה זכור כמו שמור וקדושו שלא יעשה בו מלאכה כדברי ירמיה והעונג הוא המנוחה מעמל הגוף ומצוא חפץ ודבר דבר מחפצו שלא יביאנו לעשות בו מלאכה ובכלל האזהרות (דברים י"ט:ז') ומלתם את ערלת לבבכם בכלל מצות עשה (במדבר לא) וערפכם לא תקשו בכלל לא תעשה ושאלתי גדולי הדור מה פירושם ותשובתם לדחות בקנה רצוץ כחוקם עם תלמידיהם שאין להם לב לבחון בין האמת ובין השקר

והנה בעלי האזהרות דומים לאדם שסופר כמה הוא מספר העשבים הכתובים בספר רפואות והוא לא יכיר מה תועלת בכל אחד מהם ומה יועילו לו שמותם: ויש מהם נזכרים בספר בשני שמות והוא חושב כי שנים הם כמו (דברים ט':ז') זכור אל תשכח. ועוד אפשר לך הפסוק במקום הראוי. וככה מצות רבות כתובות בתורה ואין איש שם על לב.

שער ג

יש מצוה שהיא העיקר ויש לה גדרות כמו הנזיר שיזיר מיין ושכר כל ימי נזרו כי היין מרבה התאוה בהסירו הדעת והנה דניאל התענה ולא שתה יין בפסח כי מדרבנן הוא לשתות והנה השם אסר עליו החומץ ומשרת ענבים וחרצנים וזג ותער לא יעבור על ראשו שלא ייפה עצמו לנשים והנה הטעם אם הוא נדר להיות נזיר מן היין לבדו לא יהיה קדוש לשם שלם רק יהיה עם אלה המצות

באדם ובמין הבהמה גם העוף בכללה דבר על ההווה יותר כמו
(בראשית ח':א') ויזכור א-להים את נח ואת כל החיה והבהמה כי הם נכבדים
שנולדו עמו ביום אחד וכן (שמות כ"א:ל"ג) נפל שמה שור או חמור בהווה
שנמצא יותר וככה משפט הסוס והפרד והגמל. גם אסור בנקבה כשאיננו
מהמין כמו הבהמה גם איסור במין לעולם באשת האב והאחות והבת גם
איסור בחיי אחר כאשת איש והיבמה ואשה אל אחותה גם איסור באשה כאשר
איננה מעם השוכב עד שתשוב לתורתו כי ערפה שבה אל עמה ואל אלהיה
ורות אמרה (רות א) עמך עמי וא-להיך א-להי והשוכב עמה ואיננה מתקדשת
מטומאתה ליחד השם הנכבד נותן מזרעו לע"ז גם יש איסור במוכנת להיות
אשתו כבתולה ואלמנה גם יש איסור באשתו כל ימי נדת דותה וימי שבתה
בדמי טומאה לזכר ולנקבה:

ויש פרשיות שהם כדמות מצות ואין אחת מהן מצות חיוב כאשת יפת
תואר לא התירה הכתוב לקחתה לו לאשה עד עשותו כל התנאים הנזכרים.
ואל תתמה בעבור שאמר הכתוב (דברים כ"א:י"א) וחשקת בה ולקחת לך
לאשה כי הטעם במחשבה כדבר פרעה (בראשית י"ב:י"ט) ואקח אותה לי
לאשה כפי מחשבתו שחשב וככה על בלק (במדבר כ"ב:י"א) וילחם בישראל
והראיה הגמורה שאמר (דברים כ"א:י"ג) ואחר כן תבוא אליה ובעלתה והיתה
לך לאשה. והיו התנאים שיביאנה אל תוך ביתו ולא יניחנה ברשות אחר אחרי
שיש במחשבתו שיקחנה וגלחה את ראשה ועשתה את צפרניה כמו המצורע.
ואין צורך להזכיר שתתחטא במי נדה כי כתוב במקום אחר (במדבר ל"א:י"ט)
אתם ושביכם. (דברים כ"א:י"ג) והסירה את שמלת שביה מעליה שעבדה בהם
ע"ז ככתוב (בראשית לה) והחליפו את שמלותיכם. (דברים כ"א:י"ג) ובכתה
את אביה ואת אמה אם נהרגו או אם הם חיים וכל זה האיחור אולי לא יקחנה
והלוקח בת ישראל שלא יעשה לה אלה התנאים טוב מזה החושק ואין בפרשה
כולה מצות חיוב רק (דברים כ"א:י"ד) לא תתעמר בה. וככה יש בברכות שאנו
חייבין לברך על מצות חיוב:

ויש שיברך השם שהתיר זה בתנאי זה כמו על השחיטה. והנה אם יברך
ככה בשחיטת הפסח היא מצות חיוב כמו על המילה והשם לא צונו מצות חיוב
לשחוט רק איסור לאכול בשר חי עד שישפך דמו בשחיטה לבדה לא בדרך
אחרת והנה זאת הברכה כברכת נשואין שהזכיר שאסר העריות והארוסות
והתיר את הנשואות והנה המברך על השחיטה ובודק ומסיר החלב והגידים
ומברך השם אחר אכילתו הנה שכרו אתו ואם לא אלה כל יעשה כל אלה יש עונש עליו
והנה כל אלה אינם מצות חיוב כי העיקר איננו כן ואין ספק כי המתענה ומונע
עצמו מאכול בשר כאשר התענה דניאל שכר יקבל מהשם וככה המתענה
בכל יום ואיננו מברך ברכת המזון. וככה הנזיר איננו חייב לקדש ולהבדיל

בלב ובפה ובמעשה שהם עקרים או זכר להם. ומלת (דברים י"ד:כ"ג) ליראה
את ה' כוללת כל מצות לא תעשה והיא יצאה במלת עשה והטעם כשומר עצמו
מגעת אל ערוה בעבור יראתו מה' כעבד שירא מאדוניו לעשות רע והוא רואהו
בעיניו כי יש אחרים הנמשכים אחר תאותם שלא יפחדו בעבור המלך אולי יודע
הדבר לו או בעבור שם רע ודופי וחרפה ומלת (דברים י"ג:ה') אחרי ה' א-להיכם
תלכו כוללת לעשות חסד וצדק ולאהוב שלום. ואמר הנביא ע"ה (מיכה ו':ח') כי
אם עשות משפט ואהבת חסד וזה כולל כבד את אביך ולא תרצח ולא תנאף ולא
תגנוב ולא תענה ברעך ולא תגזול ולא תחמוד ולא תכחשו ולא תשקרו ומדבר
שקר תרחק ולא תהדר פני גדול ולא תקח שוחד ולא תעשוק את רעך מאזני
צדק ולא תלין ולא תקום ולא תטור ואיפה ומצות לעני ולגר אם כסף תלוה
את עמי כל אלמנה ויתום לא תענון ורבים ככה והצנע לכת כולל כל
דרך וחוק ותורה שהורנו השם: ויש מצות רבות עברו ומה צורך לספרם בשש
מאות כמו אגודת אזוב ואתם לא תצאו אל יצא איש ממקומו ללקוט מן ולא
תותירו ממנו היו נכונים ומעשה המשכן ונסיעתו והדגלים ושלוח הטמאים ויד
ויתד במחנה וצאת על האויב שכלה זכרם והברכה והקללה ומזבח בהר עיבל
ולסיד האבנים ולכתוב התורה וערי מקלט ומלחמת עמלק:

ויש שהיו מצות על משה לבדו כמו מזבח אדמה שכרת ברית עם ישראל
ולפסול הלוחות ולהקים המשכן ושבעת ימי המלואים ולמשוח המשכן ואחיו
ובניו ולתת האורים והתומים על החושן ולשים לוחות הברית בארון ודבר נחש
נחשת וככה מצות אחרות כמו רקועי פחים ושיתנו הכהנים התורה מצד הארון
מחוץ ורצנצנת המן ומטה אהרן:

ויש מצות שיש להם כלל גבוה כמו (ויקרא י"א:ח') איש איש אל כל שאר
בשרו והשפל ערות אב ואם והחל אמך הוא על כן הוא אומר שאר אביך שאר
אמך היא וסופרי המצות ספרו כל לאו בעריות בעבור שיש בהם שמשפטם
משונה בבית דין. ומלת כרת כוללת הכל. והנה חשבו איסור כל בהמה טמאה
ועשרים מיני עופות וכל שרץ הארץ ושרץ העוף ושקץ המים מצוה וידענו כי
טומאת השמונה שרצים חמורה ובעבור שיש סימן אחד כשר לחזיר ולשפן
ולארנבת ולגמל הוצרך לומר (ויקרא י"א:י"א) ובנבלתם לא תגעו והטעם כי
אתם קדושים אל תגעו בכל נבלה שהיא טמא אתכם וככה בדג (ויקרא יא) ואת
נבלתם תשקצו והנה הזכירם כשאר הנבלות ואין על הנוגע כרת ולא מלקות:

ויש מצות לא תעשה שאם תעברו הלאו עשה זה והפטר כמו (שמות י"ב:י')
לא תותירו ממנו עד בקר אם תוכלו ואם נותר ישרף באש ואם לא יותירו אז
יותר טוב. וככה (דברים כח) יבמה יבא עליה איננה מצות חיוב רק אם ייבם אז
טוב לו לקבל שכר ואם לא יחפוץ ליבם אז יכריחנו בית דין.

ויש דרך כלל אחר בעריות יש אסור במין ויש שאינינו מהמין כמשכב זכר

שער ב

מה נכבדה חכמת המבטא וראשיתה דעת המלות החמש. כי יש כלל גבוה כולל כללים שפלים ופרטים והנה נקרא הכלל השפל הקרוב אל הכלל הגבוה מין גבוה והקרוב אל הפרטים מין שפל. והנה הכלל הגבוה כמו גוף כולל האבנים והכוכבים והמתכות והצמחים והחיים. והנה החי מין גבוה כולל העוף והבהמה והאדם והדג. והאדם מין שפל כולל ראובן ושמעון. ומצאנו מספר העוף האמורה בפרשת שמיני עשרים ובפרשת ראה אנכי אחד ועשרים וקדמונינו אמרו ראה זו דאה וכן זו דיה. ורבי מרינוס הקשה אם איה היא דיה מה טעם לספרה פעמים. וחכמינו אמרו כי הזכירה הכתוב בשתי לשונות שלא ליתן פתחון פה. אם כן יזכיר שמות כל עוף בכל לשון והשם לא דבר רק לשון שבינו העם וזהו האמת. ותירוץ זאת הקושיא מחכמת המבטא כי איה שם מין גבוה כולל דיה ודאה כמו (בראשית ט"ו:י') ואת הצפור לא בתר כולל תור וגוזל או שיאמר הכתוב (עמוס ז':ט') ונשמו במות ישחק ובמקום אחר (הושע י':ח') ונשמדו במות און ועוד כי שתי אותיות נלקחות מן דאה. על כן בכל חכמות ובכל אומנות אין אדם מבקש לדעת הפרטים כי אין כח באדם לדעת תכליתם וכמה מספרם כי לא יעמדו רגע אחד על מתכונת אחד לעולם כי יאבדו תמיד והכללים עומדים לעולם.

וצורך גדול היה לי להזכיר דבר הכלל קודם שאדבר על המצות בעבור שראיתי כמה חכמים סופרים שש מאות ושלש עשרה מצות על דרכים רבים.

יש מהם שספר בשול גדי פעם אחת ויש שספרו בג' מצות כנגד שנכתב ג' פעמים וחכמינו דרשוה ורבות ככה. ויש מי שיספור הכללים והפרטים. ויש שסופרים פעם הכללים לבדם ופעם הפרטים לבדם. ויש שסופרים מצוה אחת שבאה בשתי לשונות והטעם אחד.

ועל דרך מחקר האמת אין קץ למספר המצות כאשר אמרו המשורר לכל תכלה ראיתי קץ רחבה מצותך מאד. ואם נספר העיקרים והכללים ומצוה שהיא עומדת לעד אין המצות עשירית משש מאות ושלש עשרה. והשם הנורא יודע תום לבבי כי לא חברתי זה הספר להראות כי עמדתי על חכמות ונגלו לי סודות להתפאר גם להשיב על הקדמונים כי ידוע ידעתי שהיו חכמים ויראי השם ממני גם בדור הזה חכמים גדולים מאד רק חברתיו לנדיב שלמד לפני ספרים שחברתי לו ומרוב אהבתי אותו הוגעתי נפשי לכתוב לו ספר במצות כי ראיתיו כי הוא איש אמת וירא את ה' מרבים:

יש כלל גבוה כמו (דברים י':י"ג) לשמור את כל מצות ה' כולל עשה ולא תעשה. ומלת (ויקרא כג) ועבדתם את ה' א-להיכם כוללת כל מצוה עשה שהם

(במדבר כב) ארה לי והוא קבה לי. ובדברי משה (במדבר כא) וישלח מלאכים אל סיחון אעברה בארצך לא נטה בשדה ובכרם ומשה שינה ואמר לא נעבור בשדה. וכתיב (שמות לב) ועתה הניחה לי ויחר אפי בהם ואכלם ומשה שינה ואמר הרף ממני ואשמידם ואמחה את שמם וכהנה רבות. והנה בעשרת הדברים (שמות כ) זכור (דברים ה) ושמור (שמות כ) ולא תחמוד (דברים ה) ולא תתאוה (שמות כ) ועד שקר (דברים ה) ועד שוא. אבני שהם בלא וי"ו ומשה שינה שיהא בוי"ו. גם לא תנאף ככה ותוספת ומגערת והמשכיל יבין.

ויש הוגה בתלמוד להתפאר על כן כל עסקיו בסדר נזיקין גם הוא מקבל שכר להורות הפתאים וליישר המעוותים רק אם היו כל ישראל צדיקים לא היו צריכים לסדר נזיקין.

ועוד כי יש מצות שאינם חיוב לכל רק אחד לבדו יכול להוציא את הרבים כמעביר שופר ביום הכפורים ויום הזכרון ועולת התמיד ומוספים ופרשת הקהל וככה שופט אחד יספיק ליישר כל מעוות במקום רבים והאדם חייב לתקן עצמו ולהכיר מצות השם שבראוהו ולהבין מעשיו אז ידע בוראו. וככה אמר משה (שמות לב) הודיעני נא את דרכיך אדעך. והנביא אמר (ירמיהו ט':כ"ב) אל יתהלל חכם בחכמתו איזו חכמה שתהיה כי אם בזאת לבדה ומה היא השכל וידוע אותי וכתיב בתורה (דברים י"א:ב') וידעת היום והשבות אל לבבך. ואמר דוד (דברי הימים א כ"ח:ט') דע את א'להי אביך ועבדהו אחר כך כי בעבור זה נברא האדם. ואחר שתקן עצמו יתקן אחרים אם יוכל והנה קדמונינו ז"ל היו יודעים סוד המרכבה ושיעור קומה וחלילה חלילה שדמות יערכו לו רק דבריהם צריכים פירוש כדברי התורה (בראשית א':כ"ו) נעשה אדם בצלמנו כדמותנו. ובנבואת יחזקאל (יחזקאל א':כ"ו) כמראה אדם עליו מלמעלה ואמר ממראה מתניו ולמטה ובסוף זה הספר ארמוז לך זה הסוד

ויש מהגאונים שחבר ספר וקראו ספר היחוד על דעת אנשי המחקר ומעטים הם הדברים הנכונים בו כי פירוש חכם לעצמו כאומר לא ידענו כי היודע איננו דעת ולא ידוע גם כבד שהשם ברא העולם בחפץ מתחדש והכלל איך יחפש אדם לדעת נשגב ממנו והוא לא ידע מה נפשו ומה גויתו. רק היודע חכמת התולדות וכל ראיותיה וחכמת המבטא לדעת הכללים שהם שומרי החומות וחכמת המזלות בראיות גמורות מחכמת החשבון וחכמת המדות וחכמת הערכים אז יוכל לעלות אל מעלה גבוהה לדעת סוד הנפש ומלאכי עליון והעולם הבא מהתורה ודברי הנביאים ומדברי חכמי התלמוד ויחכם ויבין סודות עמוקים שנעלמו מעיני רבים וקצתם אפרש והגאון רבינו סעדיה חבר ספר באמונות ויש בו שערים שאין שעור לדבריו.

ועתה אשוב לדבר על המצות על פי אשר תשיג יד דעתי. והשם יורני בדרך הישרה ומי כמוהו מורה:

י

אם לא ילמוד בתחלה חכמת המדות כי היא כמו סולם מוצב ארצה וראשו מגיע
השמימה ובעמדו על המזלות והתקופות אז יכיר מעשה השם הנכבד וככה
אמרו ז"ל (שבת עה, בשינוי לשון) כל מי שאינו חושב בתקופות ומזלות עליו
הכתוב אומר (ישעיהו ה':י"ב) ואת פועל ה' לא הביטו. ועוד אם לא ידע חכמת
המדות לא ידע ראיות המדות בעירובין גם ארבעים ותשעה מדות של ר' נתן.
ולא יבין המשכיל איך תדמה נשמת האדם אל בוראה בחמשה דברים אם לא
ילמוד חכמת הנפש ולא ידענה אם לא ילמוד בתחלה חכמת תולדות השמים
והארץ והיא עמוקה מאד. גם צורך יש למשכיל שידע חכמת ההגיון כי היא
מאזני כל חכמה וכבר הזהירונו קדמונינו (אבות ב':י"ד) הוי שוקד ללמוד תורה
ודע מה שתשיב לאפיקורוס:

ויש בדברי רבותינו דברים רבים צריכים ראיות ופירוש כמו (אבות ג':ד)
הנעור בלילה (פסחים קי"א) ו[ה]שתה מים זה מחכמת התולדות. ודבר אגרת בת
מחלת ממשפטי המזלות. ודבר הלבנה שהלשלישיה על החמה מחכמת המזלות.
וככה דברים רבים במקרא צריכים פירוש כמו שהזכיר קהלת הארבעה שרשים
שהם שמים וארץ ורוח ועפר והנה (קהלת א) וזרח השמש כנגד שמים (קהלת
א) והארץ לעולם עומדת (קהלת א) וסובב סובב הולך הרוח ואיננו בא בכלל
(קהלת א) וכל הנחלים הולכים אל הים ואלה ארבעתם נזכרים בפרשת בראשית
(בראשית א) את השמים ואת הארץ ורוח א-להים מרחפת על פני המים. וככה
(ישעיהו מ) מי מדד בשעלו מים ושמים בזרת תכן כל בשליש עפר והארץ מי
תכן את רוח ה'. וככב (תהלים קד) נוטה שמים כיריעה יסד ארץ על מכוניה
עושה מלאכיו רוחות המקרה במים. וככה (תהלים לג) כונס כנד מי הים יראו
מה' כל הארץ וככה הזכיר (תהלים לג) בדבר ה' שמים נעשו וברוח פיו כל צבאם
וככה (איוב כח) לעשות לרוח משקל ומים תכן במדה כי הוא לקצות הארץ יביט
תחת כל השמים יראה. וככה (משלי ל) מי עלה שמים וירד מי אסף רוח בחפניו
מי צרר מים בשמלה מי הקים כל אפסי ארץ. וככה כתוב (איוב יא) ארוכה מארץ
מדה ורחבה מני ים. וכתוב אחר אומר (איוב לה) התכוננת עד רחבי ארץ והכל
נכון למשכיל. וככה דברים רבים כאשר נזכר בסוף ספר תהלות. כי אש וברד
מהארץ וזה אמת בראיות ברורות וככה המים על השמים ואיך הם המאורות
והכוכבים ברקיע אחד והכל אמת. וחכמי התלמוד בדורנו על דרכים רבים. יש
הוגה בו לדעת האיסור וההתר ויש מי שידע המדרשים גם הוא יחדש אחריהם
ויבקש טעם לכל מלא וחסר. ועתה אומר כלל. דע כי הנביאים אינם שומרים
המלות בעצמם בשנותם הדבר רק הטעמים שומרים לבדם שהם העיקרים כדברי
אליעזר (בראשית כד) הגמאיני השקיני. ויצחק אמר לעשיו (בראשית כז) בעבור
תברכך נפשי בטרם אמות ורבקה אמרה ואברככה לפני ה' לפני מותי. ובחלום
(בראשית מא) יפות מראה ויפות תואר ובפתרון לא נאמר כך ונאמר לבלעם

שבעל פה כי כתוב בשבת (שמות כ':י') לא תעשה כל מלאכה ומי יפרש לנו
כמה מלאכות ותולדותיהן ומדות הסוכה וכמה היא האונאה והכלל כל המצות
צריכות פירוש מקבלת האבות ואף כל המועדים אם הם תלוים במולד הלבנה
האמצעי או המתוקן או על פי המרחק שהלבנה נכונה להראות או על פי מראה
העין והשנויים רבים מפאת האורך והרוחב וקשת המראה כפי מרחב הארץ וכפי
גלגל נטות הלבנה לימין קו המזלות או לשמאלו ועל איזה מקום הוא חשבון
המולד כי הנה הוא בין ירושלם ובין זו זו האי ד' שעות ישרות שהשמש זורחת עליהם
בתחלה כראיות גמורות מחכמת המולדות ועוד מצות רבות לא נדע פירושם מן
התורה כי אם סברא כמו (דברים י':ט"ז) ומלתם את ערלת לבבכם גם טוב הוא
לדעת המקרא כי מצות רבות נלמוד מדברי המקרא כמצות (ויקרא י"ט:כ"ו)
לא תאכלו על הדם מדברי שאול (דברים כ"ד:ט"ז) ולא יומתו אבות על בנים
מדבריה אמציה רק קטון הוא התועלת כנגד היגיעה לדעת שמות ערי ישראל
ודברי השופטים והמלכים ובנין הבית הראשון והעתיד להיות ודברי הנבואה
שעברו קצתם ויש מהם עתידות שנוכל לחקרם ויש שנגשש בהם כעורים בקיר
זה אומר בכה וזה אומר בכה ואילו היינו יודעים ספר תהלות שהוא כולו זמירות
ותפלות אף על פי שנאמר ברוח הקודש אין בו נבואה לעתיד וככה איוב וספרי
שלמה ע"ה והמגלות ועזרא וככה לא נוכל לדעת מספר דניאל מתי יגיע הקץ
כי הוא לא ידעו כאשר פירשתי במקומו ואם נביט יומם ולילה בכל אלה לא
תעלה בידינו דעת מצוה שנוכל לנחול בעבורה חיי העולם הבא על כן אמרו
(בבא מציעא לא) על לימוד המקרא מדה שאינה מדה רק טוב הוא למשכיל
שיתבונן סוד לשון הקדש מהמקרא כי ממנו תוצאות חיים להבין יסוד התורה
וסוד המורא גם התרגום מועיל אף על פי שאיננו כולו על דרך פשט:

ויש חכמים רבים שלא למדו מסורת גם דיקות הלשון בעיניהם הבל גם לא
קראו מקרא אף כי הטעמים רק מימות הנעורים למדו התלמוד שהוא פירוש
המשנה והם על דרכים רבים וכולם על דרך נכונה כי מהתלמוד נדע כל המצות
אשר יעשה אותם האדם וחי בהם רק אין נכון למשכיל להיותו ריק מחכמת
המקרא כי כאשר ימצא בתלמוד כתוב שנאמר לא ידע באיזה ספר הוא ואם הוא
על דרך פשט או דרש או אסמכתא בעלמא כי מרוב חכמתם ופלפולם יוציאו
דבר מתוך דבר והם ידעו הפשט יותר מכל הדורות הבאים אחריהם. והנה מי
שלא למד המקרא לא ידע לקרות הפסוק גם צריך הוא שידעו דיקות הלשון כי
הוא ידריכנו להתבונן בתורה דברים רבים שלא פירשום קדמונינו שהיו חכמים
גדולים בכל חכמה והבאים אחריהם לא יבינו רק דבריהם המפורשים. גם יש
בתלמוד דברים לא ידעו פירושם כמו במסכת ראש השנה שבא פעמים בארוכה
וסוד נולד קודם חצות ולדידן ולדידהו. ואין יכולת במשכיל לדעת כל זה אם
לא ילמוד חכמת המזלות וידע מהלכי החמה והלבנה גם לא ידע חכמת המזלות

שער א

יש ממשכילי ישראל שכל חכמתם בדעת דברי המסורת וסימניהם הנכבדים
ורמזיהם היקרים וכל סתום ופתוח וקרי וכתיב וחסר ויתר ואותיות גדולות
וקטנות ותלויות ונקודות עליהם ומספר הפסוקים והתיבות והאותיות בכל ספר
וספר והאמת כי יש שכר לפעולות בעלי המסורת שהם כשומרי חומות העיר
כי בעבורם עמדה תורת השם וספרי הקודש על מתכונתם בלי תוספת ומגרעת
וטוב הוא למשכיל שיבין קצת דבריהם וישים לבו להתבונן טעמי הספרים כי
התיבות כגויות והטעמים כנשמות ואם לא יבין הטעמים כל יגיעו שוא ועמל
ורוח והוא נמשל למי שיש בידו ספר רפואות והוא מיגע עצמו לספור כמה
דפין בספר וכמה טורים בכל דף ודף וכמה אותיות בכל טור ומזאת היגיעה
לא יוכל לרפאת מזור והנה חכם המסורת שלא למד חכמה אחרת דומה לגמל
נושא משי והוא לא יועיל למשי גם המשי לא יועילנו.

ויש אחרים שחכמתם דיקות הלשון לדעת הבנינים ומחלוקותיהם והאותיות
המשרתים והשרשיים והשמות והפעלים העומדים והיוצאים שהם על דרכים
רבים ואותיות הטעמים והמלות ואיך ידביקו הפעולים ובאמת כי היא חכמה
מפוארה כי ידעו בעליה לדבר לשון צחות במכתבו או בחרוזיו גם טעמים
רבים הם מפורשים מדרך הלשון גם מצוה כמו (ויקרא י״ט:י״ח) ואהבת לרעך
כמוך שאיננו כתוב את רעך כמו (דברים ו׳:ה׳) ואהבת את ה׳ א־להיך והעד
הנאמן שהוא כתוב על הגר (ויקרא י״ט:ל״ד) ואהבת לו כמוך ואין להשיב
(דברים י׳:י״ט) ואהבתם את הגר כי אין שם כמו והטעם דבק כמכתוב למעלה
כאשר פרשתיו במקומו והאמת כי טוב הוא למשכיל שילמוד מזאת החכמה
רק לא יתעסק בה כל ימיו לקרוא ספרי ר׳ יהודה המדקדק הראשון וי׳ ספרי
ר׳ מרינוס וכ״ב ספרי ר׳ שמואל הנגיד ועל כאלה אמר שלמה (קהלת י״ב:י״ב)
עשות ספרים הרבה אין קץ.

ויש אחרים שהוגים תמיד בתורה ובנביאים ובכתובים גם תרגומם בלשון
ארמית והם חושבים בלבם בעבור שיחפשו טעמים כפי יכלתם שעלו אל
מדרגה עליונה והאמת כי התורה מקור חיים והיא יסוד כל המצות רק אין כח
במשכיל לדעת מצוה אחת תמימה מן התורה אם לא יעמוד על דברי תורה

שיר פתיחה

שיר לרבי אברהם ן' עזרא

אחד בלי ראשית הכל מלא הודו. אך מרומם על פי איש להגידו:
ידע לבב משכיל בוראו במעבדו. כי כל מכחש בו הוא באמת עדו:
ולעם בראהו שמו ולכבודו. הראה בהר סיני אשו ולפידו:
אכן תמונה לא ראו ולפקידו. ציר נאמן נתן דתו ותלמודו:
ואני נכה רוח בנתי בנקודו. ואמצאה כתוב סודו ומוסדו:
בית לתורתו אבנה ועמודו. יראת אלקינו שתי להעמידו:

הקדמה

רְאֵה סֵפֶר שְׁמוֹ נִקְרָא. יְסוֹד מוֹרָא וְסוֹד תּוֹרָה.

לְאַבְרָהָם בְּנוֹ מֵאִיר. סְפָרְדִי אַבֶּן עֶזְרָא.

אמר אברהם המחבר הנה נא הואלתי לדבר ורצוני להאריך, כי ליסוד מוסד אני
צריך, ובעזר משפיל ומרים, אסדר שנים עשר שערים.

ואומר בתחלה, כי אין מותר לאדם מן הבהמה, כי אם בנשמה העליונה החכמה,
היא שתתשוב אל השם הנכבד אשר נתנה, כי למען הראותה הובאה בגויה ללמוד
מעשה אדוניה ולשמור מצותיו. וכל חכמה תחיה את בעליה, והחכמות הם
רבות, וכל אחת מועלת וכולם כמעלות הסולם לעלות אל חכמות האמת, אשרי
מי שנפקחו עיני לבותם, ונהרו אל השם ואל טובו באחריתם:

ה

ספר

יסוד מורא וסוד תורה

חברו החכם הכולל הפילוסוף האלקי

רבנו אברהם אבן עזרא ז"ל

KODESH PRESS

ספר

יסוד מורא

להרב

אברהם בן עזרא

כולל

הערות נכבדות

על

התורה והמצות

<hr>

פראנקפורט ת"ר לפ"ק ·

· על ידי ה' יוסף באר ·

נדפס האדון בעניאמין קרעבם ·

Printed in the USA
CPSIA information can be obtained
at www.ICGtesting.com
LVHW090852011123
762326LV00002B/45